Marianne Moore and the Visual Arts

Marianne Moore and the Visual Arts

PRISMATIC COLOR

LINDA LEAVELL

LOUISIANA STATE UNIVERSITY PRESS

Baton Rouge and London

Library of Congress Cataloging-in-Publication Data
Leavell, Linda, 1954–
    Marianne Moore and the visual arts : prismatic color / Linda
Leavell.
        p.   cm.
    Includes bibliographical references and index.
    ISBN 0-8071-1986-5 (cl)
    1. Moore, Marianne, 1887–1972—Knowledge—Art.   2. Art and
literature—United States—History—20th century.   3. Colors in
literature.   I. Title.
PS3525.05616Z686   1995
811'.52—dc20   95-1959
                                                                                      CIP

Unpublished materials of Marianne Moore and her family are quoted with permission of Marianne C. Moore, Literary Executor for the Estate of Marianne Moore. All rights reserved. Unpublished materials from the Marianne Moore Papers, the Rosenbach Museum and Library, are quoted with permission of the Rosenbach Museum and Library.

    Quotations from "Granite and Steel," copyright © 1966 by Marianne Moore, "The Sycamore," copyright © 1956 by Marianne Moore, "To a Chameleon," copyright © 1954 by Marianne Moore, from *The Complete Poems of Marianne Moore* by Marianne Moore. Used by permission of Viking Penguin, a division of Penguin Books USA Inc. Quotations are reprinted with permission of Macmillan Publishing Company from *Collected Poems of Marianne Moore*. Copyright 1935 by Marianne Moore, renewed 1963 by Marianne Moore and T. S. Eliot. Copyright 1944, and renewed 1972, by Marianne Moore. Quotations are reprinted with permission of Macmillan Publishing Company from *What Are Years?* by Marianne Moore. Copyright 1941, and renewed 1969, by Marianne Moore. Quotations from *The Complete Poems of Marianne Moore* are reprinted with permission of Faber and Faber Ltd. Marianne Moore's poems from the *Lantern* are quoted courtesy of the Bryn Mawr College Archives, Canaday Library, Bryn Mawr, Pennsylvania. Marianne Moore's letter to Lola Ridge of May 25, 1920, is quoted with permission of the Sophia Smith Collection, Smith College, Northampton, Massachusetts. Henry McBride's letter to Marianne Moore of February 4, 1939, is quoted with permission of Maximilian H. Mitzlaff. Hilda Doolittle's letters to Marianne Moore of September 7, 1915, and August 29, 1917, are quoted with the permission of the agents of the Estate of Hilda Doolittle. Copyright © 1994 by the Estate of Hilda Doolittle. Used by permission of New Directions Publishing Company, agents for the Estate. William Carlos Williams' poem "Young Sycamore" is quoted with permission of the publisher from William Carlos Williams, *Collected Poems, 1909–1939. Vol. I.* Copyright 1938 by New Directions Publishing Company. Ezra Pound's poem "In a Station of the Metro" is reprinted with permission of the publisher from Ezra Pound, *Personae.* Copyright 1926 by Ezra Pound.

    Paul Strand's letters to Alfred Stieglitz of August 3, 1921, and July 25, 1922, copyright © Aperture Foundation Inc., Paul Strand Archive, are quoted with permission of the Paul Strand Archive. Unpublished letters of Marsden Hartley, Alfred Stieglitz, and Paul Strand are quoted with permission of the Beinecke Rare Book and Manuscript Library, Yale University, New Haven, Connecticut. Unpublished letters of Marsden Hartley are quoted with permission of the Yale Committee on Literary Property. The letter from Alfred Stieglitz to Arthur Dove of November 5, 1914, is quoted with the permission of Donald Gallup. The letter from Alfred Stieglitz to Paul Strand of September 16, 1920, is quoted courtesy of the Center for Creative Photography, University of Arizona, Tucson. The letters from Alfred Stieglitz to Paul Strand of September 16, 1920, and to Marianne Moore of January 14, 1914, are quoted courtesy of the Artists Rights Society and the Georgia O'Keeffe Foundation.

    The author is grateful to Oxford University Press for permission to reprint material from her article "When Marianne Moore Buys Pictures," *American Literary History*, V (1993), 250–71.

To my mother and father

CONTENTS

ILLUSTRATIONS

ACKNOWLEDGMENTS

First and foremost in the long line of teachers standing behind this book are my parents, Marjory Cretien and Frank Leavell, who have fostered my love of the word and the image in innumerable ways.

William A. Camfield's lectures on modern American painting, specifically the one on Georgia O'Keeffe, sparked my decision to pursue this study. The concept of precisionism and especially its images offered a vocabulary that seemed intuitively right for Marianne Moore, whose *Complete Poems* I had read in Terry Doody's modern American poetry class my first semester of graduate school. The relationship between modern painting and poetry had long seemed to me an intrinsic one, since my simultaneous discovery of them both at Interlochen Arts Academy years before. My adviser, Monroe Spears, along with Professors Doody and Camfield, guided this project through its dissertation phase. Among the many other teachers who have contributed in less direct but nevertheless important ways, I would like to acknowledge James Alley, Robert Baird, Morse Hamilton, and the late W. J. Kilgore.

A project such as this demands more than ideas. Fortunately for me, not one but three mentors—Ann Miller, Bill Piper, and Monroe Spears—have provided an unusually generous supply of friendship and inspiration. My profound thanks to all of my teachers. My hope is that this book will give back to them and others like them (not academics necessarily) something of what they have given to me.

Other friends and colleagues have also contributed their ideas and encouragement. Beth Collins' willingness to talk about poems helped me formulate many of my initial ideas. In addition to those already mentioned and a handful of anonymous readers, Linda Austin, Jack Crane, Elizabeth Grubgeld, Marsha Recknagel, Peter Rollins, Grace Schulman, Betty Ann Sisson, Libby Stott, Ed Walkiewicz, and Terry Zambon have provided helpful comments upon sections of this book at various stages of its long progress. Since we first met at the Marianne Moore Centennial Conference, Cris Miller and I have often exchanged ideas about Moore. To her I owe particular gratitude for reading and commenting upon the entire manuscript.

I was fortunate to have Pat Willis as my initial guide through the Rosenbach archives. The materials to which she directed me and her wealth of knowledge have shaped this project in significant ways. Others who have provided generous assistance at the Rosenbach include Eileen Cahill, Evelyn Feldman, Elizabeth Fuller, Leslie Morris, Doug Parsons, and Natania Rosenfeld. My thanks to them and also to the other Moore scholars whom I sometimes met there and who shared their knowledge with me, especially Charles Molesworth. Caroline Rittenhouse not only directed me through the archival works at Bryn Mawr College but also gave me a tour of the campus. Pat Willis, again, has been helpful in her capacity as curator of American literature at the Beinecke.

Among the many persons who helped me with copyright matters, I owe particular gratitude to Marianne C. Moore, the poet's niece and literary executor, both for granting permissions and for clarifying biographical information. Tessim Zorach has been most generous in answering my questions and providing copies of his parents' works. My thanks also to the many persons and collections that are cited in my notes and credits.

This research was supported in part by a grant from the Oklahoma Foundation for the Humanities and the National Endowment for the Humanities. Findings, opinions, and conclusions do not necessarily represent the views of the foundation or the NEH. An Andrew W. Mellon fellowship and NEH Travel to Collections grant also provided support. Oklahoma State University provided a semester-long sabbatical that allowed me to complete the manuscript, the College of Arts and Sciences provided three Dean's Incentive Grants and additional travel support, and the English Department subsidized many of my illustrations. I also want to thank my two research assistants, Neil Van Dalsem and Rikki Martin, provided through the Lew Wentz scholarship program.

I am grateful to Beverly Jarrett, formerly of Louisiana State University Press, for first taking an interest in my manuscript and to Managing Editor John Easterly for seeing it through to publication. To my mother I am again indebted for her assistance with proofreading.

One last teacher I want to thank is my husband, Brooks Garner. Without the love of my friends and family—all teachers in spirit if not by profession—this book would not exist.

ABBREVIATIONS

Works by Marianne Moore

CP	*The Complete Poems of Marianne Moore.* New York, 1981.
MMR	*A Marianne Moore Reader.* New York, 1961.
Obs	*Observations.* 2nd ed. New York, 1925.
Prose	Willis, Patricia C., ed. *The Complete Prose of Marianne Moore.* New York, 1986.
SP	*The Selected Poems of Marianne Moore.* New York, 1935.

Manuscript collections

Beinecke	Yale Collection of American Literature, Beinecke Rare Book and Manuscript Library, Yale University, New Haven.
Bryn Mawr	Miriam Coffin Canaday Library, Bryn Mawr College, Bryn Mawr, Pennsylvania.
Rosenbach	Marianne Moore Papers, Rosenbach Museum and Library, Philadelphia.

Marianne Moore and her family

JWM	John Warner Moore, the poet's brother
MM	Marianne Moore
MWM	Mary Warner Moore, the poet's mother

Marianne Moore and the Visual Arts

INTRODUCTION

When Ezra Pound first wrote to Marianne Moore in December, 1918, he had likely read more than thirty of her poems, primarily in the *Egoist* and *Others*, over the past four years. He was writing to offer his services as editor and promoter of her first book if she did not already have one—also to inquire who she was and what her influences had been. Guessing that her influences included the Greeks, the French symbolists, and himself, Pound became the first of many puzzled admirers to try to place Moore in a familiar context. She refused his offer regarding the book and politely corrected him: she had no Greek, had not heard of Ghil and Laforgue. As for himself: "The resemblance of my progress to your beginnings is an accident so far as I can see." Though she expressed admiration for the work of Pound and T. S. Eliot (both then in London), she defined her own New York milieu unequivocally: "Over here, it strikes me that there is more evidence of power among painters and sculptors than among writers."[1] This book elaborates that answer.

My purpose is not so much to describe one poet's interest in the visual arts as it is to define a particular form of modernism, to examine Moore's unique response to a turbulent aesthetic climate. And while this climate is part of the international, interdisciplinary phenomenon known as modernism, it is yet distinct from other climates, even those of William Carlos Williams and Wallace Stevens, whose interactions with the avant-garde also occurred in New York and at the same time as Moore's. I trace the development of Moore's modernism from her exposure to arts and crafts ideology during her adolescence until, as editor of the *Dial* in

1. MM to Ezra Pound, January 9, 1919, in *Marianne Moore: A Collection of Critical Essays,* ed. Charles Tomlinson (Englewood Cliffs, N.J., 1969), 17, 18. This letter, probably the only personal correspondence Moore published during her lifetime, answers Ezra Pound to MM, December 16, 1918, in *The Selected Letters of Ezra Pound, 1907–1941,* ed. D. D. Paige (New York, 1950), 141–44.

the late twenties, she became America's foremost arbiter of modernist taste. In defining Moore's aesthetic climate, I give particular emphasis to Alfred Stieglitz and the artists associated with him. Moore's visit to his famous 291 gallery in 1915 marked her debut into the New York art scene, she thereafter regularly attended the exhibits he sponsored, and her aesthetic affinities with the Stieglitz artists remained strong. Williams and Stevens, on the other hand, had closer ties at least initially to the artists who met at the uptown apartment of Walter and Louise Arensberg. Although a number of artists participated in both the 291 and Arensberg circles and there was originally no rivalry between them, the groups had distinct personalities and aesthetics.

Despite (or perhaps because of) the recent surge of interartistic studies, especially about Williams, Pound, and Gertrude Stein, considerable skepticism surrounds interartistic comparisons. To use the terminology of one discipline—*portrait* or *cubism*—to describe another seems imprecise. The theoretical discussions of Wendy Steiner and others have helped those like myself who are drawn empirically to interartistic comparisons to clarify our thinking. While I cannot do justice to the complexity of her argument here, I will briefly address two key questions: what makes interartistic comparison, in Steiner's words, "worth the candle," and which qualities of the two arts can be usefully compared?

As for the first, I agree with Steiner that "the interartistic comparison inevitably reveals the aesthetic norms of the period during which the question is asked."[2] Placing Moore in a visual arts context reveals norms of modernism that differ in some ways from those usually emphasized by literary historians: the Stieglitz era and the Pound era, though simultaneous, are not the same. While my purpose is strictly to show the usefulness of these norms for reading Moore, I hope they prove useful in reading her contemporaries as well. For Moore represented an ideal to which other poets aspired. Williams, who loathed Eliot, and Eliot, who ignored Williams, both regarded Moore as unsurpassed among their American contemporaries. Recalling the years prior to the publication of *The Waste Land*, Williams remembered her as "our saint—if we had one—in whom we all instinctively felt our purpose come together to form a stream."[3] At a time

2. Wendy Steiner, *The Colors of Rhetoric: Problems in the Relation Between Modern Literature and Painting* (Chicago, 1982), 18.

3. William Carlos Williams, *The Autobiography of William Carlos Williams* (New York, 1951), 146. Also, see T. S. Eliot, "Marianne Moore," *Dial*, LXXV (1923); and William Car-

when other poets felt themselves floundering in the wake of their own rebellion, they regarded Moore as having found a new direction, but they
were understandably reluctant to imitate what they did not fully comprehend. Thus, to recognize Moore's own concept of modernism is to recognize a modernism that inspired and perplexed her contemporaries on
both sides of the Atlantic.

The second problem is to define norms in such a way that they can
usefully and accurately apply to both verbal and visual art. Many interartistic studies claim that a writer "was influenced by" the painters or vice
versa, but because of the temptation to see influence as linear, I try to avoid
such a claim except in a few instances. Who can say whether a group of
artists influenced Moore or whether she was drawn to them because of
common concerns? Moore's role in the art world was far from passive; she
actively sought out certain individuals and publications and as decisively
avoided others. While on one hand "influence" seems too limited, I want
to describe something more precise than a general zeitgeist in which Moore
participated. I regard modernism as an interdisciplinary phenomenon of
the early twentieth century—but see it as a common set of problems rather
than a common set of solutions. The solutions—compressed perspective,
free verse—necessarily differ from one medium to another and even differ dramatically among artists of the same medium. Though Moore studied scrupulously the work of her fellow poets, the problems to which she
responded were not necessarily the same as theirs. She never despaired
over "the dissolution of communal belief,"[4] nor did she (as Pound supposed) respond to the innovations of French symbolism. Rather, her challenges were often those posed by visual artists, who had a stronger presence in her early milieu than did other leading modernist poets. But Moore's
responses to these challenges were unique and literary. She did not try,
as others did, to adapt cubism into poetry. My chapters, besides the initial
one, are organized according to problems, or challenges, that Moore shared
with avant-garde visual artists: those posed by analytic cubism, by collage,
by primitivism, and by American technology.

---

los Williams, "Marianne Moore," *Dial*, LXXVIII (1925); both are reprinted in *Marianne
Moore*, ed. Tomlinson, 48–51, 52–59. The Williams essay is also reprinted in William Carlos Williams, *Selected Essays* (New York, 1969), 121–31.

4. The phrase is Helen Vendler's in her Introduction to *Voices & Visions: The Poet in
America*, ed. Helen Vendler (New York, 1987), xxiv.

Despite the proliferation of books about Moore as well as her advocacy by such canon-shapers as Helen Vendler and Hugh Kenner, Moore's status as a major modernist remains less than assured. The monumentally inclusive *Columbia Literary History of the United States*, for example, does not give her so much as a paragraph.[5] The number of scholars poring over the Marianne Moore archives at the Rosenbach Museum and Library in Philadelphia seems disproportionate to the number of tourists who come there and have never heard of Moore. These scholars (often several at a time) overhear the Rosenbach docents pointing out Moore's recreated living room, identifying her as a poet who won many awards and who "knew everybody"—Ezra Pound, T. S. Eliot, William Carlos Williams, Wallace Stevens. Moore's academic advocates have, understandably, taken a similar approach. To account for her difficulty and to argue for her importance, they compare her with these high modernists by showing that she was both personally and professionally their peer. It has even become a point of debate among Moore critics which of the four she most resembles.[6] Although these relationships were surely important to Moore and analyses of them have contributed to understanding her poetry, belaboring these comparisons tends to reinforce her secondary status. Given the breadth of Moore's interests and modernism's self-conscious insistence upon being interdisciplinary, critics have yet to give her extraliterary contexts their due.

Indeed, critics often do acknowledge the importance of the visual arts to Moore, and a few go beyond acknowledgment. Laurence Stapleton's *The Poet's Advance* first emphasized Moore's early exposure to modern art. As former curator at the Rosenbach and editor of the *Marianne Moore Newsletter*, Patricia Willis repeatedly reminded scholars of Moore's extraliterary sources; her exhibition catalog *Vision into Verse* documents some of the many visual sources for specific poems. Charles Altieri's brief section on Moore in his *Painterly Abstraction in Modernist American Poetry* (more abstract than painterly) provides an enticing feminist reading of certain poems. Two studies by Grace Schulman and Dickran Tashjian address

5. Emory Elliott, ed., *Columbia Literary History of the United States* (New York, 1988).

6. John Slatin, *The Savage's Romance: The Poetry of Marianne Moore* (University Park, Pa., 1986), for example, places Moore in an American Emersonian tradition but finds that of her contemporaries she is closest to Eliot (11). Celeste Goodridge, *Hints and Disguises: Marianne Moore and Her Contemporaries* (Iowa City, 1989), aligns her with Pound and Stevens, arguing against the assumption of her proximity to Williams and Eliot (9).

Moore's relationship with particular artists, E. McKnight Kauffer and Joseph Cornell, respectively. The indispensable introduction to Moore's use of the visual arts, however, is a chapter in Bonnie Costello's *Imaginary Possessions*, which acknowledges the limitations of reading Moore in an exclusively literary context.[7]

The most influential book behind my own thinking is one I first encountered as an undergraduate: Bram Dijkstra's *The Hieroglyphics of a New Speech: Cubism, Stieglitz, and the Early Poetry of William Carlos Williams*. This pivotal study proves the necessity of an interartistic approach to Williams specifically and to New York modernism generally. Dijkstra argues "that the influence of Imagism, *Poetry*, and Pound was far less pervasive than it is generally made out to be, especially where poets such as Williams, Wallace Stevens, and Marianne Moore are concerned. A close study of the early writings of these poets cannot be possible without a thorough investigation of the sources presented by the visual arts of that time." Dijkstra's thesis is now assumed among Williams critics; its implications for the other two are more slowly being realized.[8]

As I point out in Chapter 1, it is important to recognize the extent to which New York writers and visual artists collaborated during the early

7. Laurence Stapleton, *Marianne Moore: The Poet's Advance* (Princeton, 1978), 6–8; Patricia C. Willis, *Marianne Moore: Vision into Verse* (Philadelphia, 1987); Charles Altieri, *Painterly Abstraction in Modernist American Poetry: The Contemporaniety of Modernism* (Cambridge, England, 1989), 259–71; Grace Schulman, "Marianne Moore and E. McKnight Kauffer: Two Characteristic Americans," in *Marianne Moore*, ed. Andrew J. Kappel, special issue of *Twentieth Century Literature*, XXX (1984), 175–80; Dickran Tashjian, *Joseph Cornell: Gifts of Desire* (Miami Beach, 1992), 65–77; Bonnie Costello, *Marianne Moore: Imaginary Possessions* (Cambridge, Mass., 1981), 186–214. Two more works deserve mention: Elisabeth W. Joyce, "Complexity Is Not a Crime: Marianne Moore, Modernism, and the Visual Arts" (Ph.D. dissertation, Temple University, 1991), which focuses on the Armory Show; and Darlene Williams Erikson, *Illusion Is More Precise than Precision: The Poetry of Marianne Moore* (Tuscaloosa, 1992), which uses visual-arts terms in an admittedly loose way (esp. 82–113). Besides a portion of the present book published previously, my own work includes a comparison of Moore and Georgia O'Keeffe as women artists: "Marianne Moore and Georgia O'Keeffe: 'The Feelings of a Woman—A Mother or a Cat,'" in *Marianne Moore: Woman and Poet*, ed. Patricia C. Willis (Orono, Me., 1990), 297–319.

8. Bram Dijkstra, *The Hieroglyphics of a New Speech: Cubism, Stieglitz, and the Early Poetry of William Carlos Williams* (Princeton, 1969), 45. In addition to numerous articles and chapters, seven more books devoted to Williams and the visual arts have followed. The first book-length study of Stevens' visual-arts connections has recently appeared: Glen MacLeod, *Wallace Stevens and Modern Art: From the Armory Show to Abstract Expressionism* (New Haven, 1993).

decades of this century: they socialized with each other, published magazines together, and shared a common mission. Moore's letter to Pound cited earlier expresses amazement at "the amount of steady co-operation that is to be counted on in the interest of getting things launched."[9] Since my purpose is to describe Moore's modernism and the context in which it developed, I give greatest attention to her career before 1929, when she ceased editing the *Dial* and moved from Greenwich Village to Brooklyn. The years from 1915 to 1929 are those of her closest interaction with the avant-garde, when she was regularly visiting galleries and meeting with artists and writers such as Alfred Stieglitz, Marsden Hartley, Alfred Kreymborg, William and Marguerite Zorach, Gaston Lachaise, William Carlos Williams, and many others. The issues Moore confronted during these years affected not only her early experimentation but also the work of her entire career.

Chapter 1 biographically describes Moore's development as a modernist, emphasizing how the visual arts contributed to that development. It draws upon the extensive Marianne Moore Papers at the Rosenbach Museum and Library, especially her notebooks and the almost daily correspondence among Moore, her mother, and her brother that began in her adolescence. One of the ironies of this famously guarded poet is that she preserved for posterity a more complete record of her life and work than is perhaps available on any other writer of her stature. Still, only a handful of the Rosenbach documents is published, and despite scholars' extensive use of this archive for nearly two decades, only one biographer has attempted a chronological synthesis of the information contained there.[10]

My second and third chapters focus on Moore's formal innovations. Chapter 2 deals with the problems posed by analytic cubism, how to realign the relationship between form and subject and how to enlarge the aesthetic experience to include as many of the senses as possible. I trace the development of Moore's rhymed syllabic stanza as a response to these issues. Unlike the lines of free verse, which typically indicate the rhythms

9. MM to Pound, January 9, 1919, in *Marianne Moore,* ed. Tomlinson, 18.

10. The one full-length biography is Charles Molesworth, *Marianne Moore: A Literary Life* (New York, 1990). Edited by Patricia C. Willis and published by the Rosenbach from 1977 to 1983, the *Marianne Moore Newsletter* contains some of the gems of the Marianne Moore collection. With Cristanne Miller and Celeste Goodridge, Bonnie Costello is editing a selection of Moore's letters.

of speech, Moore's stanzas cohere to an internal architecture at odds with her well-wrought cadence. This architecture consists of a virtually inaudible but harmonious arrangement of typographical spacing, syllables, and rhyme. Following the development of this stanza, Moore's attraction to spatial patterns, and especially to the tension between stasis and flux, becomes increasingly evident in the subject matter of her poems and even in her syntax.

Chapter 3 deals with the challenges of collage, with the shifting balance between the artist's imagination and the world of things and facts. Collage redefines art as selecting rather than making. Moore's poems become literally "a place for the genuine," a place where she can arrange all of the things that she likes. Resisting the reader's desire for unity, these things seem assembled miscellaneously as one might choose things over a lifetime to put in a living room. The mysteriousness of a miscellany—a museum, a living room, a Joseph Cornell box—draws the observer in, stimulating her to look at individual things with new interest as well as to look, if she will, at the "unintentional portrait" of a mind—a mind hidden to the casual observer by the protective shield of things.

Throughout these chapters especially I trace the development of Moore's technique. Because collections of Moore's poetry omit many early poems and arrange the pre-1935 ones nonchronologically, they give the impression that Moore was a full-blown modernist from the beginning, but in fact Moore experimented a good deal between 1915 and 1935. By focusing on the earlier poems, I do not mean to enter the fray over which period of Moore's poetry is strongest. Though it is beyond my scope to prove this except tacitly—by drawing in later poems when relevant—I find that Moore wrote valuable and complex poems at all stages of her career. Because Moore revised her poems so extensively and so continually, there is no such thing as a definitive edition of the poems, for her final revisions do not necessarily improve earlier versions and often obscure her original concerns. Just as Laurence Stapleton's and Bonnie Costello's studies compelled subsequent scholars to consult the Rosenbach, so have John Slatin's and Margaret Holley's books made us consider not just the sequential revisions in Moore's books but also the earliest publication of each poem.[11] I have examined all of Moore's pre-1935 poems in their var-

11. All four of these critics and others have noted the inadequacy of *The Complete Poems of Marianne Moore* (Rev. ed.; New York, 1981), which states, "Omissions are not accidents" (vii). Margaret Holley, *The Poetry of Marianne Moore: A Study in Voice and Value*

ious published (and often unpublished) versions and have found it impossible to quote consistently from any one source. When discussing the chronological development of the poems, I use the first published version; otherwise, I usually quote from *Observations* (1924), *Selected Poems* (1935), or, when textual variations are immaterial, the *Complete Poems* (1981).[12]

Because the modernist revolution in form is so evident in both painting and poetry and because other writers such as Williams, Pound, and Stein looked to the visual arts for new forms, I assumed when I began this study that the visual arts would most usefully explain Moore's innovations in form, which also seemed to be her greatest claim to stature among the modernists. I agreed with Geoffrey Hartman that the "message" is secondary: "Contemporary painters make everything a function of form. . . . Marianne Moore is so much in this tradition of modern art that one reads her poems less for their message (always suffused) than for the pleasure of seeing how style may become an act of the living—the infinitely inclusive and discriminating—mind."[13] But my examination of the Rosenbach archives revealed that Moore's interest in the visual arts extended well beyond formal considerations.

As Chapters 2 and 3 discuss Moore's formal solutions to the overthrow of nineteenth-century conventions, Chapter 4 examines the ethical implications of this revolution. It is in Moore's spiritual and moral values that she differs most from the other high modernists of poetry, and because of this difference, critics sometimes assume that she is merely old-fashioned. But Stieglitz's, Kandinsky's, and other artists' ideals of individualism and cultural pluralism provide a more illuminating context, one that reveals her radical resistance to aesthetic, social, and even spiritual hi-

---

(Cambridge, England, 1987) provides the most thorough analysis of development of Moore's technique, and I have found Holley's "Chronology of Moore's Published Poems" (195–202) an indispensable guide to locating the first published versions of Moore's poems. Also useful but less reliable is Craig S. Abbott, *Marianne Moore: A Descriptive Bibliography* (Pittsburgh, 1977). Moore's prose does not present the problems of multiple revisions that the poetry does; I therefore cite *The Complete Prose of Marianne Moore,* ed. Patricia C. Willis (New York, 1986).

12. I do not consider Moore's first book, *Poems* (1921), in my analysis, because it was published without her knowledge and hence without her recent revisions.

13. Geoffrey Hartman, jacket notes to *Marianne Moore Reads from Her Works,* Yale Series of Recorded Poets, n.d. [*ca.* 1960]. Hartman, however, devotes most of his attention to Moore's message.

erarchies. Unlike most of her peers, Moore tries to walk a fine line between primitivism and racism, and between pluralism and relativism. This chapter also explains the use of animals as exemplars of her pluralist vision.

Chapter 5 deals with questions that confronted American artists after World War I: how to preserve artistic expression in an industrial age and how to define a distinctly American art. These issues were divisive among American artists during the twenties, and I find that Moore, like the precisionist painters and straight photographers of the time, refused to accept a dilemma between art and technology. As Paul Strand advocated the camera as a paradigm for artistic expression in the machine age, so did Moore show that scientific methods and technical language are fundamental to artistic vision.

I conclude Chapter 5 with a discussion of Moore's 1932 sequence, "Part of a Novel, Part of a Poem, Part of a Play," which heralds her return to writing poetry after a seven-year hiatus and which in some form would henceforth introduce her major collections. This sequence, which originally included "The Steeple-Jack," "The Student," and "The Hero," reinforces the aesthetic assertions of earlier poems such as "When I Buy Pictures" and "In the Days of Prismatic Color." It explores the various ways that a writer must *see*—from superficial ironies, to intellectual discriminations, to the hero's spiritual vision, "the rock / crystal thing to see." For despite its verbal medium, Moore's is an art of *seeing*. "Language is a special extension of the power of seeing," she said, "inasmuch as it can make visible not only the already visible world, but through it the invisible world of relations and affinities." [14]

14. MM, "Some Answers to Questions Posed by Howard Nemerov," in *Poets on Poetry,* ed. Howard Nemerov (New York, 1966), 11. Moore is quoting Nemerov.

1

SOJOURN IN THE WHALE

The development of genius—how the individual talent responds to its environment—is no easy thing to assess. Marianne Moore was an intensely private person, "armored" to some extent even among those persons closest to her. Her famously impersonal poetry provides probably the clearest, albeit impossibly circuitous, revelation of her inner life. Even her copious notebooks and correspondence—including letters to intimate friends and family members—ruminate only rarely on the artistic or emotional problems with which she was struggling at the time. Her most revealing letters express rather, as her poems and essays do, "a series of enthusiasms for this fine thing and that."[1] But what the Marianne Moore Papers at the Rosenbach, and particularly the massive family correspondence, does provide is an almost daily chronicle of the outward events of this artist's life. And since from an early age Moore aggressively sought an environment that would be conducive to her artistic aspirations, a study of that environment should reveal much about those aspirations.

The rise of Moore's career can be viewed in three stages: before 1915, 1915 to 1919, and 1920 to 1929. The first is her formal and informal education, including her adolescence in Carlisle, Pennsylvania; her studies at Bryn Mawr College; and after graduation in 1909 her self-directed study, again in Carlisle, of contemporary experimentation in the arts. The year 1915, when Moore's first professional publications appeared and when

---

1. MM, April 11, 1919, Notebook 1250/24 (Rosenbach VII:10:07), 36. (The letters Moore wrote at Bryn Mawr are an exception; they openly describe her developing social and artistic identity.) Since Moore kept her notes in unpaginated, out-of-date diaries, I cite the page numbers of the Rosenbach's photocopies of her notebooks. In quoting from unpublished letters and notebooks, I have silently added punctuation that was omitted in haste, extended abbreviations for articles and prepositions, and corrected spelling. Each Rosenbach location number indicates the series, box, and file.

she introduced herself to the New York art scene, marked the end of Moore's apprenticeship and the beginning of her most experimental period as a poet. From 1916 until 1918 Moore lived with her mother and brother in Chatham, New Jersey, a short train ride from New York, so that she could regularly visit galleries and meet with Village intellectuals. By the third period, the twenties, the avant-garde's enthusiasm for mere innovation had waned, and some divisiveness ensued over the direction American artists should take—whether to flee to Europe, for instance. Moore, having by this time moved with her mother to Greenwich Village, was pursued by some of the most influential figures of the time: H.D. and her British friend Bryher pressed Moore to join them in Europe; Robert McAlmon and William Carlos Williams sought her participation in *Contact*; Matthew Josephson wanted her to edit the *Broom*; but the *Dial* won her. In 1920 its new editor Scofield Thayer solicited Moore's poems, her prose, and her friendship; by 1925 he had chosen her as his successor, an office she would hold until 1929, when the *Dial* ceased publication. There could hardly have been a more central position for any writer of the time than the editorship of its leading literary magazine. Though Moore withdrew from this centrality by moving to Brooklyn in 1929 (at age forty-one), her reputation was now well established. She would continue to visit museums and galleries as long as her health permitted; friends and artists continually sought her attention and advice.

The Moore family's almost daily correspondence, which began when Marianne was sixteen and her older brother, Warner, left home for Yale, reveals much about the dynamics of her family that were so vital to her art. Marianne never knew her father and, if the family correspondence is indicative, knew little about him. After leaving her husband a few months before Marianne's birth on November 15, 1887, Mary Warner Moore moved into the manse in Kirkwood, Missouri, near St. Louis, to keep house for her father, a Presbyterian minister, and to rear her two small children. Mary Warner Moore's own mother had died when she was an infant. When her father died in 1893, Mrs. Moore took her family first briefly to Pittsburgh and then to Carlisle, Pennsylvania, where she obtained a teaching position at the Metzger Institute for girls and saw that her children were properly educated. The family correspondence, begun in 1904 and continuing throughout the lives of the Moores, reveals an extraordinarily tight family, the bonds woven inextricably through a complex system of animal nicknames, playful fictions, and private language. And lest life with a pious Victorian mother seem too austere, the letters, especially those between Warner and Marianne, exhibit considerable wit and play. Indeed, the Moores regarded play as their sincerest form of affection.

As both of her children were becoming established in their respective careers—Marianne as a poet, Warner as a navy chaplain—Mary Warner Moore wrote to her son that "there is *nothing valuable in all the world*" but "listen[ing] week by week to great preaching and . . . hav[ing] freedom for fellowship with the great of the earth, *in books.*"[2] Her children's careers manifest these values. Though Mary Warner Moore would be her daughter's intimate companion at the forefront of modernism, the mother remained herself a Victorian. She took her role of mother quite seriously as both teacher and supporter of her adult children. Her letters advise and instruct in every particular of her children's behavior, from subjects for Warner's college themes and later for his sermons, to elaborate corrections of their English usage, to the naming of her grandchildren. A sizable portion of her letters to Warner is devoted to religion, including every week a detailed summary of Sunday's sermon. She also supported her children's education and careers, allowing her son to go to Yale and later to graduate school at Princeton and her daughter to Bryn Mawr rather than to the local and less expensive Dickinson College, as she had originally planned. Later, when Warner had left his pastorate at Chatham to join the navy, she moved with her daughter to Greenwich Village rather than returning to her friends in Carlisle.

There can be no doubt, as Marianne Moore herself repeatedly said, that her family contributed significantly to her poems. Mrs. Moore would often help revise her daughter's poems and essays, and one can recognize many of the poetry's characteristic images—waves and spectrums, for example—as well as exact phrases from the poems, in Mrs. Moore's letters. Upon reading some of his sister's poems in the *Dial,* Warner praised them for being "expressed . . . in our own special 'language' but so marvelously handled that the 'aliens' could & can understand them & enjoy them."[3] Moore's family was not only an inspiration but also a deliberate audience for her poems. The care with which Mrs. Moore monitored her son's sermons even from across a continent suggests that it would have been difficult for Moore to publish anything either as author or as editor that

2. MWM to JWM, [?] 1921 (Rosenbach VI:24:01).
3. JWM to MWM and MM, May 1, 1920 (Rosenbach VI:23:19).

did not meet with her mother's approval. Moore writes that she "painfully and reluctantly scrapped" certain poems that did not meet with such approval.[4] Certainly, however, Marianne Moore respected her mother's criticism far more than she resisted it, if she resisted it at all. If Mary Warner Moore was a rigid censor, she was by no means an illiterate or stupid one. Rather than liberating her daughter's talent, her death in 1947, if anything, enervated it.

Moore's eagerness to publish her poems and to find an artistic community shows that her family was not, however, her only audience. In contrast to most aspiring poets of the time, including her Carlisle friends and neighbors William and Laura Benét, Moore chose the most radical community she could find, a group of artists whose perhaps sole united purpose was to overthrow the nineteenth-century absolutes to which Mrs. Moore held so firmly. Thus, Marianne Moore might be accused of duplicity—of writing for two audiences with contradictory expectations and values. The two audiences must surely have read her poetry quite differently. The wit and irony that make her poems so enigmatic and that she had mastered in family letters would be a great aid in such duplicity. Yet Moore was no reactionary—neither to her mother's pieties nor to the modern bohemian life-style so abhorrent to her mother. Her purpose seems rather to transcend the provinciality of both—to demonstrate the stability of certain values (not necessarily her mother's) in an age that resists stability.

The books that her mother loved so dearly were an important part of Moore's early education, but so was training in the other arts. As a student at the Metzger Institute in Carlisle, she studied piano, voice, and drawing. Though she did not practice music as an adult, throughout her life Moore made pen and ink drawings, especially of small creatures and artifacts, and watercolors, one of which she prized enough to hang in her living room.[5] In addition to her formal education, the family of the Moores' minister in Carlisle, Dr. George Norcross, enlarged Moore's cultural awareness. Late in life she recalled that this family was "a main influence on my life as a writer," specifically because of their "unfanatical innate love of books, music, and 'art,' [which] made Blake, Rembrandt,

4. MM to JWM, June 19, 1921 (Rosenbach VI:24:07).
5. Many of Moore's drawings have been reproduced in the *Marianne Moore Newsletter*. The watercolor of a house is in Moore's living room at the Rosenbach.

Figure 1 Marianne Moore, *Malaclemys terrapin*

1936. Drawing done at Norfolk, Virginia. Marianne Moore Papers. The Rosenbach Museum and Library.

Giotto, Holbein, D. G. Rossetti and Christina Rossetti, Turner, Browning, Ruskin, Anthony Trollope, George Meredith, household companions." She also recalls that the three Norcross daughters who graduated from Bryn Mawr inspired her to follow their example (*Prose*, 571–72).

The youngest of the Norcross daughters, Mary Jackson Norcross, ten years Marianne's senior, was so close to Mary Warner Moore as to be virtually a parent to Marianne and Warner during their adolescence. Never again would a fourth person be so thoroughly absorbed into the Moores' intimate system of fictions and nicknames.[6] She assumed family responsibilities—from routine housekeeping, to paying Marianne's doctor bills, to buying drapes at her own expense for the Moores' living room, to tutoring Marianne daily in German and composition for her Bryn Mawr en-

---

6. JWM to Mary Jackson Norcross, March 5, 1905 (Rosenbach VI:11a:03), written on the occasion of Norcross' birthday, provides an especially vivid account of the family's fictional relationships.

trance exams. Though Mary Norcross did not regularly sleep at the Moore home, Warner's room after he moved out became her "loom room," where she practiced her weaving. Mary Norcross was an enthusiastic participant in the American arts and crafts movement and took weaving lessons in Boston, where the Boston Society of Arts and Crafts, the first and most prominent of its kind in America, had been established in 1897. After a summer trip to Monhegan Island in Maine in the summer of 1904, Mary Norcross and Mrs. Moore decided to buy property there. Although the expense of sending Warner to Yale led them to postpone the purchase, during the following year they ordered house plans from *Craftsman*, Gustav Stickley's magazine, as well as catalogs on raising chickens, vegetables, and bees. Mary Norcross planned also to establish "a learning home" there when her father retired. The house in Maine never materialized, but in the spring of 1908, Mary Norcross did acquire woodland property at Sterrett's Gap, nine miles from Carlisle, and built a crafts house there. Perhaps she never gave up the idea of making this home a school and recreation center, but because of a lack of money, her mother's prolonged illness, and her own poor health, her plans were never realized.[7]

Arts and crafts ideology held a firm grip on the Moore household while Marianne was preparing for Bryn Mawr. In her letters to Warner, Mrs. Moore repeatedly expresses concern over the quality of furnishings Warner purchased for his dormitory room. She writes, "I want you by your Junior year to have a beautiful room; and *the best we can command* will be for your room and Sissy's." She disapproves his choice of a desk chair but offers to refer it to "our authority on furnishings, the Beaver [Mary Norcross], and hear what she has to say." Mrs. Moore's objection to his desk is even stronger: "I should rather have a deal kitchen table. You do not guess how offensive to my taste are those commercial looking desks."[8] She wrote to a crafts community, Roycrofters in East Aurora, New York, to inquire about a handmade desk for her son—this by a mother who was canceling magazine subscriptions to save money.[9]

Marianne did not share Mary Norcross' enthusiasm over "her learn-

7. This history is documented in the Moore family correspondence—they called Norcross' house the Mountain—and in Marianne Moore's obituary for Mary Norcross in the *Bryn Mawr Alumnae Bulletin*, XVIII (June, 1938), 27–28 (Bryn Mawr).

8. MWM to JWM, September 27, 1904 (Rosenbach VI:10:70); October 16, 1904, and October 22, 1904 (Rosenbach VI:10:71).

9. MWM to JWM, February 2, 1905 (Rosenbach VI:11a:02); verso of MWM to JWM, April 3, 1905 (Rosenbach VI:11a:04). Mary Norcross made drapes and other accessories

ing home"[10] and perhaps for other aspects of the arts and crafts movement (she was persistently skeptical of "movements"), but certain values that she learned either from Norcross or at Bryn Mawr, where arts and crafts enthusiasm also ran high, became fundamental to her aesthetic and even political sensibility. Most obviously, she maintained a keen sensitivity to "people's surroundings," as indicated by her poem on the subject, and a democratic appreciation for crafts regardless of whether society accords them the status of art. She believed in the sanctity of work and that work should be the honest expression of the worker and his or her materials. Her telling a classmate's father that she is a "Socialist . . . but not a Marxian" may stem directly from William Morris' and other craftsmen's political views.[11] And Moore's and her mother's participation in the suffrage campaign certainly resulted from their relationship with Mary Norcross. The connections between woman suffrage and the arts and crafts movement in this country deserve recognition, for many arts and crafts enthusiasts were women, and like Judy Chicago and other recent feminists, they sought a higher status for practical arts, often made by women, in resistance to the hegemony of fine arts, traditionally made by men.

The resistance to hierarchies and presumptuousness—implicit in arts and crafts ideology and later central to Moore's modernist aesthetic—is evident in the letters she wrote home from Bryn Mawr. Regarding a friend's seeing a man of whom others disapproved, she retorts: "I think it's a very inartistic way of looking at life to have scandal suggested to one by unconventions. . . . By artistic I mean with a view to the relations of things, with a respect for the main issues of life and a sort of contempt for hard and fast definitions."[12] She admires one professor for being as "kind as possible but very cruel in humiliating the presumptuous," and another for "cast[ing] an eye on trivial and important things alike with an unconsciousness of mien which pleases me exceedingly."[13] Already she has a clear

---

for both Warner's and Marianne's college rooms. The desk Mrs. Moore bought for Marianne on her twentieth birthday is in her living room at the Rosenbach.

10. MM to JWM, March 22, 1905 (Rosenbach VI:11a:03).

11. MM to her family, February 2, 1909 (Rosenbach VI:15a:03). After Marianne went to college, the family letters were circulated round-robin fashion between Carlisle, New Haven, and Bryn Mawr. Most of Moore's college letters are addressed to "family," which included her mother, her brother, and Mary Norcross.

12. MM to her family, November 29, 1908 (Rosenbach VI:14:11).

13. MM to her family, December 17, 1908 (Rosenbach VI:14:12); March 4, 1909 (Rosenbach VI:15a:04).

sense of her own likes and dislikes; she writes home detailed reviews of the plays and concerts she saw on campus and in Philadelphia. In the winter of her senior year she visited several galleries in New York City with her classmate Hilda Sprague-Smith and scorns all the paintings she saw there except those by the American impressionist Childe Hassam.[14] She dislikes the poems favored by the editor of the Bryn Mawr literary magazine about "Spiritual aspiration, love and meditation" and favors instead—and writes—what she calls "critical poetry, the informal Browning kind, picture-comment and music analysis etc.," because it is "the most impersonal and unforced."[15]

It is clear from comments such as these that by her senior year Moore already regarded herself as an artist (and a remarkably modernist one), but she was uncertain about her future. She writes home: "About next year I am certainly up a tree—I know you feel no unworthy pressure on me but if I paint, or if I write, or if I fool time, all of which I shall probably do, I ought to make some money first. . . . It's silly for me to paint, when I couldn't make a cent at it and when I'd do it badly if I knew I *had* to make a cent at it."[16] At this time she was writing stories, too, but by the spring of her senior year seemed most inclined toward poetry rather than fiction or painting both because she could "dash off poems" and because she received encouragement from a Greek professor who reportedly lectured on the rhythm of her poem "Ennui" for half an hour to his class.[17]

Moore's first brush with the New York avant-garde occurred virtually by chance during the month before her graduation. She was leaving the Bryn Mawr library when she met and began conversing with a young woman, a Miss Haviland, who happened to be visiting her aunt and uncle near the campus. Moore learned that Miss Haviland's cousin Paul Haviland shared a photography studio in New York on Fifth Avenue with "an Alfred Stieglitz." As with all important events, Moore describes this

14. Mrs. Charles (Isabelle Dwight) Sprague-Smith, Hilda's mother, was prominent in the New York art scene and had studied under the influential antiacademic painter Robert Henri. Moore mentions going to the Montross and Macbeth galleries and seeing the work of Arthur B. Davies (MM to her family, February 4, 1909, Rosenbach VI:15a:03); the Macbeth had held the famous exhibition of "The Eight," organized by Henri, the previous year. Moore later recalled that during this visit she "got a sense of what was going on in New York" (*MMR*, 255).

15. MM to her family, February 22, 1909 (Rosenbach VI:15a:03).

16. MM to her family, February 24, 1909 (Rosenbach VI:15a:03).

17. MM to her family, March 15, 1909, and March 16, 1909 (Rosenbach VI:15a:04).

encounter in great detail, including Miss Haviland herself, the appearance of her aunt and uncle's house, and that of Miss Haviland's room, where they eventually went. Of the photography studio, she writes: "they don't work for the public and they don't take personal photographs—they take people outdoors and children and Swedes etc. They took that photograph of Rodin that everybody likes so much." The Little Galleries of the Photo-Secession, or 291, as it was called, was actually a gallery rather than a studio, but a photography *gallery* was quite unheard of at this time; the Rodin she refers to is by Eduard Steichen, a leading member of the Photo-Secession. Miss Haviland took Moore to her room to see two numbers of *Camera Work*, a publication of the gallery. Moore reports:

> I was shown the books "peaches" surely. I was taken by storm for I thought they would be common garden photographs on dull paper— they are satisfactory in every particular—way beyond pictures (painted)— One was called the bubble, a girl crouching over a stream with her arm out, holding a big crystal ball—thin glass or soap bubble of some sort on it and there was another of a nymph under the shadow of a tree or bank; splashed all over with sun and spray so you could barely make her out—they were most refined in every particular— Mr. Haviland had articles in each of the books which I read. They are both [Haviland and Stieglitz] very spirited and young enthusiasm-ists—In very good taste—[18]

Miss Haviland then showed Moore a new dress, and they agreed to go sketching together sometime. She urged Moore to visit the studio on her next trip to New York. Moore wrote down the address in her notebook:

> Paul Haviland
> 291 Fifth Ave.
> Alfred Stieglitz [19]

When Moore finally did visit 291 six and a half years later, she still expected to find a studio where Stieglitz's photographs were exhibited.

She may have seen the Rodin photograph and possibly other photographs from *Camera Work* in the lecture room of Georgiana Goddard King, under whom Moore was studying prose writing when she met Miss

18. MM to her family, April 4, 1909 (Rosenbach VI:15a:05). When Moore memorialized Stieglitz nearly forty years later, she called him "an en'thus'iast" (*Prose*, 646).

19. MM, Notebook 1250/1 (Rosenbach VII:01:01).

Figure 2 Annie W. Brigman, *The Bubble*

1908 photograph published in *Camera Work*, XXV (January, 1909). The Royal Photographic Society, Bath.

Haviland. Moore appreciated Miss King enormously, especially her acute criticism, and called her "the best teacher I have had here (for my hobby)."[20] King, who would later become a prominent art historian, was hired to teach English during Moore's senior year and did not actually teach courses in art history until several years after Moore had graduated. King was, however, a friend of Gertrude Stein and had probably seen the Steins' collection of modern paintings in Paris as early as 1906, when Gertrude's brother Leo was just beginning to collect Picassos, Matisses, and Cézannes. It is probable that King had also visited 291 in New York by the time she began teaching at Bryn Mawr. She subscribed to *Camera Work* and regularly posted photographs of contemporary art from it and other periodicals in her lecture room.[21]

20. MM to her family, February 25, 1909 (Rosenbach VI:15a:03).

21. These could be the photographs Moore showed to some campus visitors along with a Rossetti and some Blakes (MM to her family, January 10, 1909, Rosenbach VI:15a:02). For my information about King, I am indebted to Stapleton, *The Poet's Advance*, 6; and Susanna Terrell Saunders, "Georgiana Goddard King (1871–1939): Educator and Pioneer in

But what must have influenced Moore's development as an artist and a modernist even more profoundly than anything she could have learned at this time about photography or French painting is the example set by King, and no doubt by other teachers at Bryn Mawr, of educating oneself. Years later she would write: "The net result of my experience at Bryn Mawr was to make me feel that intellectual wealth can't be superimposed, that it is to be appropriated; my experience there gave me security in my determination to have what I want."[22] One of the reasons for Bryn Mawr's founding in 1885 was to provide women with an opportunity for graduate study in all departments, since few graduate programs at that time accepted women. Although King, for example, received a master's degree from Bryn Mawr in philosophy and political science and did some graduate work in English, most of her education, and all of her training in art history, she earned by traveling and especially by reading widely. Like King, Moore learned that for a woman to hold her own intellectually, she must take wholehearted responsibility for educating herself. In 1915 Moore wrote to her brother, who was then doing graduate work in theology at Princeton, about their mother's response to H.D.'s suggestion that Marianne come live in London: "*Your letter writings* are as nothing to what ensued. I told her you were to be 'educated' and I might get in a little grown up wigwagging on the side."[23] Such "wigwagging," which was to continue for the rest of her life, included voracious reading and note-taking in all the respectable fields of art and science as well as sports and fashion, and it included visiting New York in 1915 and eventually moving to Greenwich Village in 1918.

Moore's prediction of what she would do after graduation proved to be accurate. After studying business for a year in Carlisle, she taught at the Carlisle Indian School for four years to earn money, but she continued to paint—her animal drawings earned her $2.50 at the fair in 1915[24]—and most importantly to write. From 1909 to 1915 Moore served her apprenticeship. Even before she graduated, Moore had sent home poems for Mary Norcross to type and submit to the *Atlantic*. In addition to

Medieval Spanish Art," in *Women as Interpreters of the Visual Arts, 1820–1979,* ed. Claire Richter Sherman (Westport, Conn., 1981), 209–38.

22. MM to Winifred Ellerman [Bryher], August 31, 1921, carbon (Rosenbach V:08:06).

23. MM to JWM, September 8, 1915 (Rosenbach VI:21:10).

24. MM to JWM, November 26, 1915 (Rosenbach VI:21:12).

educating herself on meter, music, and innovations in all the arts, she continued after graduation diligently to write poems, to revise, and to send them out; the Rosenbach files include typescripts of many unpublished poems of this period.

At Bryn Mawr and in the years following her graduation, Moore developed a habit of saving newspaper and magazine articles about art and also pictures of the works themselves. At first she fastidiously pieced these clippings together and pasted them into a scrapbook (along with clippings about theater, the suffrage movement, science, and literature), but later on when keeping the scrapbook became too time-consuming, she would save the clippings inside the covers of books or sometimes in envelopes. The two scrapbooks she kept from 1909 to 1915 are especially important, however, for they represent the great extent to which Moore was educating herself about modernism even before she experienced it firsthand in New York in 1915. The clippings she saved at this time are mostly from the Boston *Evening Transcript, Literary Digest, Current Opinion*, and the *Spectator* and among other topics discuss artists such as Gordon Craig, George Bernard Shaw, Rodin, John Masefield, and Nijinsky and movements such as cubism, futurism, synchromism, fauvism, and imagism. Also included are several reviews of the controversial Armory Show in 1913, the first public exhibition in America of Cézanne, Picasso, Braque, Matisse, Duchamp, and Picabia. Although more than half of the works exhibited at the Armory Show were American, the impact and controversy of the European art is evident in the titles of the articles Moore saved: "The Greatest Exhibition of Insurgent Art Ever Held," "Post-Impressionism Arrived," "The Mob as Art Critic," "Bedlam in Art," and "Mr. Roosevelt on the Cubists." [25]

In 1915 Moore found the niche she had been seeking. After repeated rejections from the established magazines of the time, Moore discovered a number of little magazines that were open to experiments like her own. In March, 1915, she read copies of *Blast*, the *Egoist*, and the *Little Review* at the Library of Congress. In April, 1915, her first poems appeared in the *Egoist*; others appeared the following month in *Poetry* and by December in the recently formed *Others*. Since it was not possible for her to go to London, where the *Egoist* was published, Moore set out for the other

25. MM, Scrapbooks 1 and 2 (Rosenbach X:01 and X:02). Costello first called attention to the importance of these scrapbooks in *Imaginary Possessions*, 188, 270.

center of modernist activity, New York, where *Others* was published. In his letter of acceptance, Alfred Kreymborg, the enthusiastic young editor of *Others*, had said that he thought Moore's work "an amazing output and absolutely original if with his 'uneddicated consciousness' he might judge." After her many rejections, Moore would certainly have welcomed Kreymborg's response, and it was partly at his urging that she decided to "direct [her] claws to New York."[26] With map, a new coat, and an appointment with Kreymborg, she set out for New York with friends from Carlisle in December, 1915.

Her trip began with a visit to 291, the morning before she was to meet Kreymborg. The lengthy, detailed description of her visit to New York, which Moore wrote afterward in "installments" to her brother and entitled "Sojourn in the Whale," gives a vivid impression of Stieglitz and 291.

Wednesday morning I went to "*291*" to see, as I thought, some of Alfred Stieglitz's photography. He had an exhibition up of Bluemner, a modern architect. Mr. Stieglitz was exceedingly unemotional, and friendly and finally after telling me how he was hated, said I might come back and look at some of the things standing with their faces to the wall in a back room. I enjoyed them. He has a magnificent little thing of the sea in dark blue and some paintings of mountains by a man named Hartley, also some Picabias and Picassos and so on. He told me to come back and he would show me some other things.[27]

Two days later she does return. Though Stieglitz has nothing new to show her, he gives her *Camera Work* "to cut and look at." Moore compliments him on the photographs by him and by Steichen that Alfred Kreymborg has shown her in the meantime and then says to him:

I had not known there was anything in existence like Steichen's photograph of Gordon Craig—I said at all events I had never seen anything like it. "Well, there *is* nothing like it," he said. He told me to come in and take my coat off and look at the copies of Camera Work. He opened his knife and handed it to me, a plain wicked one with a ring in the end. . . . Presently Mr. Stieglitz came in with as nearly an approach to a self-conscious manner as it would be possible to at-

26. MM to JWM, October 3, 1915, and October 18, 1915 (Rosenbach VI:21:11).
27. MM to JWM, December 12, 1915 (Rosenbach VI:21:13).

Figure 3 Oscar Bluemner, *Old Canal Port*

1914. Oil on canvas. 30 ¼ x 40 ¼ in. (76.8 x 102.2 cm.). Collection of Whitney Museum of American Art. Gift of Gertrude Vanderbilt Whitney. 31.114.

tribute to him and said, "Miss Moore, Mr. Kerfoot" without however looking back at Mr. Kerfoot.[28]

After providing a lengthy description of J. B. Kerfoot, the literary critic for *Life* and a contributor to *Camera Work*, she reports their conversation, which she eventually directs to Kerfoot's recent review in *Life* of *Others*. She says to Kerfoot:

> "I thought it very generous of you to speak of Others for it is an experiment. You don't often speak of magazines do you?" "Never" he said "there has never been a notice of a magazine in Life before, so far as I know. I haven't taken any interest in poetry. This is the first time I have been able to see anything in it." I said "Of course some of it is trash, but what delights me is that the authors of it are willing to ad-

28. MM to JWM, December 19, 1915 (Rosenbach VI:21:13).

Figure 4 Alfred Stieglitz, *291—Picasso-Braque Exhibition*

1915. Platinum print. 7 ⅝ X 9 ⅝ in. (19.5 X 24.5 cm.). Alfred Stieglitz Collection. © 1994 Board of Trustees, National Gallery of Art, Washington.

mit that it might be trash." "Oh yes" he said "that must be understood. It's absolutely essential that they should admit it." . . . I asked him if he knew the Egoist, he said not . . . and we had a discussion of the word "haunting," both Mr. Stieglitz and Mr. Kerfoot downing me saying that a haunting quality was not the earmark of good art—but of bad art. I said I meant the sort of thing that annoyed you till you had to trace it to the source where you had first encountered it and he said "Oh that's a different thing—that's another sort of 'haunt.' " [29]

The detail of these descriptions, which continue for many pages, reveals the depths of Moore's enthusiasm, but none of her encounters provokes as much detail as does her meeting with Alfred Kreymborg. He gave her some back issues of *Others* and told her about various people in New York including Marcel Duchamp, Alanson Hartpence, and Stieglitz,

29. *Ibid.*

Figure 5 Eduard Steichen, *E. Gordon Craig*

1905 photograph published in *Camera Work* (April/July, 1913). The Royal Photographic Society, Bath.

who Kreymborg said had been very good to him and had given him things. He then took her by the studio of Adolph Wolf, a poet and sculptor, before taking her to his apartment for dinner and to meet his wife. Moore provides every detail of this occasion from the placement of books, typewriter, and pictures about the room, to the china, the menu, and every aspect of Gertrude Kreymborg's appearance—not to mention the conversation. They discussed Amy Lowell, Ezra Pound, the Aldingtons (Richard and H.D.), and after supper the Kreymborgs showed her "some photographs by Mr. Stieglitz and Steichen, of Shaw, Anatole France and others, that Mr. Stieglitz had given them and some of the most superb pictures of snow and engines and boats that I have ever seen." Then Alfred said to her: "Are you fond of Japanese prints? We have a hundred and one things to show you." Several days later the Kreymborgs invited her to a concert and to dinner again, at which they began calling each other by first names and Moore invited them to come see her in Carlisle.[30]

The one postcard that Moore wrote to her mother from New York (in contrast to the pages and pages she wrote later to her brother) is apparently designed to alleviate some of Mrs. Moore's anxieties and perhaps to prepare her for the invitation that Marianne, whose usual family nickname at this time was "Rat," would extend to the Kreymborgs.

> Alfred Kreymborg came to see me at 4 and took me to dinner with him and Mrs. K stopping at a sculptor's on the way. The K's are the loveliest people I ever have met—gentle and full of fun and peaceful—very poor with some beautiful things, no Bohemian fierceness—Neither of them "smokes"—and they showed me photographs and read a few poems. The photos are the most beautiful things Rat ever saw, by A. Stieglitz most of them. I've met him and he is everything ideal, sane and modest. Imperturbable and kind. He is a friend of the K's and gave them the photos and he is a friend of Kerfoot's. Kerfoot also likes the Kreymborgs and comes to the meetings.[31]

In addition to Moore's two visits to 291, she also visited the recently opened Modern Gallery "to see some Van Goghs and some of Mr. Stieglitz's magazines"[32] and twice visited the Daniel Gallery, where she saw an exhibition of paintings and embroideries by William and Marguerite Zorach. At the suggestion of Kreymborg, she introduced herself to Alanson Hartpence, an employee of the Daniel Gallery, who Moore

30. MM to JWM, December 12, 1915, and December 26, 1915 (Rosenbach VI:21:13).
31. MM to MWM, December 2, 1915 (Rosenbach VI:21:13). At this time the most frequently used family nicknames are from Kenneth Grahame's *The Wind in the Willows*: Marianne is "Rat," after the scribbler of verses.
32. MM to JWM, December 12, 1915 (Rosenbach VI:21:13).

Figure 6 Marguerite Zorach, *Waterfall*

1915. Embroidered tapestry. Original lost. Photograph from Peter A. Juley & Son Collection. National Museum of American Art. Smithsonian Institution.

says "knows the ground" and is "a positive dogmatist on art theory."[33] On her second visit there, Hartpence showed her among other things some "Man Rays, and Marins and things by a man named Manigault, and a Prendergast."[34]

Although Kreymborg encouraged Moore to introduce herself to Hartpence and to tell Stieglitz that she knew him, Moore's motivation for visiting these three galleries was quite her own. In fact, after her first visit to 291 when Kreymborg asked her if she had mentioned his name to Stieglitz, Moore said, "No, I didn't know he knew Mr. Kerfoot or you or any of the men who are interested in poetry."[35] The community Moore discovered in New York well suited her own diverse interests.

Eight months after Moore's trip to New York, she and her mother moved from Carlisle to live in a parsonage in Chatham, New Jersey, where Warner had been assigned as a Presbyterian minister. Moore was now only a short train ride from New York—she called this her "Middle Pullman Period"[36]—so that she could regularly visit the New York galleries and participate in the meetings with Kreymborg and other experimental writers and artists. The fragments of conversation she recorded in the notebooks she kept for this purpose and especially the poetry she wrote indicate that these must have been crucial years for her, although since she was living with her brother, there are few letters to document them. While Moore's notebooks from 1916 to 1919 provide an impressive scattering of names—William Carlos Williams, Lola Ridge, Skipwith Cannell, Mark Tobey, Alfred Kreymborg, Alanson Hartpence, Mary Carolyn Davies, the Zorachs, Wallace Stevens, Mina Loy, Stieglitz, and Maxwell Bodenheim—they do not chronicle the nature of the gatherings or even of the discussions, for these entries, many of them unrelated to art or writing and some of them incoherent and all but illegible, were never intended for other readers.[37] More readable accounts of the meetings are provided in Williams' *Autobiography* and Kreymborg's *Troubadour,* which capture the energy and enthusiasm of these years as well as providing vivid portraits of various personalities.

33. MM to JWM, December 19, 1915 (Rosenbach VI:21:13).

34. MM to JWM, December 26, 1915 (Rosenbach VI:21:13).

35. MM to JWM, December 12, 1915 (Rosenbach VI:21:13).

36. MM, Notebook 1250/23 (Rosenbach VII:10:06), 47.

37. See esp. MM, Notebook 1250/23 (Rosenbach VII:10:06); see also MM, Notebook 1250/24 (Rosenbach VII:10:07). Some of the names, notably that of Wallace Stevens, appear in comments made about the person.

Although Kreymborg had collaborated with his roommate Man Ray in publishing the *Glebe*, the first issue of which was titled *Des Imagistes: An Anthology*, the publication which was most successful in bringing the new poets together was *Others*. Once *Glebe* began publishing too many Europeans for Kreymborg's taste, he abandoned it, but in 1915 upon meeting a willing and wealthy sponsor, Walter Conrad Arensberg, he eagerly initiated *Others*, the manifesto of which after much cutting read simply, "The old expressions are with us always, and there are always others." To begin they could get poems from two friends of Arensberg's—his Harvard classmate Wallace Stevens and an Englishwoman named Mina Loy who knew the Italian futurist F. T. Marinetti and whose subject matter was shockingly (for those days) uninhibited—but they soon received manuscripts from such unknowns, or virtual unknowns, as T. S. Eliot ("Portrait of a Lady" via Pound), Carl Sandburg, William Carlos Williams, and Marianne Moore. These writers not only began to meet in print, but those who lived in or near New York and were so inclined began to meet in person.

One of the most popular meeting spots was the Kreymborgs' cottage in Grantwood, New Jersey, on the slopes of the Palisades, where poets and some painters would gather on Sunday afternoons. Williams writes of these gatherings: "We'd have arguments over cubism which would fill an afternoon. There was a comparable whipping up of interest in the structure of the poem. It seemed daring to omit capitals at the head of each poetic line. Rhyme went by the board. We were, in short, 'rebels,' and were so treated." [38] Besides the Kreymborgs, the regulars included Orrick and Peggy Johns, Williams, Horace Holley, Skipwith and Kitty Cannell, Arensberg, Man Ray, Mary Carolyn Davies, Robert Alden Sanborn, Alanson Hartpence; occasionally Marcel Duchamp (brought along by Arensberg), Mina Loy, and Malcolm Cowley also attended. "Now and then," according to Kreymborg, Mary Carolyn Davies would be accompanied by "an astonishing person with Titian hair, a brilliant complexion and a mellifluous flow of polysyllables which held every man in awe." [39]

Because of the Moores' practice of neither working nor socializing on

<hr />

38. Williams, *Autobiography*, 136.

39. Alfred Kreymborg, *Troubadour: An Autobiography* (New York, 1925), 238–39. MM, Notebook 1250/23 (Rosenbach VII:10:06), 44–45, confirms that Davies visited Moore, around November, 1916, to invite her to the meetings, though not necessarily to Grantwood.

Sunday, it is unlikely that Moore made appearances even "now and then" at Grantwood. But she did appear in Greenwich Village. Williams recalls that Grantwood spawned evening gatherings along Fourteenth Street, especially at the Kreymborgs' and at Lola Ridge's apartments. And in his autobiography the sculptor William Zorach recalls the poets' meeting at his and Marguerite's place.

> In those days we knew lots of young poets, and they spent much of their time with us. They would meet at our place to discuss poetry and what could be done with it. They would plan little magazines and publicity and places to get poetry published. We would all read poems and discuss them; Alfred Kreymborg, whose plays we produced, William Carlos Williams, Marianne Moore, Maxwell Bodenheim, Lola Ridge, Wallace Stevens, and Orrick Johns. . . .
>
> Marguerite and I both wrote poetry . . . and the modern young poets liked what I wrote. They liked the naiveté, the simplicity, and the direct expression of a mood. They published some of our poems in *Others*. . . . When I became more proficient and began editing and shifting words and working over my poems, the poets lost interest.[40]

Lists of names can, however, be misleading, for even though Loy and Stevens, for instance, often appear on the lists of Village regulars from these years, Moore did not meet Stevens until 1943 and by 1921 had met Loy only once, before a performance of Alfred Kreymborg's *Lima Beans*, in which Williams, Loy, and William Zorach played the leading roles.[41] But Moore's notebook indicates that during the winter and spring of 1916–17 Moore was coming into contact with a good many new faces and new ideas. While Moore's conversation, and no doubt her poetry as well, "held every man in awe," she must have been equally awed by what she saw and heard, for she wrote: "Many of these things which I like I don't thoroughly understand & that brings me to a standstill experimentally"; and on another occasion, "I came away so loaded down with ideas I could hardly keep the sidewalk."[42]

40. William Zorach, *Art Is My Life: The Autobiography of William Zorach* (Cleveland, 1967), 55.

41. Moore describes her first meeting with Stevens at Mount Holyoke College in *Prose*, 582, and her meeting with Loy in MM to Hilda Doolittle [H.D.], November 1, 1921 (Rosenbach V:23:32).

42. MM, December 19, 1916, and April 9, 1917, Notebook 1250/23 (Rosenbach VII:10:06), 50, 57.

Since some of the longest of the conversations she recorded are with Alfred Stieglitz and Alanson Hartpence, she surely attended exhibitions at 291 and the Daniel Gallery. Particularly notable are the several pages of minute handwriting that she devotes to Stieglitz's story of the failure of his first marriage and his disgruntled remarks about the Independents Show. This conversation, which Moore dates May 12, 1917, took place at 291 two days before it closed forever; the final exhibit was of paintings by Georgia O'Keeffe, who would not move to New York until the following year. After quoting Stieglitz, Moore adds: "Hartley came in and he also dragged in mountains. Said these things were so common (of Miss O'Keeffe's)—he wanted to feel the way he felt when he was on a mountain." To this Moore adds the remark (probably her own), "I don't see the commonness." [43]

Almost as pertinent as determining with whom Moore did associate in New York is determining with whom she did not associate, though the latter task has obvious difficulties. There is no evidence that I know of that Moore ever set foot in the West 67th Street apartment of Walter and Louise Arensberg, which not only housed a major collection of works by such moderns as Duchamp and Picabia (now at the Philadelphia Museum of Art) but also served as a kind of salon for artists and writers. [44] Although Arensberg did help finance *Others*, he withdrew from active involvement in it after the first issue. Thus, the *Others* group, with which Moore did associate, was not identical to the Arensberg circle despite their initial ties. Gatherings at the Arensbergs' apartment differed in style from their counterparts in the Village, for the Arensbergs served lavish amounts of food and drink and were hosts to several French artists such as Duchamp and Picabia (who would often speak in their native tongue) as well as to American artists such as Man Ray, Charles Demuth, Arthur Dove, Marsden Hartley, Morton Schamberg, Joseph Stella, Stuart Davis, Charles Sheeler, and occasionally Stieglitz. In addition to the poets who sometimes came there—Loy, Williams, Stevens, Kreymborg, Amy Lowell—were such celebrities as Isadora Duncan, the boxer Arthur Cravan, and the Baroness Elsa von Freytag Loringhoven. But whereas Stieglitz was the acknowledged

43. MM, May 12, 1917, Notebook 1250/23 (Rosenbach VII:10:06), 58–60. The parentheses indicate Moore's insert.

44. For more information about the Arensberg circle, see Abraham A. Davidson, *Early American Modernist Painting, 1910–1935* (New York, 1981), 74–120. The distinctions he draws between the Arensberg circle and the Stieglitz group are especially helpful.

high priest of 291, the dominating personality of the Arensberg circle was not Arensberg himself but Marcel Duchamp, whose *Nude Descending a Staircase* had in 1913 attracted almost as much controversy as the rest of the Armory Show put together.

While there seems to have been no competition between the Stieglitz and Arensberg groups (for instance, Stieglitz described Kreymborg to Moore as "one of my children,"[45] yet Kreymborg collaborated with Arensberg in publishing *Others*), the groups had distinct personalities. In general, the Arensberg circle was more iconoclastic and cerebral than the Stieglitz group, whose aesthetic principles could assume a fervent moral tone, and such artists as Dove, Hartley, and Demuth who included themselves in both groups had correspondingly diverse, but not necessarily conflicting, values. Duchamp's readymades epitomize in some ways what the Arensberg circle stood for. Having been more or less rejected by the cubist "establishment" in Paris, Duchamp gave up painting in 1913 and in 1915 moved to America, where his *Nude Descending a Staircase* had earned him an attractive notoriety and where he had an immediate friend and patron in Arensberg. Not disappointing those who expected outrageousness, he submitted for display in the Independents Show of 1917 a urinal, which he entitled *Fountain* and signed "R. Mutt." Although the urinal was banned from the show, the controversy it spurred was to make *Fountain* the most famous of Duchamp's readymades—which were commercially manufactured objects that he selected, displayed, and titled. Another well-known readymade is the snow shovel he hung from the ceiling of his studio and entitled *In Advance of the Broken Arm*. Among the Americans who employed the readymade concept were Morton Schamberg, who attached a piece of plumbing to a wooden base and called it *God*, and Man Ray, whose assisted readymades, or "objects," include *Gift*, a flat iron with tacks projecting from its surface. Duchamp and certain members of the Arensberg circle—the precursors by fifty years of conceptual art—were to form the nucleus of New York dadaism.

Regardless of whether or not Marianne Moore actually met Duchamp at this time or visited the Arensbergs' apartment, she seems not to have been affected by Duchamp and his iconoclastic notions of art, as Williams admittedly was. After recording some impressions of Arensberg and other members of this circle in his prologue to *Kora in Hell* (1920), Williams specifically juxtaposes Moore as "a North" "in contradistinction to their

45. MM to JWM, December 19, 1915 (Rosenbach VI:21:13).

South."[46] Moore had friends among the Arensberg circle, notably Williams and Kreymborg, and admired certain of their works, such as Man Ray's, but her aesthetic principles have closer affinities with those generally upheld at 291.[47]

As Marianne Moore was to discover early in her career and to recall later, 291 was the "acropolis" of American modernism (*Prose*, 646)—not only in its mythic stature but also in its sense of spiritual purpose. Having studied photography in Europe and gained some recognition there as an art photographer, Stieglitz's first crusade upon returning to America in the 1890s was to raise the status of photography from a hobby to a fine art. In 1902 he broke away from the New York Camera Club, of which he had been the leading member, and gave the name "Photo-Secession" to the progressive "pictorial" photographers he fostered. In 1903 he began publishing *Camera Work*, devoted at this time to publishing high-quality reproductions of pictorial photographs and articles about photography, and in 1905 founded the Little Galleries of the Photo-Secession at 291 Fifth Avenue. Although the emphasis of both *Camera Work* and 291, as the gallery became known, soon shifted away from photography exclusively, this mission remained important to Stieglitz even after *Camera Work* had ceased publication and 291 had closed. In 1922 he published a special issue of *MSS.*, a short-lived successor to *Camera Work*, in which he asked a wide variety of not-necessarily-sympathetic contributors to respond to the question, "Can a photograph have the significance of art?"

But the mission that would make 291 an "acropolis" was educating Americans about modern art. (In fact, 291 was never a commercial gallery; Stieglitz neither advertised nor accepted commissions.) In 291's third season, Stieglitz exhibited drawings and paintings for the first time. Over the next few years 291 would show more and more nonphotographic exhibits. *Camera Work* diversified too, publishing Gertrude Stein, Mina Loy, and

46. Williams, *Selected Essays*, 5–7.

47. Though Williams did associate with the Stieglitz group later, the common assumption that he was a regular at 291 is at best an exaggeration. Williams and Moore did not meet personally until shortly after 291 closed in 1917, and scholars have found no evidence that he ever visited 291. For discussion of Williams' and Stieglitz's relationship, see Dijkstra, *The Hieroglyphics of a New Speech*, esp. 82–88, 108; Dijkstra's Introduction to *A Recognizable Image: William Carlos Williams on Art and Artists*, ed. Bram Dijkstra (New York, 1978), 30, 33–36; and William Marling, *William Carlos Williams and the Painters, 1909–1923* (Athens, Ohio, 1982), 2–6. Moore's recollection of a luncheon with Duchamp and Stevens decades later does not indicate whether she already knew Duchamp personally (*Prose*, 582).

other experimental writers. Until the Armory Show in 1913, Stieglitz's gallery was virtually the only place in America where one could see the works of Cézanne, Matisse, Picasso, and other avant-garde Europeans. After the Armory Show had given these artists wide exposure, Stieglitz devoted his efforts primarily to supporting American painters such as Max Weber, John Marin, Arthur Dove, Marsden Hartley, Georgia O'Keeffe, and eventually the photographer Paul Strand. Among these and other 291 regulars there was much talk of the "spirit" of 291. Hartley called 291 "a kind of spiritual family—working together with a common bond." [48] Above all else this bond consisted of an openness to new forms of expression and a fervent individualism. Stieglitz differed from most European modernists, for example, in his distrust of movements and manifestos, which in his mind opposed individualism. In 1917, partly because of the war, 291 closed and *Camera Work* ceased publication. In subsequent decades Stieglitz continued his support of American artists, primarily "the seven"—Marin, Hartley, Dove, O'Keeffe, Stieglitz, Strand, and the variable "X"—in a series of galleries—the Anderson Galleries, the Intimate Gallery, and An American Place.

Stieglitz's third crusade, for "straight photography," is indebted to the other two and would have far-reaching effects in American art. In order to demonstrate the artistic potential of photography, Stieglitz had originally advocated that pictorial photographers manipulate their negatives and prints freely in order to achieve a painterly effect, one that would resemble symbolist and pre-Raphaelite painting. They would, for example, scratch their negatives or smear them with gum bichromate. But Stieglitz's exposure to cubism and other developments in European painting made the misty landscapes and ethereal maidens of the pictorialists seem old-fashioned; thus, in 1910 he began his crusade for "straight," or "pure," photography. As a technique, straight photography meant sharp focus and little if any manipulation of the negative (Stieglitz had practiced this himself even during his pictorialist phase), but as an aesthetic, it defined a new way of seeing that had ethical as well as aesthetic implications. According to Sarah Greenough, "In objective or pure photography, the photographer expressed his creativity not through manipulation or expressive printing techniques, as in pictorial photography, but through his seeing, his distinctive and decisive vision of the world." [49]

48. Marsden Hartley to Alfred Stieglitz, February [?], 1913 (Beinecke).
49. Sarah Greenough, "Alfred Stieglitz and 'The Idea Photography,'" in *Alfred Stieglitz:*

The development of the Stieglitz ideology was, however, by no means the work of Stieglitz alone. Rather it was the accomplishment of a variety of talents. *Camera Work* and 291 provided an outlet and a context for the more formal ideas. And if the point is to be made that the visual arts were important to poetry, it must be acknowledged that writing was a major activity of the Stieglitz circle. Few of the artists supported by 291 found only one medium to be adequate. In the early years the Mexican caricaturist Marius de Zayas was one of the more important theorists of the group, as was later Paul Strand. Max Weber and Marsden Hartley each published several volumes of poetry as well as numerous essays. Arthur Dove also wrote poetry, as did Charles Demuth, and Stieglitz himself. John Marin kept poetrylike notebooks. Many wrote elegant, even poetic, letters to one another.

Marianne Moore was never part of Stieglitz's inner circle, which in the twenties came to include writers such as Sherwood Anderson, Waldo Frank, and Paul Rosenfeld (Moore's friend and colleague at the *Dial*) as well as "the seven" painters and photographers he sponsored. But beginning with her 1915 visit to 291, Moore regularly visited Stieglitz's galleries. As editor of the *Dial*, Moore devoted the second of her "Comment" columns to the 1925 "Seven Americans" exhibit at the Anderson Galleries, Stieglitz's first major exhibition since the closing of 291, and in her official capacity attended numerous exhibitions and met with artists. A 1938 letter from Stieglitz to "My dear Marianne Moore" thanks her for "the evening you gave us" (O'Keeffe and himself), indicating that Moore and Stieglitz socialized well beyond their early acquaintanceship. The letter urges Moore to see O'Keeffe's current show and accompanies a book of Dorothy Norman's poems. Moore answered Stieglitz's letter and thanked him for the book. The previous year Moore had asked Norman, Stieglitz's close companion and business manager, about publishing a book of Bryher's. Upon Stieglitz's death, Norman asked Moore to contribute to a memorial portfolio. Moore's short but laudatory contribution (*Prose*, 646) stands in marked contrast to Williams', which was so insulting that Norman omitted it.[50]

Photographs & Writings, by Sarah Greenough and Juan Hamilton (Washington, D.C., and New York, 1983), 21.

50. Alfred Stieglitz to MM, January 14, 1938 (Rosenbach V:64:04); MM to Alfred Stieglitz, January 28, 1938 (Beinecke); and MM to Winifred Ellerman [Bryher], July 4, 1937 (Rosenbach V:08:06). Dijkstra provides the history of Williams' essay "What of Al-

A 1937 letter reports that Stieglitz telephoned Moore regarding Marsden Hartley, whom Stieglitz had advised to seek Moore's advice about publishing some poems.[51] Hartley subsequently paid a long visit to Moore's apartment, apparently for the first time, and though Moore expresses annoyance at his insensitivity to her mother's illness, she forgives him this "once" and expresses willingness to help him. Moore and Hartley had known each other for at least twenty years (the letter calls him Marsden), and they admired each other's work. Moore owned four of Hartley's books of poems, two of them inscribed from him. Hartley wrote a poem titled "Marianne Moore" that praises her "genteel cool perspicacity."[52] In the summer of 1937 he wrote to his and Moore's mutual friend, Isabel Lachaise, in whose vacation home he was staying, to ask her to bring along Marianne Moore's poems (the only book mentioned), as he "would so like to read them here where there is quiet and space in the mind."[53] Moore did help Hartley by sending off his poems to various publishers and after his death in 1943 by encouraging the publication of his *Selected Poems*. The publisher sent her an advance copy in appreciation for her share in the book's publication (there seems to have been talk at one time of her writing an introduction), and she responded characteristically by complimenting the printing, "the blacks and whites" that are "strong as Marsden Hartley's work has always seemed."[54]

In addition to Hartley, Rosenfeld, and Stieglitz, Moore knew other members of this circle and of course was well acquainted with their work. To name a few other documented examples, her friend Bertram Hartman (also an artist) took her to visit Paul Strand's studio in 1921, where she saw Strand's "photographs—very fine things of people ships rocks, hands feet, porcelain skyscrapers etc." In 1923 Williams took Moore with him to visit the painter Charles Demuth (often Stieglitz's "seventh" during the twenties) at a sanatorium in Morristown, Pennsylvania, where he was being treated for diabetes.[55] Moore's letters and notebooks indicate sev-

---

fred Stieglitz?" in his Introduction to *A Recognizable Image*, 33–36, and publishes it for the first time in the same volume (177–79).

51. MM to JWM, January 30, 1937 (Rosenbach VI:34:15). Gail R. Scott points out that Hartley devoted as much time to his writing as to his painting in her Preface to *The Collected Poems of Marsden Hartley*, ed. Gail R. Scott (Santa Rosa, 1987), 21.

52. Hartley, *Collected Poems*, 225.

53. Marsden Hartley to Isabel Lachaise, June 14, 1937 (Beinecke).

54. MM to B. W. Huebsch, October 28, 1945 (Rosenbach V:67:16).

55. MM to JWM, September 10, 1921 (Rosenbach VI:24:10); MM to JWM, April 8,

eral occasions when she met Georgia O'Keeffe, whom Moore thought "very handsome."[56] But Stieglitz's influence extended far beyond his inner circle. He assisted many artists not necessarily identified with him, such as Gaston Lachaise, the French-American sculptor whom Moore came to know in the early twenties, and William and Marguerite Zorach, whom she first knew through *Others.* The Lachaises and Zorachs were close to one another and also to the Strands and to Hartley—all of their names appear in Moore's notebooks of the late teens and twenties.

In early 1925 both Marguerite Zorach and Gaston Lachaise made portraits of Moore. *Observations* had just appeared in late 1924 followed by the announcement of Moore's winning the *Dial* award in January; she would assume the duties of acting editor of the *Dial* the following June. Moore's appointment book shows three meetings with Marguerite Zorach in February, 1925, and another notebook records conversations that took place at these sittings, at which Gaston and Isabel Lachaise, William Zorach, and the Zorachs' son Tessim were sometimes present.[57] Though Moore is not on a first-name basis with the Zorachs, she and Marguerite, born less than two months apart, have a remarkable empathy for one another. Both Zorachs had studied painting in Paris, where they witnessed the advent of fauvism and cubism firsthand. They were among the earliest members of the New York avant-garde to achieve recognition, and both had works in the Armory Show. Moore admired the Zorachs' paintings and embroideries she saw in 1915: "the pictures gave me a chill they were so good. They have one waterfall and arrangement in stripes, that is as rhythmical as a zebra and as realistic as De Maupassant."[58] As subsequent chapters will show, their work probably inspired two of her poems, "In the Days of Prismatic Color" and "New York," the only poems of which I am aware that respond to the work of visual artists in her circle. Marguerite Zorach made at least three portraits of Moore, two pencil sketches (one of which appeared in the *Dial*) and a

<hr />

1923 (Rosenbach VI:26:05). Demuth's sanatorium could very well be the "contagious hospital" in Williams' poem "Spring and All," written around this time.

56. MM, December 8, 1924, Notebook 1250/25 (Rosenbach VII:11:01), 83; see also MM to JWM, December 7, 1923 (Rosenbach VI:26:13).

57. MM, Daily Diary 1925 (Rosenbach VIII:01:07); MM, February, 1925, Notebook 1250/25 (Rosenbach VII:11:01), 85–90.

58. MM to JWM, December 19, 1915 (Rosenbach VI:21:13).

Figure 7 Marguerite Zorach, *Marianne Moore and Her Mother*
1925 [dated 1919]. Oil on canvas. 40 ¼ x 30 in. (102.2 x 76.2 cm.). NPG. 87. 217. National Portrait Gallery. Smithsonian Institution.

double portrait in oil of Moore and her mother.[59] The oil shows a stalwart, confident Marianne with bright orange-red hair and a pensive, guarded mother in muted tones just behind her. It captures with remarkable perception the relationship between mother and daughter, for the juxtaposition of the two faces and their strong resemblance suggests, besides a portrait of mother and daughter, a double portrait of Marianne. The portrait conveys Marianne's paradoxical dependence upon and resistance to

59. Zorach's drawing appears within Williams, "Marianne Moore," *Dial*, LXXVIII (1925), after p. 396. Tessim Zorach told me of another pencil sketch, now in the collection of the Brooklyn Museum.

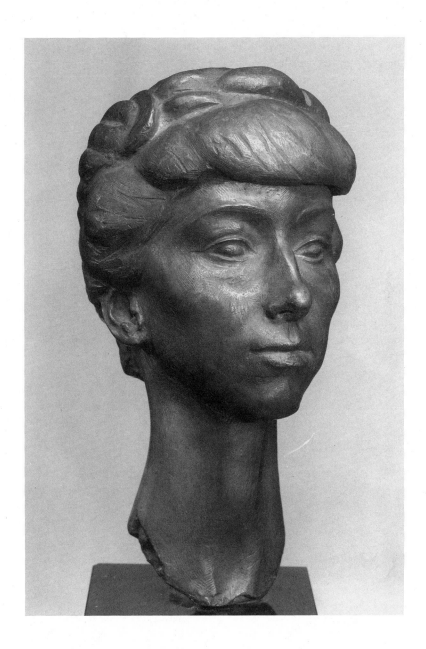

Figure 8 Gaston Lachaise, *Marianne Moore*

1925, cast in bronze 1946. 13⁷⁄₈ in. x 9¹⁄₂ in. (35.2 x 17.8 x 24.1 cm.). All rights reserved, The Metropolitan Museum of Art. Gift of Lincoln Kirstein. 1959. (59.156).

her mother's presence and the complexity of that presence as both censor and muse to her daughter's art.[60]

It was apparently Lachaise's wife Isabel who engaged Moore to sit for her husband; Gaston Lachaise came in during Moore's first sitting at the Zorachs' and Mme. Lachaise told him Moore had agreed to sit for him beginning the following Friday. These sittings overlap with the Zorach ones and continue several times a week through April until just before Moore begins work at the *Dial*. Lachaise's most famous works are large-scale nude statues of his wife. When Moore inquires what she should wear for her sitting, Lachaise says: "Nothing"; Mr. Zorach interjects: "Nothing. I guess he'd like you not to wear anything at all"; and Lachaise: "Nothing special—what you like."[61] Lachaise also made numerous portrait busts and had already done those of several *Dial* personalities, including Scofield Thayer and E. E. Cummings. Moore's notebook reveals a particular fascination with Isabel Lachaise, both her observations about people and theirs about her. After her husband's death, Isabel Lachaise had the unfinished plaster mold cast in bronze and gave the bust to Moore. Moore was overwhelmed at this generous gift and wrote in her letter of thanks: "How well I remember [Lachaise's] saying, 'I believe in a large amount of work!' I tell this to myself over and over and am helped not to tire."[62]

The years of Moore's absorption into New York's avant-garde (also the years of America's involvement in World War I) were anxious ones in the Moore household. After being in Chatham less than a year, Warner en-

60. For further information about Marguerite Zorach, see Roberta K. Tarbell, *Marguerite Zorach: The Early Years, 1908–1920* (Washington, D.C., 1973). The oil portrait of Moore and her mother is dated 1919, but because of a letter (MWM to JWM, November 19, 1919, Rosenbach VI:23:12) saying that only one person (not Zorach) had completed a portrait of Moore at that time and because the Zorachs left New York in late 1919 for more than a year, the painting is likely misdated. The weekly appointments with Mrs. Zorach in Moore's 1925 diary surely suggest a sitting, but the conversation Moore records at the first of these meetings does not indicate that Mrs. Moore was present. Patricia Willis' notes at the Rosenbach helped date the painting.

61. MM, February 9, 1925, Notebook 1250/25 (Rosenbach VII:11:01), 85.

62. MM to Isabel Lachaise, April 13, 1946, quoted in Carolyn Kinder Carr and Margaret C. S. Christman, *Gaston Lachaise: Portrait Sculpture* (Washington, D.C., 1985), 84. In *"The Dial:* A Retrospect," Moore devotes nearly a whole paragraph to Lachaise, in which she also recalls this statement (*Prose,* 362). For further discussion of Moore and Lachaise's relationship, see Gerald Nordland, *Gaston Lachaise: The Man and His Work* (New York, 1974), 89–93; and Carr and Christman, *Gaston Lachaise,* 84.

listed for active duty in the navy. A few months later, in November, 1917, he surprised his mother and sister by announcing his engagement to Constance Eustis. For a mother accustomed to giving advice on every particular of her children's lives, this was indeed a shock. The old bonds of family unity seemed threatened irrevocably. Warner's letters over the following months and years reveal his attempts both to establish his independence—at first he stopped using family nicknames—and also to reestablish family ties under new conditions. His resignation from his pastorate and his marriage in 1918 made it necessary for his mother and sister to find new living quarters. Marianne, too, was struggling with independence. In a rare moment, she confided to her notebook in the summer of 1918: "Well, there are reasons why it is better to live away from home—You want to go somewhere—come in at an unusual hour, or you don't want to eat, you want to be alone—my mother comes in 16 times a day bringing me apples & things to eat, and if you can't eat, she doesn't understand, the whole house is upset. Send for the doctor, insist on an exam. Oh my—Well—I can't have it." [63] Mary Warner Moore sincerely wanted what was best for her children and was still considering in the fall of 1920 allowing Marianne to live alone. (They would live together until Mrs. Moore's death, when Marianne was almost sixty.) But she continually spoke of her daughter's frailty and saw herself as protecting "Mr. Rat" from the "big cats." [64] The move to Greenwich Village itself required sacrifice on Mrs. Moore's part, separating her from friends in Carlisle and putting her in proximity to a life-style she found loathsome. Several months after their move Moore recorded her mother's comments: "I had no more idea of an artist or of these people you go among from time to time than I have now of people in an almshouse or an insane asylum gathered together into a group and treated kindly—not half so good an idea." [65] And Moore may truly have needed the protection, at least of her time, for the Moores often had visitors from breakfast until bedtime. While Mrs. Moore's letters of 1919 attribute her daughter's aloofness to the hurt of Warner's betrayal (as she perceived it), it may also be true that Moore was simply rechanneling her creative energies—her "play"—into her art, for her letters to

63. MM, Summer, 1918, Notebook 1250/23 (Rosenbach VII:10:06), 67.

64. Like Moore's other family personae, Rat is male. Why? Perhaps as a means of allying herself with Warner; in the early letters they are both "uncles" to their mother, Baby Fawn. Later Marianne became "Uncle Rat" to Warner's children.

65. MM, June, 1919, Notebook 1250/24 (Rosenbach VII:10:07), 34.

Warner at this time are relatively infrequent, brief, and newsy, in marked contrast to her earlier letters and the playfulness of her poems of the period. Her mother reported one night that Marianne was at an *Others* party "where many read poems and criticize one another. . . . It seems to be the only thing in life nowadays that occasions real spontaneity in her." [66]

Moore's long preoccupation with freedom and restraint takes on new meaning in light of these family relationships. (In 1923, for example, she would study freedom within the confines of "Marriage," in 1940 within the confines of mortality in "What Are Years.") In March, 1919, she published a poem about a carrot. Since she was a redhead and was at the time emerging as a "radical" artist, "Radical" could easily be read as a self-portrait. The title is a pun; literally "root," "Radical" may also be read as first line, contrasting with "conserving."

RADICAL

Tapering
to a point, conserving everything,
   this carrot is predestined to be thick.
     The world is
     but a circumstance, a mis-
        erable corn-patch for its feet. With ambition, imagination,
                                  outgrowth,
nutriment,
with everything crammed belligerent-
   ly inside itself, its fibres breed mon-
     opoly—
     a tail-like, wedge-shaped engine with the
       secret of expansion, fused with intensive heat to color of the
                             set-
ting sun and
stiff. For the man in the straw hat, standing still and turning to look back at it,
     as much as
     to say my happiest moment has
       been funereal in comparison with this, the conditions of life
                             pre-

66. MWM to JWM, April 23, 1919 (Rosenbach VI:23:05).

determined
slavery to be easy and freedom hard. For
   it? Dismiss
agrarian lore; it tells him this:
      that which it is impossible to force, it is impossible
         to hinder. (*Obs*, 48)

Not even the "miserable corn-patch," however, may be read as self-pity-
ing. Moore must have valued spontaneity and individuality at least in part
because they were so difficult for her.

Despite the frequent discussion of religion in both her mother's and
brother's letters, Moore's letters, even as an adolescent, virtually never
mention such matters. When once during the traumatic year following
Warner's marriage, she does say "out of a clear sky" that she thinks Warner's
problem is a "*lack of faith*," her mother is stunned: "Marianne's saying
this, was a wave passing over my soul, after it had banged against me.
For Marianne herself has never professed to have faith;—has almost *said*
her soul was dim with darkness and utter lack of faith. Life has come to
her in great surging waves this past year however; I know that; but she has
made no motion; no show of that fact; so I have not said I knew."[67] Moore's
reticence on the subject allowed Mrs. Moore to view her daughter as a
missionary, and even martyr, among the bohemians: "The Dial has a heinous
way of having its contributors entertained socially one at a time after each
contribution, and on Monday Ratty was laid on this altar, whence for an
hour her precious essence went up in smoke to make fragrant the Bene-
dictine apartment of Mr. Thayer. . . . Rat's influence for good is tremen-
dous; for he does not put forth his notions ever. Puritanic they would be
called. But he makes all 'that set' aware of them; and he never having mentioned them, they of course cannot refute them." On another occasion:
"Rat writes all the time when at home; *diligent in business he surely is*,
and I feel sure he will be blessed of God. For the work is as wearisome to
him as mine has ever been to me." And again: "Rat has been sought after;
much pursued by class mates and the literary group here . . . and the
true reason is, *his true religion and its visible outcome*. Little do his adher-
ents and suppliants think this preposterous thing; they would refuse to believe it but *that is* the attraction. Rat himself admits it." Mrs. Moore would
surely have smiled at Williams' remembering Moore years later as "our

67. *Ibid.*

43

saint."[68] (Nor can she be blamed for reading into her daughter's work her own convictions; recent critics disagree to the extent that some regard Moore's beliefs as Victorian pieties and others as postmodern deconstructionism.)

As one can imagine, there was considerable tension between Mrs. Moore and many of her daughter's associates. Some, such as H.D., Bryher, Scofield Thayer, and Monroe Wheeler, sought ways to appease the gatekeeper even while, in H.D.'s and Bryher's case, trying futilely to lure Moore away from home.[69] Others, such as Robert McAlmon and Williams, were less diplomatic. Moore's notebook records a conversation between Williams, Anthony Wrynn, her mother, and herself on Sunday, June 2, 1923, which concludes: "[MM] Perhaps I didn't tell you (that we don't accept invitations for Sunday or ask our friends to come Sunday). [WCW] Yes you did tell me but what could I do? May I come again? [MM] Of course not for a long time."[70] Years later Williams recalled: "[Moore's] loyalty to the [*Others*] group and to her mother was unflagging. It irritated us somewhat, the mother thing, but there was nothing to do about it."[71]

Before the publication of *The Waste Land* in 1922, Moore was arguably the most esteemed of the modernist poets. Her early publishers, Richard Aldington in London and Alfred Kreymborg in New York, were of course among the first to admire her. When Moore's poems first appeared in the *Egoist*, H.D. wrote to Moore to introduce herself (they had been classmates at Bryn Mawr but knew each other only by sight) and to express her husband's admiration: "R[ichard Aldington] has spoken often of your work:—We both think you have achieved a remarkable technical ability! R. says it is quite the finest that he has seen from America!" Two years later H.D. calls Moore's work "more rare, more fine than any modern I know."

68. MWM to JWM, February 1, 1921 (Rosenbach VI:24:03), March 17, 1921 (Rosenbach VI:24:04), April 22, 1921 (Rosenbach VI:24:05); Williams, *Autobiography*, 146.

69. Mrs. Moore's objections to bohemian life-styles did not extend to same-sex couples. For instance, despite her annoyance at Glenway Wescott, she tolerated him because he was Monroe Wheeler's "beloved" (MWM to JWM, January 10, 1924, Rosenbach VI:27:01). What she found most offensive was vulgarity—making public what, for her, ought to be private.

70. MM, June 2, 1923, Notebook 1250/25 (Rosenbach VII:11:01), 61.

71. William Carlos Williams, *I Wanted to Write a Poem: The Autobiography of the Works of a Poet*, ed. Edith Heal (New York, 1958), 20.

At a party in 1919 a few months after Pound had written Moore for the first time, Kreymborg introduced Moore to Harriet Monroe as "the 'infant terrible' of all New York"; Monroe replied, "Yes, and of all poets; the one whom Ezra Pound is adjuring us all to imitate—a thing utterly impossible to do." Robert McAlmon also reports on Moore's reputation across the Atlantic: "Some things you ought to know: That T. S. Eliot has asked many questions about you and thinks you the person who has most definitely established an individual, unique, beautiful and musical rhythm, with intellectual content. He rates you more highly than anybody he has spoken of and we have talked of about everybody. . . . Wyndham Lewis likes your things very much too."[72]

Still, Moore received her most consistent and ardent admiration from her own side of the Atlantic. In his autobiography Williams describes Moore in the early twenties as "a rafter holding up the superstructure of our uncompleted building . . . one of the main supports of the new order," and implies that it is this new order, this uncompleted building that *The Waste Land*, "the great catastrophe," blasted.[73] Though Eliot and Moore admired each other and never acknowledged such a rivalry, Williams' loyalty to Moore over the years is part of his resistance to the academic, "foreign" modernism of Eliot and Pound. He repeatedly praises her in superlatives, as he does in 1932: "there is no work in verse being done in any language which I can read which I find more to my liking and which I believe to be so thoroughly excellent."[74]

Another significant admirer at this time was Scofield Thayer. According to Kreymborg, Moore became "the first of 'the old guard' to be accepted by the new magazine" after Thayer heard her read "England" and "induced her to part with it."[75] Because of Thayer's unabated admiration for Moore and her work, her relationship with the *Dial* was to become increasingly significant during the twenties.[76] From the 1920 publication of "England" and "Picking and Choosing" until 1924, the *Dial* published

72. Hilda Doolittle [H.D.] to MM, September 7, 1915, and August 29, 1917 (Rosenbach V:23:32); MM to JWM, February 7, 1919 (Rosenbach VI:23:03); Robert McAlmon to MM, April 12, 1921 (Rosenbach V:40:06).

73. Williams, *Autobiography*, 146.

74. William Carlos Williams to MM, June 2, 1932, in *The Selected Letters of William Carlos Williams*, ed. John C. Thirlwall (New York, 1957), 122.

75. Kreymborg, *Troubadour*, 333.

76. See Nicholas Joost, *Scofield Thayer and "The Dial": An Illustrated History* (Carbondale, Ill., 1964), 83–102.

fourteen of Moore's poems, and from 1921 to 1926 it published nineteen signed book reviews as well as a great many unsigned "Briefer Mention" reviews by her. In 1924 Thayer decided with Sibley Watson, officially the "president" of the *Dial* but actually more of a coeditor, to give the prestigious *Dial* award to Marianne Moore. The announcement of the award appeared in the January, 1925, issue and in each of the successive issues for February, March, and April appeared a "Comment" devoted to Moore's poetry. These unsigned editorial tributes to Moore's poetry (written by Thayer) were followed in June of the same year by a tribute to Moore's discernment—an announcement that Moore would assume the duties of acting editor. A year later came the announcement of Thayer's official resignation and of Moore's assumption of the duties of editor—a position to which she would devote virtually all of her creative energies until the *Dial* ceased publication in June, 1929.

After the first World War, dissent arose among the modernists. As I will discuss in Chapter 5, the differences between the Stieglitz group and Arensberg circle (evolving now into dadaism) no longer remained friendly, and there was resentment between those artists who chose to live abroad and those who stayed home. Many expressed disgust with the art world generally. A letter from Bertram Hartman to Moore about "that celebrated chess player Marcel Duchamp" is typical: "There's too much of the Oh so precious *ART* with psychological apologia & aesthetics talked around in New York. BULL BULL."[77] Unlike in the previous decade, rivalry between the magazines was often vicious. Moore worked some at the *Broom* in early 1923 and socialized with its staff, but when Matthew Josephson approached her about editing it, they had what Moore called "a real carnage of skin & fur for 2 hours or more."[78] The fight, witnessed by Mrs. Moore, began with an argument over a recent story in *Secession*; when Josephson broached the subject of Moore's working for the *Broom* by asking her if she should hate to have it given up, she replied, "Well—*no* . . . I am interested in good photographs, and I read Dr. Williams's articles, but if it came to no more, I shouldn't feel bereft." The report continues, "Rat admitted that there was nothing in the *Broom* that he could not spare; the *Dial* too for that matter; that *Secession* had no interest for him; that *The Natural History Magazine* he could not do without, nor the *Spectator*, nor some others but that in the matter of the kind of modern

77. Bertram Hartman to MM, January 17, 1925 (Rosenbach V:25:04).
78. MM to JWM, May 10, 1923 (Rosenbach VI:26:06).

caviare that seasons new writing he was sure; there was but one verdict concerning it."[79] Because of her similar low regard for *Contact*, she resisted Williams' and McAlmon's persistent attempts to publish her book even though a few months later she complied with the Dial Press's request to do so.[80] Despite her disparagement of the *Dial* to Josephson, her conversation notebook shows her repeatedly defending it: "in comparison with the Dial," she tells someone, "the L[ittle] R[eview] seems to me like a Woolworth [handkerchief] in comparison with one of Belfast linen."[81] Long before her association with the *Dial* became official, she was part of its inner circle attending the teas and dinners Thayer hosted at its offices.

Moore never derided the other magazines in print, and she contributed a little to all of them, but her strong alignment with the *Dial* was itself a public statement. The policy of the *Dial* was not to take sides, a position that could be and was criticized. This pluralist stance along with the *Dial*'s high critical standards and uncompromising appearance appealed to Moore. Although she had praised *Others* in 1915 for publishing what might be "trash," by the second decade of modernism, selectivity—"picking and choosing"—had become integral to her aesthetic. The appearance of the written word had always been important to Moore, and thus the quality of the *Dial*'s paper, layout, and printing, made possible by Thayer's and Watson's private funds, were for her essential rather than incidental features. And as with earlier publications such as *Camera Work*, Thayer and Watson insisted upon integrating verbal and visual expression and continued to print fine reproductions of drawings, sculptures, and paintings even when it became financially disadvantageous to do so. While Moore's editorial responsibilities did not originally extend to the art work, as Thayer's health deteriorated, Watson gave her greater authority in selecting pictures.[82] A few she solicited, but many came from the "Living Art" folio Thayer had assembled and from the extensive private collections of Watson and Thayer. Except for her resistance to nudes, Moore's taste generally concurs with that of Thayer and Watson: she liked sculpture and caricature; she preferred representational works to abstraction. Later Moore

79. MWM to JWM, May 8, 1923 (Rosenbach VI:26:06).
80. MWM to JWM, May 26, 1924 (Rosenbach VI:27:06).
81. MM, August 2, 1921, Notebook 1250/25 (Rosenbach VII:11:01). The word after *Woolworth*, possibly an abbreviation for *handkerchief*, is illegible.
82. MM to JWM, January 16, 1927 (Rosenbach VI:28:02).

recalls the works and artists most memorable to her: "Among the pictures, as intensives on the text, were three verdure-tapestry-like woodcuts by Galanis; Rousseau's lion among lotuses; 'The Philosophers' by Stuart Davis; Adolph Dehn's 'Viennese Coffee House'; and Kuniyoshi's curious 'Heifer'—the forehead with a star on it of separated whorled strokes like propeller fins; Ernest Fiene, Charles Sheeler, Arthur Dove, John Marin, Georgia O'Keeffe, Max Weber, Carl Sprinchorn, the Zorachs, and Bertram Hartman; Wyndham Lewis, Brancusi, Lachaise, Elie Nadelman, Picasso and Chirico, Cocteau line drawings, and Seurat's 'Circus'" (*Prose*, 358). She respected the opinions of the *Dial* art critic, Henry McBride, who was one of modernism's earliest and staunchest champions, and was willing to reject criticism by the prominent but less progressive Thomas Craven.[83]

In response to a playful birthday letter from Warner to Marianne imagining her role as editor, Mrs. Moore responds in kind (Moore's upstairs *Dial* office is the "Palm Tree").

> There are a good many shoving and hollering about it [Rat's Palm Tree], and eyeing the thick leaves above, but those beasts are not the giraffes. Rat 'rastles hisself diligent to 'lure those lofty creatures— but either they've "got" something bad, or they won't feed near when they are all right; and as for seeing the hitched mouse [Mrs. Moore], they don't know there is a mouse. But these facts don't bother the Rat; the Palm Tree's the thing—I doubt that there's any rat in the world that so affectionates its Tree. It pores over its "pieces"; it "wonders?" it *believes* it's got something that with "fixing" will "*do*"! Very jubilant. Then it writes; tick-tacks; sends to "doctor" [Watson]; sends to the author;—sends to press; reads and re-reads in proof; alters; sends to author. Then when the mag is out? O me! Every ad and paragraph is scrutinized and read. It is held off and held near. It is now an exaltation—now a depth of endless descent into woe and disgrace. Were the Dial a human creature it would be honored in having such unending solicitude bestowed upon it.[84]

Moore's "fixing" things annoyed some contributors. Years later Donald Hall described Hart Crane's objections to her changing one of his poems and asked if she asked revisions of many poets; she responds: "We had an inflexible rule: do not ask changes of so much as a comma. Accept it or re-

83. MM to JWM, February 21, 1927 (Rosenbach VI:28:03).
84. MWM to JWM, December 1, 1927, (Rosenbach VI:28:13).

ject it" (*MMR*, 267). If there was such a rule, Moore broke it more than once. A rule to which she did adhere, however, was to consider the merits of the work rather than the author; for example, she rejected a piece by James Joyce (over Watson's protests) and a "Comment" by former managing editor Alyse Gregory.[85] Moore's standards of obscenity, which seem to resemble her mother's more than her peers', were also controversial: she sometimes objected to nudes and, for instance, asked Llewellyn Powys to remove a paragraph mentioning syphilis.[86] But she is obviously open-minded on the matter, for there is no shortage of nudes in the issues she edited (indeed, nudes typify the work of Blake, Lachaise, and the Zorachs, among Moore's favorite artists). It constitutes an ironic confession when, in "*The Dial*: A Retrospect," she quotes D. H. Lawrence's letter to her: "I knew some of the poems would offend you. But then some part of life must offend you too." (*Prose*, 360)

When the *Dial* ceased publication and Moore moved with her mother to Brooklyn in 1929, she had attained considerable prestige as an arbiter of taste. She continued to attend museums and galleries and maintained close ties with the art world. Monroe Wheeler, who befriended Moore in early 1923 and became a regular visitor in her home, remained close to Moore until her death. He joined the staff of the Museum of Modern Art in 1935 and served as the head of its department of exhibitions and publications from 1941 until 1967. Over the years Moore often accompanied Wheeler to museum and gallery openings and through him met a number of artists.[87] During the thirties her interest in surrealism drew her to galleries such as the Julian Levy that exhibited such works.[88] In the forties

85. MWM to JWM, March 15, 1927, and March 17, 1927 (Rosenbach VI:28:04); and MWM to JWM, August 16, 1927 (Rosenbach VI:28:09).

86. MWM to JWM, December 23, 1926 (Rosenbach VI:27:25). Mrs. Moore's strong objections to what she deemed obscenity in modern literature recur frequently in her letters, and she probably exaggerated the importance of the issue for her daughter. While Marianne surely shared these objections to some degree and would not openly offend her mother, the artistic merits of a work are her primary concern. Moore's letter to Sibley Watson (quoted in entirety in MWM to JWM, March 15, 1927, Rosenbach VI:28:04) confirms this. It is also likely that Moore's objections were not mere prudery—that she saw nudes as degrading a person's (usually a woman's) individuality. She took extensive notes from an article by W. A. Gill in the June, 1907, *Atlantic* that criticizes Rodin's nudes for shifting attention away from the individual to the species. MM, Notebook 1250/1 (Rosenbach VII:01:01), 134–36.

87. Monroe Wheeler to the author, August 7, 1988. (Wheeler died on August 14, 1988.)

she developed friendships with the commercial artist and illustrator E. McKnight Kauffer and also with the sculptor Malvina Hoffman.[89] But while the friendships Moore formed with Kauffer and Hoffman surely sustained her both personally and professionally, they did not effect new directions in her work as did the art she had encountered earlier in her career. In any case, the degree of Moore's personal intimacy with an artist is not necessarily a measure of aesthetic affinity.

Moore's most public role in the art world in later years was as advocate for aspiring artists. Her files contain correspondence with a number of artists including, in many cases, drafts of her letters of recommendation. Among the artists she recommended for various honors and fellowships are the watercolorist Robert Andrew Parker, who illustrated a special edition of Moore's poems published by the Museum of Modern Art; her favorite portrait photographer, George Platt Lynes; the naive painter Loren MacIver; Dudley Huppler, whose animal drawings Moore admired and considered using as tail pieces for her translation of the *Fables of La Fontaine*,[90] and, the most famous of these, Joseph Cornell. In addition, she exchanged a brief but warm correspondence with Robert Motherwell also regarding the possibility of illustrations for her *Fables*.

Her correspondence with Cornell, sixteen years younger than she, is especially rewarding, revealing a deep, aesthetic intimacy. Moore and Cornell, whom Monroe Wheeler called "kindred artists,"[91] had much in common besides their art: both lived their adult lives with their mothers, and neither, as Moore wrote of Handel, "was known to have fallen in love" (*CP*, 25). Their most obvious affinity, however, is their love of assemblage. Both hoarded words and images as sources for their art. Cornell first wrote

---

Wheeler was in his early twenties when he met Moore; he published "Marriage" in his serial *Manikin* several months later. During the early thirties he lived in France, where he published books by artists such as Picasso and Chagall. He is known for his high standards of art-book design and, especially, for initiating and developing the Museum of Modern Art's publication program.

88. Moore's fliers from these galleries are preserved in vertical files at the Rosenbach.

89. See Schulman, "Marianne Moore and E. McKnight Kauffer," in *Marianne Moore*, ed. Kappel, special issue of *Twentieth Century Literature*, 175–80; and Malvina Hoffman, *Yesterday Is Tomorrow: A Personal History* (New York, 1965), 321–23, which includes Hoffman's pencil drawing of Moore.

90. I am grateful to Patricia Willis and Charles Molesworth for calling my attention to these relationships.

91. Interview with Monroe Wheeler in "Marianne Moore," *Voices & Visions,* a television series produced by the New York Center for Visual History, 1987.

Figure 9 Joseph Cornell, *Nouveaux contes de fées* (*called "Poison Box"*)
1948. Painted, paper-covered, glazed wooden box for a construction of wood, paint, velvet, mirror, paper-covered boxes and metal latches and hinges. 32 x 26 x 14.9 cm. The Lindy and Edwin Bergman Joseph Cornell Collection, 1982.1857 recto. Photograph © 1994 The Art Institute of Chicago, All Rights Reserved.

to Moore in 1943 after she had praised his "The Crystal Cage (Portrait of Berenice)," an assemblage of text and images published in *View* magazine.

51

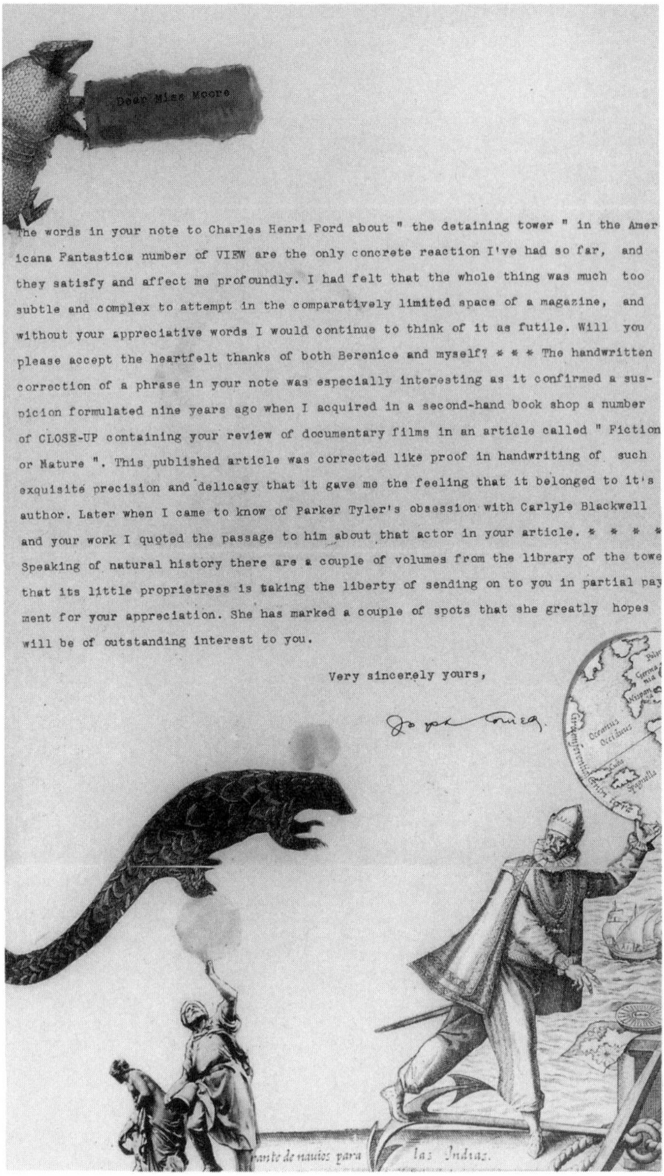

The words in your note to Charles Henri Ford about " the detaining tower " in the Amer
icana Fantastica number of VIEW are the only concrete reaction I've had so far, and
they satisfy and affect me profoundly. I had felt that the whole thing was much too
subtle and complex to attempt in the comparatively limited space of a magazine, and
without your appreciative words I would continue to think of it as futile. Will you
please accept the heartfelt thanks of both Berenice and myself? * * * The handwritten
correction of a phrase in your note was especially interesting as it confirmed a sus-
picion formulated nine years ago when I acquired in a second-hand book shop a number
of CLOSE-UP containing your review of documentary films in an article called " Fiction
or Nature ". This published article was corrected like proof in handwriting of such
exquisite precision and delicacy that it gave me the feeling that it belonged to it's
author. Later when I came to know of Parker Tyler's obsession with Carlyle Blackwell
and your work I quoted the passage to him about that actor in your article. * * * *
Speaking of natural history there are a couple of volumes from the library of the towe
that its little proprietress is taking the liberty of sending on to you in partial pay
ment for your appreciation. She has marked a couple of spots that she greatly hopes
will be of outstanding interest to you.

                              Very sincerely yours,

Figure 10 Letter from Joseph Cornell to Marianne Moore, March 23, 1943
Marianne Moore Papers. The Rosenbach Museum and Library (V:12:11).

Nearly all of his letters to her have cutout engravings pasted on them; one letter has blue pockets on it, each with an animal inside. He also sent her books and excerpts of books from among his collections. For Cornell, the older artist was a source of inspiration: "In going over your poems again this week," he writes, "the lines 'it tears off . . . the mist the heart wears' gave me considerable stimulus and consolation amidst a too familiar and too protracted period of sluggish groping trying to find in my various collections of notes and documents not the proverbial 'needle' but a 'star.' " [92] Cornell afforded Moore the opportunity to watch a younger artist succeed, and sometimes fail, at methods well known to her. Her letter recommending him for a Guggenheim says:

> Although some of his studies do not—in my opinion succeed—those that do, I feel have a poetic associative force hard to rival; for instance, the Tower of Berenice and typescript accompanying in *View.* His use of early masters and engravers, the sense of design in his wall-paper specimens, and of romance in his choice of woodcuts, his consistent rigor of selection, constitute, it seems to me, a phase of poetry. Working in a category that easily becomes specious, he is the more instructive,—as teaching one to "see," to avoid temptations to which imaginative workers are subject. This is a kind of initiation in originality.[93]

If anything, Cornell is the more "poetic" of the two artists, surely the more romantic. His "imaginary gardens" are more apt to have real butterflies in them than toads.[94]

Although Moore had published only one piece of art criticism prior to becoming editor of the *Dial*,[95] an essay about Alfeo Faggi's sculpture (*Prose*, 73–75), once she acquired the protective shield of anonymity pro-

---

92. Joseph Cornell to MM, November 1, 1946 (Rosenbach V:12:11). The Moore-Cornell correspondence at the Rosenbach lasts from March, 1943, through February, 1950.

93. MM to Guggenheim Foundation, September 19, 1945, carbon on verso of Joseph Cornell to MM, August 17, 1945 (Rosenbach V:12:11).

94. For further discussion of Moore and Cornell's relationship, see Tashjian, *Joseph Cornell,* 65–77.

95. A possible exception is a brief newspaper announcement of an exhibit at the Metzger Institute of drawings by George W. Plank, who would years later illustrate Moore's *The Pangolin and Other Verse* (London, 1936). Moore saved this unsigned clipping in her Notebook 1250/1 (Rosenbach VII:01:01); the close description could well be Moore's, written around 1910. I thank Charles Molesworth for this suggestion.

vided by the "Comment" section, she seems to have eagerly taken up the task of writing about art. The second "Comment" she wrote is devoted to Stieglitz's "Seven Americans" show; her third, to an exhibition of children's drawings at the Worcester Art Museum (291, incidentally, had been the first gallery to present children's art seriously). Later "Comments" treat Dürer, Audubon, Blake, and such art-related topics as maps, book illustration, and advertising (*Prose*, 149–223).

The art criticism Moore published in later years is primarily about the work of friends: E. McKnight Kauffer, Robert Andrew Parker, and Malvina Hoffman. There is also the short tribute to Stieglitz. Moore's papers at the Rosenbach reveal that some of her most ambitious art criticism went unpublished. Around 1916 she wrote two paragraphs on the cartoonist F. G. Cooper. A year or so later she uses the painting of Arthur B. Davies as a key example of "understatement."[96] Anticipating her later role as advocate for under-recognized artists, in early 1922 she wrote a description of drawings and paintings by Gaston Lachaise's stepson, Edward Nagle, for an exhibit that apparently never took place.[97] In 1937 she sent the *Globe* a four-page review of the important "Fantastic Art, Dada, Surrealism" exhibition at the Museum of Modern Art and then sent a revised version to the *Saturday Review*. There are at least two unpublished reviews of art books, including one of Mai-Mai Sze's *The Tao of Painting*.[98] Perhaps the editors who rejected these pieces were seeking something more critical and less descriptive, for Moore writes almost exclusively about art that she likes, and she generally expresses her admiration, as she does in poetry, through a rigorously detailed description of the work itself.

The number of art books in Moore's library indicates not only that Moore's interest in art persisted from her Bryn Mawr years until her death in 1972, but also that throughout her life friends regarded an art book

---

96. MM, "F. G. Cooper" (Typescript in Rosenbach II:02:15); MM, "Understatement" (Typescript in Rosenbach II:07:02).

97. This mysterious typescript (Rosenbach II:02:09) contains no titles, artists' names, nationalities, or dates, but Moore's notes in MM, Notebook 1250/25, Rosenbach VII:11:01, 38–42, correspond with works described in the typescript and indicate that in January, 1922, Nagle asked her to write a catalog description for a possible exhibit in London. Nagle was Isabel Lachaise's son and had been a friend of Sibley Watson and E. E. Cummings at Harvard. Several of his drawings appeared in the *Dial*.

98. MM, "Concerning the Marvelous" (Typescript in Rosenbach II:01:30); MM, "The Tao of Painting" ["Tedium and Integrity"] (Typescript in Rosenbach II:06:12); MM, "Art Books" (Typescript in Rosenbach II:01:12).

to be an appropriate gift. While Moore's library reflects considerable appreciation for the work of her contemporaries, it also reveals an interest in such diverse forms as jewelry-making, illuminated manuscripts, Persian art, Gothic architecture, printmaking, Chinese calligraphy, and antique automatons. And her reading diaries as well as her poems show a life-long interest in the arts; during the thirties, for instance, she regularly took notes from the "Page for Collectors" in the *Illustrated London News* on such topics as Irish cut glass, unicorns, caricatures, Persian bronzes, and mummified cats.[99]

In describing Moore's involvement in the art world of her contemporaries, I have not emphasized sufficiently her love of museums and travel, nor her interest in the art of previous centuries, all of which contributed to her aesthetic and inspired numerous poems. Subsequent chapters will bring forth some of these interests. Whereas Moore's interest in the arts grew and diversified over the years, the aesthetic values that she formed early in life, at home and at Bryn Mawr, and during her years in the Village were to stay with her. And the qualities she valued in painting, sculpture, and photography were to remain inseparable from those she valued in poetry and prose. "When I Buy Pictures" is as much about poetry as is "Poetry" about art generally. Her praise of E. McKnight Kauffer in 1949 could not more precisely describe her own work: "Instinctiveness, imagination, and 'the sense of artistic difficulty' . . . have interacted till we have an objectified logic of sensibility as inescapable as the colors refracted from a prism" (*Prose*, 427).

99. MM, Notebook 1250/6 (Rosenbach VII:02:02).

2

SURFACES AND SPATIAL FORM

Marianne Moore was once asked in an interview, "Is the visual pattern [of a poem] not as important as the spoken?" She replied: "No. Not at all as important, although I do think of it. I like to see symmetry on the page, I will confess." She then removed from the wall a framed poem and carefully dusted the glass with a cloth that she kept in a vase on a tall chest. Later in the interview, after responding to a question on the conversational quality of her poems, her attention returned to the frame she was still holding and to the wood engraving printed directly below her poem. "Laurence Scott framed it," she said speaking of the page, "leaving more of a margin below than above, and all are carefully mitred. I made a mistake there [indicating a line in the poem] and I put a patch over it. It's just newsprint, so it has to be under glass."[1] Although Moore assures her interviewer that the spoken quality of a poem is her chief concern, Moore's actions here (duly recorded) reveal her devotion to the poem's visual, physical presence.

This devotion indicates a certain disregard for conventional distinctions in genre. In addition to many of Moore's friends' being, like herself, wielders of both pen and brush (Williams, Cummings, Hartley, the Zorachs), she especially appreciated writers who could observe like painters and painters who could observe in writing. "The direct influences bearing on my work," which Moore lists to Ezra Pound—"Gordon Craig, Henry James, Blake, the minor prophets and Hardy"[2]—include two artist-writers, Blake and Craig, and two writers whose visual quality she admired: of Hardy she writes, "there are in his work certain unmistakably distinctive traits of eye, an awareness of architecture" (*Prose*, 132), and of James she says, "I could visualize scenes, and deplored the fact that Henry James

1. MM, "Conversation with Marianne Moore" (Interview with Grace Jan Schulman), *Quarterly Review of Literature*, XVI (1969), 158, 165.
2. MM to Pound, January 9, 1919, in *Marianne Moore*, ed. Tomlinson, 17.

had to do it unchallenged" (*MMR*, 254). Moore likewise recognizes the verbal precision of certain painters; she praises Whistler's "perfect diction" and Audubon's "faithfulness to the scene" (*Prose*, 165, 178). Often, too, she identifies avant-garde writers and artists together, as she does in a *Dial* "Comment" that defends contemporary American writers—an editorial "us"—against attacks such as Theodore Roosevelt's "fearless effacing of futurism and cubism" (*Prose*, 191). In a letter to Robert Motherwell she calls his paintings "poetry of the brush" and explains: "It is all one, isn't it? I do not see how there can be categories."[3]

When Moore's critics insist on categories—describing her poems as either "rhetorical conversations" or mute, numerical grids—they obscure one of her greatest achievements as a modernist, her synthesis of the verbal and the visual, the dramatic and the spatial.[4] In response to, among other factors, the revolution in European painting during the first decade of this century, American poets broke free from the "metronome" of iambic pentameter but soon found themselves wanting not mere freedom but a new form, one that would accommodate the irregularities of speech yet still provide order. In London, Pound studied the Chinese ideogram and the sculpture and painting he labeled vorticist to learn how to incorporate spatial form into poetry. In New York, poets along with painters and photographers sought ways to respond to the Armory Show of 1913, especially to the cubist paintings exhibited there. Williams wrote in his *Autobiography*: "There was . . . a great surge of interest in the arts generally before the First World War. New York was seething with it. Painting took the lead. It came to a head for us in the famous 'Armory Show' of 1913."[5] Williams, however, would not find a satisfactory form until the forties, when he "discovered" the variable foot. Marianne Moore did not join Pound's and Williams' public plea for new forms—because by 1916 she had found one. Her invention is modern poetry's most underrated

3. MM to Robert Motherwell, December 1, 1945, carbon (Rosenbach V:42:34).

4. Two critics who do so are nevertheless among Moore's most perceptive readers: Grace Schulman emphasizes the conversational quality of Moore's poems, and Hugh Kenner views Moore's visual idiom as a pivotal discovery of her age. See Schulman's *Marianne Moore: The Poetry of Engagement* (Urbana, 1986), 43–75, 97–116, and Kenner's *A Homemade World: The American Modernist Writers* (New York, 1975), 91–118.

5. Williams, *Autobiography*, 134. Actually, the "surge of interest" began with the Armory Show—hence its fame. An art work mentioned in this paragraph, Duchamp's *Fountain*, indicates that Williams is confusing the Armory Show with the less famous Independents Show of 1917.

achievement: a stanza that splits and then realigns the poem's "architecture" and its "tune."[6] To see the stanza Moore developed as a response to cubism is to recognize an original response to one of the early modernists' most perplexing challenges.

During the decade after World War I both European and American painters retreated from their most radical experiments with cubism and abstraction. Moore likewise moved away from her formal innovations. She first abandoned her stanza for free verse and then from 1925 to 1929, while editing the *Dial,* published no new poems. Her prolific prose of this period, however, reveals her continued fascination with the appearance of the page (hence anticipating her return in the thirties to her stanzaic form). The topics she chose for her *Dial* "Comments" include book illustrations, maps, handwriting, and typography. In one "Comment" she writes: "The subtleties and atmospheric depth of naturalistic painting and drawing are disturbing in a book, says a writer on Text and Illustration in the Printing Number issued with a *London Times Literary Supplement,* since 'in reading type you look "at" the page; in looking at a realistic illustration you look "through" it'" (*Prose,* 198).[7] One could argue that in quite another sense one looks "through" a page of text to the meanings beyond the words rather than "at" the type itself. Indeed, most contemporary publishers choose type that is as unobtrusive as possible in order to facilitate looking "through" the page. Moore realizes, as does the *Times* reviewer she quotes, that this was not always the case, and both praise "the wonderful series of books designed and produced by William Blake, in which a method of engraving invented by himself produced a unity comparable to that of early illuminated manuscripts" (quoted in *Prose,* 198). As a book reviewer Moore is rarely remiss in looking only "through" and not "at" the page. Her review of Gertrude Stein's *The Making of Americans* praises the "chiseled typography"; her review of Glenway Wescott's *Natives of Rock* politely finds fault: "Although there are typographical errors as ingeniously undetectable as the book is decorative, such errors recede" (*Prose,* 128, 139).

The sometimes odd-looking poems of Williams, Loy, Pound, and Cummings attest that Moore was not the only writer of her time concerned

---

6. Describing her composition process, Moore said, "If the phrases recur in too incoherent an architecture—as print—I notice that the words as a tune do not sound right" (*MMR,* 263).

7. I have added the word *type,* which was inadvertently omitted from the reprint.

Figure 11 Paul Cézanne, *Village of Gardanne*

1885–86. Oil. 36 1/4 x 29 3/8 in. (92 x 74.5 cm.). The Brooklyn Museum 23.105. Ella C. Woodward Memorial Fund and the Alfred T. White Fund.

with the appearance of the page. But this awareness of surface that to some extent characterizes many of the poems of Moore's generation is perhaps the single most pronounced characteristic of modern painting since

Figure 12 Pablo Picasso, *Standing Female Nude*

1910. Charcoal. $19\,1/16 \times 12\,5/16$ in. All rights reserved, The Metropolitan Museum of Art. The Alfred Stieglitz Collection. 1949. (49.70.34).

the time of the impressionists. During the nineteenth century, most teachers at the École des Beaux-Arts in Paris, which had dominated the Western art world since the seventeenth century, taught its students to paint finely polished, photographlike surfaces upon which one could detect neither the texture of the paint nor the activities of the brush. Like readable type, such a surface enhances the viewer's ability to look "through" rather than "at" the canvas and thus maintains the illusion, which had prevailed in Western art since the Italian Renaissance, of a painting's being a window through which to view a particular scene. When certain artists began to question the dictates of the Academy in the mid-nineteenth century, at first only the evidence of brushwork and actual paint blurred the clear view through the window. But as the influence of Japanese prints became evident in paintings such as those of Degas and Whistler and the space behind the surface of the canvas became more and more compressed, observers became conscious of flat planes of color that existed both in the illusion of space behind the canvas and in the compositional space upon the canvas. The first great painter to understand and utilize fully this spatial tension was Cézanne. Particularly evident in Cézanne's landscapes are rectangular areas of color that function both as roof tops or planes of rock in the illusion of distance and as parallel strokes of paint in the abstracted composition on the canvas. Even more radical than Cézanne's patches of paint were the areas of bare canvas or paper that he left exposed, thus making explicit that a canvas can be at once the foreground behind which valleys sink and mountains rise and the background upon which paint is brushed.

Taking Cézanne's experiments with space a significant step further, Picasso and Braque began using geometrical surface planes to describe faces, nudes, and guitars, subjects that, unlike roof tops and rocks, are not readily defined by geometrical planes. The result, cubism, created an image that for the first time in European art bore little resemblance to the appearance of the subject it was supposed to represent. By exaggerating the surface planes and "hermetically" fixing them together, the cubists virtually eliminated the illusion of depth behind the picture plane and eventually came very close to eliminating illusion itself. In the "analytic" phase of cubism, which lasted from 1909 to 1912, the image appears broken up, or analyzed, into geometrically shaped planes that lie at various angles to each other in a shallow but still three-dimensional space behind the surface of the canvas; in the later and most abstract works of analytic cubism, called "hermetic" cubism, there is so little background or negative space behind the cubist planes that one gets the impression of a hermetically fused and impenetrable surface some few inches behind the picture plane.

This illusive surface was finally brought flush with the canvas in 1912, when Picasso and Braque began to apply to the canvas materials like newspaper, wallpaper, bottle labels, and cigarette paper wrappers in a collage technique. Although one might expect to find that "synthetic" cubism at last papers over the traditional "window," destroying illusion forever, illusion proves itself indomitable and thus all the more intriguing. I have oversimplified the movement "forward" from Cézanne's roof tops to Picasso's and Braque's collages in order to emphasize that artists were becoming aware of the surface of their medium; actually what artists were becoming increasingly aware of is the complex spatial relationship between the illusion behind the canvas and the physical fact of the canvas itself. When part of a still life, a newspaper clipping will more readily maintain its two-dimensional identity than will a stroke of paint. But what does one make of a piece of wood-grained wallpaper pasted upon a canvas that in turn has objects pasted or painted on top of it so that it gives the illusion of receding into the picture like a tabletop? Or what does one make of a similarly placed piece of paper that has been painted by the artist to give the illusion of wood-grained wallpaper? Picasso, Braque, and Juan Gris delighted in the intrigue and wit of such visual puns.

And as Robert Rosenblum has pointed out, they delighted in verbal puns, too. Well aware of the problem Moore noted in the *Dial* of looking "at" a page of type versus looking "through" a naturalistic picture, cubists frequently incorporated words and fragments of words in their paintings and collages to encourage the viewer to look "at" as well as "through" the surface. And while their concerns were, of course, primarily visual, their choice of words, letters, and even of typography often evoked verbal meanings as well. For instance, the title—nearly always fragments of the title— of the French newspaper *Le Journal* frequently appears pasted, stenciled, and painted in the works of Picasso, Braque, and Gris. Fragmenting such a familiar word (and image) clearly coincides with other familiar images the cubists shattered but also creates unexpected new meanings and implications. The isolated letters JOU, for example, could suggest *joie* (joy), *jouer* (to play), and *jouir* (to enjoy or to come, in sexual slang).[8]

8. Robert Rosenblum, "Picasso and the Typography of Cubism," in *Picasso, 1881–1973,* ed. Roland Penrose and John Golding (London, 1973), 49–75 (quotation on 51).

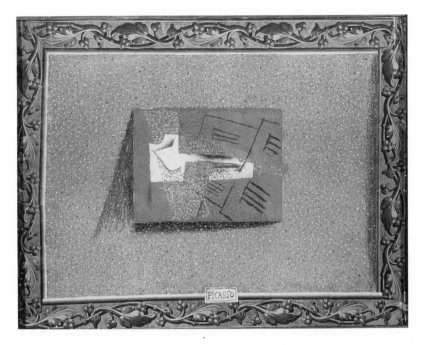

Figure 13 Pablo Picasso, *Pipe and Sheet Music*
1914. Gouache and graphite on pasted paper. 27 ¾ x 34 x 1¾ in. The Museum of Fine Arts, Houston. Gift of Mr. and Mrs. Maurice McAshan.

Rosenblum notes, too, the diverse signatures of the synthetic cubists that appeared after several years of Picasso's and Braque's leaving their cubist works unsigned. Juan Gris, for instance, found his name in a *Le Journal* headline and included the clipping in a collage still life. But Picasso was the master of the collage signature, including in one work a letter addressed to himself, but not of course in his handwriting, and in another a mock name plate on a mock frame: "Together with the decorative paper border, which parodies the baroque carved frame of a traditional masterpiece, the name plate ennobles, as if in a museum display, the modest little Cubist still-life of pipe and music score. . . . And as a further complication, the printing on the name plate, though nominally impersonal in its block letters, is nevertheless sufficiently irregular to suggest that it, unlike the decorative frame, is handmade, not machine made, so that all facts and fictions are cast into doubt."[9]

9. *Ibid.,* 67.

In exploring the surface of their medium with words, painters found their concerns suddenly very like those of writers. If one could imagine a mirror image of the painters' movement "forward" from behind the picture plane to the surface domain of words and type, she might see the writers, like Marianne Moore, moving from "behind" the referential meanings of their words to meet the artists on the visual domain of the printed page.

While there were some artists like Max Weber and some writers like Gertrude Stein who purposefully tried to adapt the principles of cubism to poetry and prose,[10] Moore did not. Her scrapbooks and notebooks indicate she read as widely as she could about the Armory Show and various movements in modern art. In one article on cubism, for instance, Moore noted the following statement: "the aesthetic emotions are not stirred by the imitation of natural objects, but by the creation of formal design out of those objects."[11] But probably Moore understood cubism no better than did the American critics and painters at that time—which is to say that she was stimulated by the spirit of innovation and by the aesthetic questions cubism raised but that she with other Americans perceived European art to be more advanced than their own. In later years she praised E. McKnight Kauffer for expressing "what we all felt" about the Armory Show when he wrote, "I didn't understand it but I certainly couldn't dismiss it."[12]

Moore's early exposure to the pre-Raphaelites, however, especially to Dante Gabriel Rossetti's paintings, may have prepared her for the dense surfaces and compressed space of cubism. Through her friendship with the Norcross family, Moore developed an appreciation for the pre-Raphaelites and their advocate John Ruskin before she went to college, and when she traveled to Paris and the British Isles in 1911 she saw and admired pre-Raphaelite paintings by Millais and Rossetti and paintings and a tapestry by Burne-Jones.[13] Though the movement toward the surface of the can-

10. See Max Weber, *Cubist Poems* (London, 1913); and, for example, Gertrude Stein, "Picasso," *Camera Work*, special number (August, 1912), reprinted in *Camera Work: A Critical Anthology*, ed. Jonathan Green (Millerton, N.Y., 1973), 223–25.

11. "A Gospel of Art," *Spectator*, July 18, 1914, pp. 97–98. Moore saved this article in her Scrapbook 1 (Rosenbach X:01).

12. MM to E. McKnight Kauffer, April 1, 1950, carbon (Rosenbach V:32:21).

13. Moore's visits to galleries in Scotland and England are recorded in MM to JWM, June 20, 1911, July 5, 1911, and July 16, 1911; all in *Marianne Moore Newsletter*, VI (1982), 10, 11, 19–20.

vas took less extreme forms in England than in France and had less impact on American modernist painters, it nevertheless anticipated cubism in several ways. (The expatriate American James McNeill Whistler, also a favorite of Moore's, through his friendship with Rossetti in London and with Degas in Paris was the only significant link between the two movements.) At the same time that the realists on the Continent first departed from academic conventions in 1848, the pre-Raphaelites likewise rebelled against academic conventions such as Renaissance perspective—hence the name pre-Raphaelite. The early works of the original Pre-Raphaelite Brotherhood—William Holman Hunt, John Everett Millais, and Rossetti—have a compressed, sometimes ambiguous, perspective. And like the cubists, Rossetti occasionally used words to emphasize the flatness of a painting; indeed, some of Rossetti's paintings are so dense with figures and detail to warrant the appellation "hermetic." [14] The close relationship between pre-Raphaelite poets and painters of course also anticipates the modernists. But whereas in France the compressed perspective of postimpressionists like Degas and Cézanne led eventually to cubism, in England it led via William Morris to the arts and crafts movement, specifically to the designing of wallpaper, textiles, and other ornamental surfaces. Morris also effected a strong interest in book design in England and America, which through Mary Norcross probably contributed directly to Moore's interest in book illustration and typography.[15]

Also through the Norcrosses and probably through her reading of Rossetti, Moore developed an ardent, lifelong appreciation for one of her admitted influences, William Blake, whom Rossetti considered his forebear. In Moore's recreated living room at the Rosenbach three of Blake's *Job* illustrations hang framed above her desk.[16] It must be partly because of Blake's own flattened perspective (he also rebelled against the Academy) that his illustrations and text appear so unified—a quality that, as already noted, Moore especially admired.

14. See Timothy Hilton, *The Pre-Raphaelites* (New York, 1970), 31–46, 97, 175.

15. For thorough discussion of the theoretical and actual importance of surfaces in late nineteenth-century English and American taste, see Catherine Lynn, "Decorating Surfaces: Aesthetic Delight, Theoretical Dilemma" and "Surface Ornament: Wallpapers, Carpets, Textiles, and Embroidery"; for discussion of the importance attached to book design in America, see Doreen Bolger Burke, "Painters and Sculptors in a Decorative Age"; all three essays are in Burke *et al.*, *In Pursuit of Beauty: Americans and the Aesthetic Movement* (New York, 1986), 52–109, 316–19.

16. These were a birthday gift from her mother in 1919.

Far removed from pre-Raphaelitism but not so far removed from cubism is another of Moore's early interests, cartoons. In the same scrapbook where she kept clippings on modern art are a great many cartoons and caricatures, many of which predate the Armory Show. When she met J. B. Kerfoot during her 1915 trip to New York, she inquired whether he knew the cartoonist F. G. Cooper (since both published in *Life*).[17] And around this time she wrote a short review of Cooper (unpublished) in which she admires the dialogue of his cartoons both for its conversational qualities and for its decorative qualities, that is, for its part in the visual design. She says that certain colloquial expressions he uses "are not so much jokes as they are the legs and angles of a sort of aesthetic geometry which will not brook modification or infraction. They are manifestations of the modern spirit, which are ready to stand or fall on their merits as art." She devotes the second of two paragraphs to his signature: "Clean cut work is often marred by a signature. In F. G. Cooper's work, instead of destroying the unity of the picture, the signature in a sense *is* the picture. Impersonating an impartial observer, the 'g' strikes an attitude and presents in itself, a complete version of the story. We have in this letter, the Utopian who may see himself as others see him, without needing to wish that he had been cast for a more significant part."[18] Moore's concern with the integration of words into a visual design and with the animation of the signature, not to mention the verbal wit, are cubist in spirit if not in form. Other modernists shared her interest in cartoons, most notably Marius de Zayas, a regular at 291, whose caricatures and drawings incorporating words appeared in *Camera Work, 291,* and other publications.

But for all Moore's interest in the appearance of the written word, she apparently never experimented with making pictures out of words in the manner of Apollinaire's *calligrammes* or, later, concrete poetry. When she said in the interview from which I quoted at the beginning of this chapter that the visual pattern of a poem is not as important as the spoken, she was not lying, for she was a poet acutely concerned with the rhythm and diction of spoken language. She had as keen an interest in dialects as she had in typography and in her scrapbooks collected many articles on theater alongside those on painting. One can assume that the quality she admired in F. G. Cooper was her ideal: the "integration" of conversa-

17. MM to JWM, December 19, 1915 (Rosenbach VII: 21:13).
18. MM, "F. G. Cooper" (Typescript in Rosenbach II:02:15).

66

The Standpatter

Figure 14 F. G. Cooper, *The Standpatter*

Drawing published in *Collier's,* May 16, 1914. Marianne Moore copied this into her notebook (Rosenbach VII:01:01).

tion with visual design. Her professed indebtedness to Gordon Craig corroborates this ideal, for Craig's innovative production theories and set designs made drama a more visual and thus a more unified aesthetic experience. Moore's notebooks indicate that one of her first perceptions of modernism was that it synthesized the arts. Studies of colors being heard and of sounds having colors fascinated her; following her notes on one article about such matters, she writes, "The aim of the new century seems to be to make the art of olfactory harmony, phonetic harmony and chromatic harmony one."[19]

Like Gordon Craig and William Blake, Marianne Moore made a traditionally auditory genre a more visual one; she did so through her unique use of the stanza as a structural unit.[20] Because readers of English poetry are more accustomed to counting feet than to looking "at" the page, they have called Moore's stanzas "syllabic verse," which means that each stanza has exactly as many syllables as every other stanza in the poem. In English poetry, at least, such a form seems a rather arbitrary alternative to iambic pentameter or to free verse. Williams' variable foot, for instance, because it is based on the breath of speech, seems less arbitrary.[21] But the term *syllabic verse* ignores the readily apparent visual spacing of the stanza as well as its often unapparent pattern of rhyme. Moore herself continually protested the term; insisting that she composed in "rhymed stanzas" rather than lines, she used "pattern," "mathematics," "symmetry," "arrangement," and "architecture" to describe these stanzas.[22] This architectural symmetry is internal, not merely external. While Moore's original typescripts have few overrun lines (she used elite type and narrow margins and occasionally turned the paper sideways), the many overruns in her published poems prevent the stanzas' appearing perfectly symmetrical. Without capitals to signal new lines, it becomes difficult to distinguish the overruns from indented lines without counting the syllables.[23] If Moore had

19. MM, Notebook 1250/1 (Rosenbach VII:01:01), 87. This remark follows her notes on I. Goldberg, "Are You a Pseudochromesthesiast? Colors Are Heard," Boston *Evening Transcript,* June 3, 1914.

20. For much of my understanding of Moore's stanzas I am indebted to Holley, *The Poetry of Marianne Moore,* especially her excellent discussions of rhyme (20–22) and the syllabic stanza (83–89).

21. Henry M. Sayre, *The Visual Text of William Carlos Williams* (Urbana, 1983), argues that the variable foot *is* arbitrary (2–4).

22. MM to Thomas P. Murphy, May 21, 1950, in *Marianne Moore Newsletter,* V (Fall, 1981), 15; MM, "Conversation with Marianne Moore," 156, 158; *MMR,* 263.

23. In response to Pound's suggestion, Moore stopped using initial capitals in 1919. After 1951 she moved overruns to the right of the page to prevent this confusion (*Prose,* 506). In at least one poem, "Critics and Connoisseurs," what should, according to the syllabic, rhyme, and typographical scheme, be an overrun becomes an asymmetrical seventh line in each stanza (*CP,* 38–39).

been aiming for appearance alone, she would have used shorter lines. Moore's stanzas are architectural, spatial forms made from an internal mathematics of syllabism and rhyme.

While syllabic meter is more audible in nonstressed languages such as Japanese and French than in stressed Germanic languages such as English, still syllabic meter and rhyme are usually aural qualities, not visual ones. But in Marianne Moore's poetry the more the rhyme and syllabic meter separate themselves from the rhythmic and syntactic flow of the sentence, the more spatial they become. Like the juvenilia of her contemporaries, Moore's earliest poems, the ones she wrote while a student at Bryn Mawr, have regular stressed rhymes, accentual (though not always regular) meters, and syntax that conforms to line length.[24] At the time of Moore's first professional publication in April, 1915, she had been writing poetry for eight years. Though she continues to publish conventionally rhymed, metered verses along with her experimental poems until the end of 1915, one may witness the evolution of her stanza in the poems she published from April, 1915, until July, 1916.

One of the two poems published in the *Egoist* in April, 1915, "To a Man Working His Way Through the Crowd," reveals the transition from metered to syllabic verse (rhyme and syllable count are indicated to the right).

To Gordon Craig: Your lynx's eye	*a* 8
Has found the men most fit to try	*a* 8
To serve you. Ingenious creatures follow in your wake.	13
Your speech is like Ezekiel's;	*b* 8
You make one feel that wrath unspells	*b* 8
Some mysteries—some of the cabals of the vision.	13
The most propulsive thing you say,	*c* 8
Is that one need not know the way,	*c* 8
To be arriving. That foreword smacks of retrospect.	13
Undoubtedly you overbear,	*d* 8
But one must do that to come where	*d* 8
There is a space, a fit gymnasium for action.[25]	13

24. See [Patricia C. Willis, ed.], "Marianne Moore's Poems Written in Early Youth," *Marianne Moore Newsletter,* V (Spring, 1981), 17–19.

25. MM, "To a Man Working His Way Through the Crowd," *Egoist,* II (April 1, 1915), 62.

Here the first two lines of each stanza are metered both accentually and syllabically; since these two lines are iambic tetrameter, they necessarily have eight syllables per line, four of which are stressed. The third line carries the iambic rhythm forward briefly until a strong caesura interrupts it. Though the position of the caesura is neither syllabically nor accentually regular and the section of the line after the caesura does not maintain the iambic meter, the third line does maintain a consistent pattern of thirteen syllables. Moore's break with conventional meter in the third line of her stanza implicitly praises Gordon Craig's break with convention and thereby expresses Moore's indebtedness to him. The poem portrays Gordon Craig as "wrath[ful]," "overbear[ing]," and "propulsive," the last quality reinforced by the "wake" he creates, by his "working his way through the crowd," and by the propulsive iambic meter. All of this energy arrives, however, in the last line at a "space" (emphasized in each stanza by the caesura)—one that nevertheless is "a fit gymnasium for *action*." The gymnasium, a space where action is formed and controlled, is, of course, Gordon Craig's stage. Parallel to the space-action duality in the poem are Craig's eye and his speech, the two qualities that Moore isolates for praise and that resonate elsewhere in "vision," "say," and "retro*spect*." This synthesis of space with action and of eye with speech anticipates Moore's own stanza, to which *she* is still arriving. In Moore's poetry one witnesses a sentence "making its way through" the stanza.

The third line of these stanzas exhibits the first of Moore's stanzaic innovations: typographical indentation and a move from accentual to syllabic meter—that is, to a meter that does not interrupt or compete with the natural rhythms of the sentence as, for instance, accenting "to" does in the penultimate line. The other poem published just below this one, "To the Soul of Progress" (later retitled "To Military Progress"), is altogether syllabic and also has the last line of a three-line stanza indented.

Her next innovation, evident in "To Browning," published in August, 1915 (later "Injudicious Gardening"), is a move to unstressed rhymes. Though she had used feminine (two-syllable) rhymes before, in the second stanza of "To Browning" only the final unstressed syllables of the second and fifth lines rhyme. Also in the second and fifth lines one can see what would eventually become a consistent practice: within a stanza rhymed lines are not equal syllabically but do begin typographically at the same point.

However—your particular possession—	11
The sense of privacy	*a* 6
In what you did, deflects from your estate	*b* 10
Offending eyes and will not tolerate	*b* 10
Effrontery.[26]	*a* 4

That Moore continues to make rhyme lines parallel typographically (as in lines 2 and 5) but not syllabically (as in lines 3 and 4) exemplifies her use of rhyme as a structural device, not necessarily an aural one.

These early experiments culminate in two poems that appeared in *Others* in December, 1915, "To Statecraft Embalmed" and "George Moore." Both poems are longer than earlier poems and both employ unusually complex patterns of typographical spacing, syllable count, and rhyme. In "George Moore," except for the central line, which matches the fourth and tenth lines, and the second and twelfth lines that do not rhyme, the second half of the poem inversely reflects the pattern of the first half.

In speaking of 'aspiration,'	*a* 8
From the recesses of a pen more dolorous than blackness itself,	17
Were you presenting us with one more form of imperturbable French drollery,	*b* 20
Or was it self directed banter?	*c* 9
Habitual ennui	*d* 6
Took from you, your invisible, hot helmet of anaemia—	*e* 16
While you were filling your "little glass" from the decanter	*c* 9
Of a transparent-murky, would-be-truthful "hobohemia"—	*e* 16
And then facetiously	*d* 6
Went off with it? Your soul's supplanter,	*c* 9
The spirit of good narrative, flatters you, convinced that in reporting briefly	*b* 20
One choice incident, you have known beauty other than that of stys, on	17
Which to fix your admiration.[27]	*a* 8

26. MM, "To Browning," *Egoist*, II (August 2, 1915), 126.
27. MM, "George Moore," *Others*, I (December, 1915), 105–106. In quoting these

Much more so than in "To Statecraft Embalmed," in which the rhymes and syllabic repetition are audible, the pattern of "George Moore" is spatial. Here syllabic meter, unstressed rhymes, the lengthiness of some of the lines, and the distance of rhymes from each other all contribute to a mostly inaudible pattern of rhymes and syllables that must be *seen*, along with the typographical pattern, to be recognized. Although Moore's subsequent poems are never as neatly symmetrical as "George Moore," this experiment reveals her predilection for geometric design. Again the structure is appropriate to the subject, for while Moore ridicules George Moore's self-conscious aestheticism (comparable with the poem's contrived symmetry), she praises his "spirit of narrative," which like the prose of her own poem, prevails despite the contrivance.

In nearly all of the poems Moore published through 1915 it is possible to pause slightly at the end of a line without disrupting the syntactic flow of the sentence.[28] Though it becomes increasingly difficult to make Moore's syntax agree with her line breaks, it first becomes ridiculous to do so in June, 1916, when Moore ends a line of "Pedantic Literalist" with the first word of a sentence, the article "A." A month later Moore would exploit this new freedom more fully by dividing the word "battle-/ship" at the end of a line. "Critics and Connoisseurs," published in July, 1916, contains the first fully realized Moore stanza, for here she has not only a typographical and syllabic pattern consisting of rhymed and unrhymed lines but, most significantly, a syntax liberated from stanzaic form, which allows her to write longer poems and to write more straightforward, naturally fluid prose sentences. Following are the first two stanzas:

There is a great amount of poetry in unconscious		14
Fastidiousness. Certain Ming		*a* 8
Products, imperial floor coverings of coach		12
Wheel yellow, are well enough in their way but I		
have seen something		*a* 16
That I like better—a		6
Mere childish attempt to make an imperfectly		
ballasted animal stand up,		*b* 20

poems with long lines, I follow Moore's late practice of moving overruns to the right in order to avoid confusing overruns with new lines.

28. There is one early exception: "My Lantern," *Lantern*, XVIII (Spring, 1910), 28 (Bryn Mawr).

A determination ditto to make a pup	*b* 12
Eat his meat on the plate.	6
I remember a black swan on the Cherwell in Oxford	14
With flamingo colored, maple-	*c* 8
Leaflike feet. It stood out to sea like a battle-	12
ship. Disbelief and conscious fastidiousness were the	
staple	*c* 16
Ingredients in its	6
Disinclination to move. Finally its hardihood	
was not proof against its	*d* 20
Inclination to detain and appraise such bits	*d* 12
Of food as the stream [29]	5

Like the cubists, Moore learned to pull form and content apart in order to draw attention to each; that is, she made form abstract. She made meter distinct from cadence in order to draw attention both to the spatial design of a poem and also to the dynamic rhythm of its prose. Although I am emphasizing her spatial design, the prose was probably her greater concern. Moore often expressed indebtedness to prose stylists such as Dr. Johnson, Sir Francis Bacon, Sir Thomas Browne, and Henry James and was fond of quoting, both as a principle and as an example of style, Ezra Pound's statement: "Say nothing—nothing—that you couldn't in some circumstances, under stress of emotion, actually say" (*Prose*, 592, 607; *MMR*, 261). In her 1916 essay "The Accented Syllable," she quotes thirteen passages of prose in which she believes "the tone of voice" rather than the meaning "gives us pleasure," such as the following one from *Tom Jones*: "Tom when very young, had presented Sophia with a little bird which he had taken from the nest, had nursed up and taught to sing" (*Prose*, 31). Note that here she makes the cadence abstract by asking readers to enjoy the tone of voice apart from the meaning. She explains: "By the tone of voice I mean that intonation in which the accents which are responsible for it are so unequivocal as to persist, no matter under what circumstances the syllables are read or by whom they are read" (*Prose*, 32). Thus, in her own poetry Moore aimed for prose accents that would persist despite the "circumstances" of the geometric stanza in which it appeared.

Perhaps it is not coincidental that the liberation of syntax from form in Moore's poetry occurred a few months after her December, 1915, visit

29. MM, "Critics and Connoisseurs," *Others*, III (July, 1916), 4.

to New York, when she first saw the cubist and cubist-inspired works of Picasso, Picabia, Bluemner, Hartley, and the Zorachs. Although Moore may not have made a conscious connection between cubist painting and her own poems, her geometric, abstract stanzas break up the natural fluidity of prose sentences as the geometric, abstract planes of cubism break up the fluid images of nudes, faces, and landscapes. In both cases, the geometry sometimes conforms to the image or syntax but often is at odds with it. And in both cases the effect is the same. By shattering our expectations, both Moore and the cubists force us to look at the structure of language and of visual images in new and startling ways, and both call attention to the structure of their work by abstracting it. A cubist nude forces viewers to realize at once that a nude is more geometrical than they had thought and also that it is essentially not geometrical—hence many viewers' initial outrage. By breaking the fluidity of the sentence, Moore likewise made readers aware of both regular and irregular rhythms in language and moreover enhanced their aesthetic experience by providing visual as well as auditory rhythms. (What makes syntax in poetry and line in painting *seem* fluid is the familiarity of the conventions, for their relationship to the reality they describe is just as artificial as are Moore's stanzas and the cubist planes.)

Moore's most radical experiments with the stanza occur from 1917 to 1919. Her notebook from her "Middle Pullman Period" indicates frequent meetings with members of the avant-garde; the heady discussions impressed and sometimes overwhelmed her. In the late fall of 1916 she recorded some of the conversation that occurred after a performance of Alfred Kreymborg's play *Lima Beans* at the Provincetown Playhouse. She notes that Ezra Pound's "versions of Fenollosa make me think of these Chateaux on 5th Ave near the Park" and in response to the question "Didn't you think Mina Loy was beautiful?" (Loy had performed in the play), Moore answered, "I thought her *dress* was beautiful."[30] The chateaux and *a* dress appear in "Those Various Scalpels" the following spring. In this poem, which may not be a portrait of Loy or any other specific individual (who could imagine such a person?), Moore seems to question the efficacy of the radical experimentation that she was encountering in New York *and* engaging in herself. Thus, in this playful self-parody she pushes her stanza to new extremes. She had divided the compound noun, "battleship," at the end of a line in "Critics and Connoisseurs" but now

30. MM, Fall, 1916, Notebook 1250/23 (Rosenbach VII:10:06), 48.

she divides "re-/Peating" and "su-/Perior"; in both cases, the lopped off syllable serves as end-rhyme. (Moore was still using capital letters to begin new lines.) She had used a mixture of long and short syllabic lines in her stanzas before but now uses an outrageous asymmetry, a syllabic pattern of 1-18-13-26-17 (with slight inconsistencies). The one-syllable line is in all but one instance a merely connective word, not one deserving emphasis; it is also a rhyming syllable. Following are the first two stanzas:

Those	*a*	1
Various sounds, consistently indistinct like		
intermingled echoes	*a*	18
Struck from thin glasses successively at random—the	*b*	13
Inflection disguised: your hair, the tails of two		
fighting-cocks head to head in stone—like		
sculptured scimitars re-	*b*	26
Peating the curve of your ears in reverse order:		
your eyes, flowers of ice		18
And	*c*	1
Snow sown by tearing winds on the cordage of disabled		
ships: your raised hand	*c*	18
An ambiguous signature: your cheeks, those rosettes	*d*	13
Of blood on the stone floors of French chateaux,		
with regard to which the guides are so		
affirmative—the regrets	*d*	26
Of the retoucher being even more obvious: your		
other hand [31]		17

The scalpels themselves suggest the way Moore's lines dissect her sentences. The typically graceful, fluid aspects of the woman—her hair, her eyes, her cheeks, her hands, her dress—are described in "lapidary" terms. Like the "intermingled echoes" (note the euphonic alliteration and assonance) and various stones throughout the poem, certain other images echo randomly: the "flowers of ice//And/Snow" and the "rosettes/Of blood"; the "tearing winds" and the "storm/Of conventional opinion"; the "bunches of grapes" and the "vertical vineyard." This is Moore's most "cubist" poem.

31. MM, "Those Various Scalpels," *Lantern*, XXV (Spring, 1917), 50–51 (Bryn Mawr).

In Moore's final revision of "Those Various Scalpels" she removed its most extreme structural devices: the divided words, the twenty-six syllable line, all but one of the one-syllable lines. But she preserved the one-syllable line and divided word in another poem of this period. "The Fish" (*CP*, 32-33) is also playful, and again fluidity confronts stone: sea confronts cliff, sentence confronts stanza.[32] Like synthetic cubism that plays with layers of reality and illusion, "The Fish" plays with layers of sense and nonsense. The poem describes a place where the sea meets a cliff, but the sea in this poem, contrary to expectations, is "black jade"; the wave, not cliff, has barnacles encrusted upon it; and "The water drives a wedge /of iron through the iron edge/of the cliff." Is the "defiant edifice" in the sixth stanza the sea or the cliff? Perhaps, as with positive and negative space in cubism, one cannot tell the difference: the "*lack* of cornice, dynamite grooves, burns, and/hatchet strokes . . . *stand/out* on it" (my emphasis). Sea and cliff, like fluid sentence and static stanza, seem to resist each other, one creating "hatchet strokes" in the other; however, each defines the other's shape.

Except from 1921 to 1932, when Moore turned first to free verse and then to prose exclusively, she would use the stanza she developed in 1915 and 1916 for the remainder of her career.[33] This stanza differs in fundamental ways both from conventional English verse and from free verse. At the time Moore began writing poems, conventional English verse consisted of 1) accentual meter, 2) a regular pattern of accented end-rhymes, 3) line breaks that typically conformed to breaks in syntax, and 4) an appearance on the page that was different from that of prose. The imagists and subsequent practitioners of free verse rebelled against the first two of these conventions: they wanted to preserve the accent, or cadence, of verse but to abandon its syllabic regularity; they abandoned end-rhyme altogether. But practitioners of free verse exploit more fully the possibilities of line breaks and the poem's appearance than had their predecessors. Thus, poets such as Loy, Pound, Williams, and Cummings use line breaks and typographical spacing to show the reader how, in the absence of rhyme and meter, to read the poem. A word at the end of a free verse line receives

32. I thank Randy Phillis for calling my attention to this parallel.

33. Beginning in the forties, however, she would occasionally depart from a regular pattern of stanzas, and later she did so more frequently. But these departures never quite return to the free verse form of the twenties. Usually they employ end-rhyme and some typographical indentation.

as much accentual and semantic emphasis as its rhymed prototype; a word in a line by itself or surrounded by white space receives even greater emphasis.

This is not the case with Moore's stanzas. Like conventional poems, Moore's are both accentual and metrical, but in her stanzas the accent and meter are independent of each other. Like free verse poems, hers contain the irregular cadence of prose, but this cadence is superimposed on an inaudible syllabic meter. Unlike free verse, Moore's stanzas consistently have at least two end-rhymed lines,[34] but because her rhymes are so often unstressed and because they occur at spatial rather than accentual intervals, they also provide a virtually inaudible form without interrupting the cadence. Line breaks and typography perform an opposite function in Moore's stanzas than they do in free verse. Instead of defining the rhythm of the poem, they define the spatial pattern of syllables and rhyme, a pattern that would not exist without them. The poems Moore converted from stanzas to free verse, such as "Picking and Choosing," "England," and "Peter,"[35] demonstrate how thoroughly her syllabic meter and rhyme disappear when the line breaks conform to the syntax. Compare the second stanza of "Picking and Choosing" with its free verse counterpart:

upward—accomplishes nothing. Why cloud the fact		12
that Shaw is self-conscious in the field of sentiment		
but is otherwise re-	*b*	19
warding; that James is all that has been		9
said of him if feeling is profound? It is not Hardy	*b*	14
the distinguished novelist and Hardy the poet,		
but one man (*SP*, 50)		16

Now the free verse version:

---

34. No critic that I have read has acknowledged that all of Moore's syllabic stanzas (in their original state) have a pattern of rhyme. Rhyme is integral to the structure of her stanza, not an occasional adornment.

35. The free verse versions of these poems are in Moore's *Complete Poems;* the stanzaic versions are in her earlier collections, such as *Selected Poems* (New York, 1935). If one regards Williams' variable foot as based on the breath of speech, it does not differ in principle from free verse as I describe it here. Even if one accepts Sayre's argument that the variable foot is essentially spatial, it is so only to the extent that white space interrupts the syntax; the variable foot does not define an internal architecture comparable to Moore's rhyme and syllabics.

accomplishes nothing. Why cloud the fact
that Shaw is self-conscious in the field of sentiment
but is otherwise rewarding; that James
is all that has been said of him. It is not Hardy the novelist
and Hardy the poet, but one man interpreting life as emotion.

(*CP*, 45)

Moore's stanza thus manages to synthesize the order of conventional poetry with the naturalness of free verse; it is no wonder her contemporaries
were envious.

But while in principle Moore's stanzas strike an ideal balance between
the formal, regular rhythms of poetry and the natural, irregular rhythms
of prose, after 1919 Moore became dissatisfied by the balance. As readers
became more and more accustomed to the conventions of free verse, it
frustrated Moore that readers treated her stanzas as free verse and would,
for instance, break the sound of a word in the middle if a line break occurred there. She revised some poems to keep this from happening.[36] Her
many published revisions show, too, that throughout her career she sometimes inclined to the "formal" side of the balance but more often to the
"natural" side. The most radical imbalance occurred during the twenties,
when Moore began revising stanzaic poems into free verse and wrote most
of her new poems in free verse.[37] If one regards the *Dial* "Comments" as
poem substitutes, then in the late twenties Moore departs completely from
poetic form, since she published no new poems from 1925 to 1932.
Furthermore, *Observations*, published in 1924 at the height of her free
verse phase, contains a number of revised earlier poems; while most of
these retain their stanzaic appearance ("Poetry," drastically shortened in
the second edition, is the notable exception), in several poems revisions
disrupt the original syllabic and rhyme pattern, and Moore did not repair the forms (*Obs*, 41, 48, 49, 61). However, the balance tilts the other
way when Moore returned to using stanzas in the thirties. In *Selected
Poems* (1935), "Poetry" is restored to its stanzaic form (though its pattern is now imperfect), and several other poems, such as "Those Various

36. MM, "Conversation with Marianne Moore," 162; MM to Dorothea Gray, November 5, 1935, in *Marianne Moore Newsletter*, II (Fall, 1978), 11.
37. Possible exceptions are four stanzaic poems ("An Egyptian Pulled Glass Bottle in
the Shape of a Fish," "The Bricks Are Fallen Down ," "'Nothing Will Cure the Sick Lion
But to Eat an Ape,'" and "Peter") published for the first time in *Observations* (New York,
1924).

Scalpels" and "Roses Only," which appeared in imperfect patterns in *Observations,* are restored to their original, formal perfection.[38] The subsequent collections, *Collected Poems* (1951) and *Complete Poems* (1967), show further revisions of the early poems, here nearly always in the interest of prose principles such as precision, concision, and the naturalness of speech. Again, she makes little effort to repair broken patterns and even uses ellipses in some poems to show that whole stanzas are excised (*CP*, 27, 30, 100). Consequently, those who read only the *Complete Poems* have the impression that the stanzaic patterns in the *Selected Poems* section are much more irregular than they originally were.

The less severe revisions to the poems published after 1935 indicate that in her later poems Moore felt increasingly more satisfied with the balance she attained between good prose and formal design. While it is true that the disparity between syntax and line breaks becomes less pronounced in the later poems, spatial design and syntax continue to resist one another. Despite Moore's expressed uneasiness with dividing words at the ends of lines, for example, she continued to divide them. She wrote in 1950: "I regard the stanza rather than the line as a unit and sometimes divide words at the end of a line, but try not to do it since the reader's resistance to unconventionality defeats one by diverting attention from that continuity which one's unconvention is attempting to attain."[39] In the *Complete Poems,* published in Moore's eightieth year, divided words such as "about" and "piloting" still appear fourteen times, more than half of these in poems first published from 1935 to 1943, and these fourteen do not include compound words such as "seaside" and "overcome," which are divided with much greater frequency. The very late poem "Avec Ardeur" (the one Moore was holding in a frame during her interview) consists of staccato rhymed stanzas (not syllabic ones), which playfully break up the otherwise fluid progression of her sentences. The poem is addressed to "Ezra, who knows what cadence is" and includes the lines: "Without pauses,/the phrases//lack lyric/force" (*CP*, 238–39).[40] Here Moore suggests that the "pauses" are essential to the poem's "lyric force," in other words, that her unusual line and stanza breaks are what make prose cadence into poetry. Though Moore retreated from her most radical ex-

38. "Poetry" appears in its original stanzaic perfection in *Others,* V (July, 1919), 5.
39. MM to Murphy, May 21, 1950, in *Marianne Moore Newsletter,* 15.
40. Moore's framed version, entitled "Occasionem Cognosce," was taken from the *New York Review of Books,* October 31, 1963, p. 19.

periments with form, as did modernist painters, she adhered to this cubist principle.

It is important to see Moore's stanza in its historical context. She developed it from 1915 to 1919, at a time when free verse was not yet the accepted norm for modern poetry, at a time when the early enthusiasts of imagism were rejecting the formlessness of free verse. These same writers were looking to the painters—or, more accurately, looking *with* the painters—for new forms. The adulation Moore received from other poets in the late teens indicates that her stanza did represent what they were all in various ways seeking. Though other poets no doubt learned from Moore, her stanza seemed so uniquely hers that they could not altogether adopt it (and perhaps, as with cubism, they did not altogether understand it). Instead, they continued to use line breaks and white space to define the rhythm of the poem, thus teaching readers of modern poetry the conventions of free verse, which were useless to reading Moore's stanzas. The punctuation and the natural intonation of the prose sentence provide the rhythm of Moore's poems, and the typographical spacing, syllabic meter, and rhyme form an "architecture" over which and through which her carefully wrought "tune" can flow.

My analogy between Moore's stanzas and cubism implies a nearly arbitrary relationship between Moore's syntax and her line and stanza breaks. But just as a cubist would not paint an abstract design of "cubes" and then fill in the design with eyes, noses, and other portions of his subject, neither does Moore begin a poem with an abstract design of syllables and rhyme. Still, the relationship between the prose "tune" and the formal "architecture" is extraordinarily tense in her poems of the late teens. As she revised certain of these poems in the twenties, she would sometimes coordinate line breaks with syntactic pauses for emphasis, as she did by making the final, epigrammatic stanza of "In the Days of Prismatic Color" irregular, in sharp contrast to the rest of the poem, in which syntax and line breaks are so at odds that she preserved four divided words. By the same token, altering the stanzaic pattern of "The Fish" so that the line "Accident—lack" becomes the playful "ac- / cident—lack" is surely no accident.[41] At the same time painters such as Arthur Dove and Georgia

---

41. See MM, "In the Days of Prismatic Color," *Lantern*, XXVII (1919), 35 (Bryn Mawr); MM, "The Fish," *Egoist*, V (August, 1918), 95; and these same poems revised (*Obs*, 49–50, 43–44).

O'Keeffe were turning away from their early experiments with abstraction toward more conventional representation, Moore was seeking greater co-ordination between line breaks and syntax as indicated by these revisions and especially her move to free verse.

Her simultaneous but more gradual movement away from the per-sonalities that had dominated her earlier poems toward animals and other subjects from nature indicates that Moore may have been seeking a more "organic" form. Although animals had appeared in some of Moore's earliest poems, they usually serve then as metaphors for persons—"To a Prize Bird" is about George Bernard Shaw, for example—but as I dis-cuss in subsequent chapters, Moore becomes increasingly interested in the animal for its own sake, as in "Black Earth" (1918) and "Peter" (1924). Organic subjects hold a new fascination for certain painters and photog-raphers of the twenties as well. In Chapter 5 I attribute this postwar shift to functionalism, an aesthetic that arose first among architects (before the war) in response to the new materials of the machine age, glass and steel. Architects—and later other artists—looked to nature for examples of form following function as analogies to the streamlined, unadorned forms to which glass and steel lend themselves. At the same time Georgia O'Keeffe began painting New York cityscapes in the twenties, she also began paint-ing shells and her famous flowers; likewise, Paul Strand was photograph-ing close-ups of machine parts as well as close-ups of rocks, lichens, and grasses. Because of their desire to reconcile beauty and technology, these artists looked to nature for forms based on mathematical, or geo-metrical, principles—thus, their ideas of organic form differed from nine-teenth-century ones. In 1923 Moore expresses admiration for Brancusi because (repeating Ezra Pound), "without mathematics, he arrives at a re-sult which is mathematically exact."[42] The functionalist aesthetic, which dominates Moore's poems of the thirties and forties, becomes evident in her work of the twenties, in poems such as "The Labours of Hercules" and "To a Snail."

Though the French philosopher Gaston Bachelard seems unaware of Moore's poetry and she to my knowledge never read his *The Poetics of Space*, these contemporaries would have empathized with each other's at-traction to spatial form. Bachelard finds a shell intriguing because it re-veals, without explaining, the "transcendental geometry" by which it was made.[43] Not despite but indeed because of the shell's geometry, it is

42. MM to Robert McAlmon, July 5, 1923 (Rosenbach V:40:06).
43. Gaston Bachelard, *The Poetics of Space,* trans. Maria Jolas (1958; Boston, 1969), 105. Bachelard lived from 1884 to 1962.

mysterious; Bachelard quotes Paul Valéry: "A *crystal*, a *flower* or a *shell* stands out from the usual disorder that characterizes most perceptible things. They are privileged forms that are more intelligible for the eye, even though more mysterious for the mind, than all the others we see indistinctly." [44] One of the first of Moore's numerous "privileged forms" is a snail. A draft of "To a Snail" indicates that it began in stanzas probably in the mid-teens,[45] but it first appears in free verse.

> If "compression is the first grace of style,"
> you have it. Contractility is a virtue
> as modesty is a virtue.
> It is not the acquisition of any one thing
> that is able to adorn,
> or the incidental quality that occurs
> as a concomitant of something well said,
> that we value in style,
> but the principle that is hid:
> in the absence of feet, "a method of conclusions";
> "a knowledge of principles,"
> in the curious phenomenon of your occipital horn. (*Obs*, 23)

The first eight lines are virtually a treatise on functionalism. The opposition to external adornment is fundamental to the functionalist aesthetic, as is the synthesis of beauty and morality in lines 2 and 3. The last four lines express what for Moore is also the essence of organic form, that it is at once geometrical and mysterious. Like Bachelard and Valéry, she values the mystery of the shell, the "principle that is hid," the principle hid not in murkiness and imprecision but in a form that is hard, compressed. The oxymoronic "method of conclusions" indicates a mysterious, hidden "method" that makes visible the geometric "conclusions." As in "To a Man Working His Way Through the Crowd," there is tension between a dynamic process and its spatial destination. Although both snail and, by implication, poet possess "a knowledge of principles," principles such as "compression" and what Bachelard calls the "teachings of a transcendental geometry," such principles can be recognized but not explained. Hid-

44. *Ibid.*, 105–106. Because of the affinities he perceived between Valéry and Moore, E. McKnight Kauffer urged Moore to read Valéry and sent her a copy of his essays.

45. Bonnie Costello reproduces an early stanzaic draft of "To a Snail" and discusses the sources of its quotations in "'To a Snail': A Lesson in Compression," *Marianne Moore Newsletter*, III (Fall, 1979), 11–15.

den in their "conclusions," these principles are as mysterious, as shy, as seductive as the snail's occipital horn.

According to Bachelard, a shell is one of several "primal images" of refuge, along with houses, nests, and even color; such images, he claims, are primal and universal because "whenever life seeks to shelter, protect, cover or hide itself, the imagination sympathizes with the being that inhabits the protected space."[46] He quotes the painter Vlaminck: "The well-being I feel, seated in front of my fire, while bad weather rages out-of-doors, is entirely animal. A rat in its hole, a rabbit in its burrow, cows in the stable, must all feel the same contentment that I feel."[47] If one accepts the universality of Bachelard's primal images, Moore becomes the archetype, not the oddity, among poets, for her poems overflow with images of animal well-being. Her favorite animals tend to be the burrowers, the nest and shell builders, and the armor bearers. Vlaminck's statement suggests, for instance, the nicknames that the Moore family chose for each other from *Wind in the Willows*: all burrowers, Marianne is "Rat," Warner is "Badger," and Mrs. Moore is "Mole." Among the animals of the poems, the jerboa "honors the sand by assuming its color" and "leaps to its burrow"; the plumet basilisk runs, flies, and swims "to get to/his basilica"; the frigate pelican "finds sticks for the swan's-down-dress/of his child to rest upon"; the ostrich "builds his mud-made/nest in dust"; the "strongly intailed" pangolin has not only the famous armor but also a "nest/of rocks closed with earth from inside, which he can thus darken" (*CP*, 14, 15, 20, 25, 100, 117–18); the dragon and jellyfish both have invisibility; and the paper nautilus is shell, nest, and armor all at once. And such "protected shapes" are not exclusive to animals. A *Dial* "Comment" shows Moore's predilection for "protected shapes" extending even to signatures and typography: "The secrets of Dürer, however, are not easily invaded, the clearness and simplicity of his signature in the adjusted yet natural housing of the D beneath the medievally prominent A, being a subtlety compared with the juxtaposed curves of the modern monogram, the printing of letters backward, or the variously arranged inverting of duplicates" (*Prose*, 203).

When Moore returned to writing stanzas in the thirties, she was not abandoning organic form. Rather, she seems to have reconceived her own stanza as organic. Two descriptions of her composition process illustrate

46. Bachelard, *The Poetics of Space*, 132.
47. *Ibid.*, 91.

this shift in thinking. In early 1919 Moore describes the process to Ezra Pound: "I have occasionally been at pains to make an arrangement of lines and rhymes that I liked, repeat itself, but the form of the original stanza of anything I have written has been a matter of expediency, hit upon as being approximately suitable to the subject."[48] In 1961 she similarly describes this process to Donald Hall, except that she substitutes for "expediency" as an explanation for the original stanza an analogy from nature: "Words cluster like chromosomes, determining the procedure." As in "To a Snail," Moore implies that the origins of the geometrical form are mysterious, even to the poet herself: "Spontaneous initial originality—say, impetus—seems difficult to reproduce consciously later" (*MMR*, 263). Margaret Holley concludes from examining Moore's stanzas of the thirties and forties that Moore was at this time balancing "organic" and "mechanical" forms: the first stanza composed (not necessarily the first in the poem) bears an organic relation to the syntax, and the rest of the stanzas mechanically repeat the pattern of the model one with apparent disregard for syntax. Holley locates an organic "model stanza" in virtually all the poems of these years.[49] That such a stanza cannot be readily identified in the stanzaic poems before 1930 indicates that organic form was a relatively late concept in the development of Moore's stanza. It was, however, a persistent and important one. Her growing attraction to geometrical patterns and rhythms in nature corroborates this. The poems of the thirties and forties celebrate "eight green/bands . . . painted on/the tail— as piano keys are barred/by five black stripes across the white," "close-//laid Ionic chiton-folds/like the lines in the mane of/a Parthenon horse" (*CP*, 22, 122), among many other such patterns.

Of course, Moore does not admire such patterns merely for their aesthetic appeal. She may have imagined her geometrical stanzas as her own form of protective armor, "scale/lapping scale with spruce-cone regularity," as her own "mirror-of-steel uninsistence" (*CP*, 117, 152). For Moore's stanzas do in a sense protect her "knowledge of principles" from even her most sympathetic admirers. Early on she stumped Ezra Pound, who wrote her, "I oughtn't to be too lazy to analyze your metric; but . . ."[50] And even

48. MM to Pound, January 9, 1919, in *Marianne Moore*, ed. Tomlinson, 17.

49. Margaret Holley, "The Model Stanza: The Organic Origin of Moore's Syllabic Verse," in *Marianne Moore*, ed. Kappel, special issue of *Twentieth Century Literature*, esp. 184.

50. Pound to MM, December 16, 1918, in *Selected Letters of Ezra Pound*, ed. Paige, 144.

now after years of knowing that Moore wrote in syllabic stanzas, most of her readers have not realized how thoroughly rhyme pervades those stanzas. For by using syllabism and unaccented rhyme, Moore chose forms that least resist the natural rhythms of speech and that therefore can long go undetected. Note, for instance, how unobtrusively the pattern persists in poems such as "The Sycamore," reprinted below, where the rhyme scheme—nearly all slant rhymes except for the emphatic central epigram—is *axabbxaa axabbxaa axabbxaa*. That Moore often did not mend broken stanzaic patterns as she revised her poems indicates further that she wished to preserve the original, organic forms, the mysterious "impetus"; as in broken shells, the "method of conclusions" remains visible.

One of Moore's strongest ties to other modernist poets is her love of visual detail. Just as Pound used "hardness" to describe H.D.'s poems when he was first promoting imagism, one can also call Moore's images "hard." H.D. did so herself in an early review, calling Moore's work "frail, yet as all beautiful things are, absolutely hard." Williams describes Moore's poetry as a "brittle, highly set-off porcelain garden." Hugh Kenner calls it "the language flattened, the language *exhibited*."[51] It seems difficult to describe Moore's distinctive imagery without spatial analogies. But neither her images nor their "hardness" is imagist, even in the broadest sense of the term. And while Moore is both descriptive and visual, she is never painterly, as Williams often is and as H.D. and Stevens can be. A comparison of Williams' "Young Sycamore" and Moore's "The Sycamore" demonstrates this difference.[52] First, Williams' "Young Sycamore":

> I must tell you
> this young tree
> whose round and firm trunk
> between the wet
>
> pavement and the gutter
> (where water

51. Hilda Doolittle [H.D.], "Marianne Moore," *Egoist*, III (August, 1916), 118; Williams, *Selected Essays*, 124; Kenner, *A Homemade World*, 106.

52. Although Williams' poem was first published in 1927 and Moore's in 1955, I maintain that the characteristics of Moore's poetry that I discuss here are evident at least as early as the twenties.

is trickling) rises
bodily

into the air with
one undulant
thrust half its height—
and then

dividing and waning
sending out
young branches on
all sides—

hung with cocoons—
it thins
till nothing is left of it
but two

eccentric knotted
twigs
bending forward
hornlike at the top.[53]

Now, Moore's "The Sycamore":

Against a gun-metal sky
I saw an albino giraffe. Without
leaves to modify,
chamois-white as
said, although partly pied near the base,
it towered where a chain of
stepping-stones lay in a stream nearby;
glamor to stir the envy

of anything in motley—
Hampshire pig, the living lucky-stone; or
all-white butterfly.

53. William Carlos Williams, *The Collected Poems of William Carlos Williams*, ed. A. Walton Litz and Christopher MacGowen (2 vols.; New York, 1986), I, 266–67.

A commonplace:
there's more than just one kind of grace.
  We don't like flowers that do
    not wilt; they must die, and nine
    she-camel-hairs aid memory.

    Worthy of Imami,
    the Persian—clinging to a stiffer stalk
      was a little dry
thing from the grass,
in the shape of a Maltese cross,
    retiringly formal
      as if to say: "And there was I
      like a field-mouse at Versailles." (*CP*, 167)

Both poets describe something they have seen, both use imagery, but, whereas Williams presents a single picture, Moore presents multifarious visual facts. Both trees are leafless sycamores, and both are specific trees; that one is young and next to the gutter of a city street while the other is old and next to a stream with stepping-stones is less significant than that Williams' tree seems to be part of everyday experience while Moore's, through association with an "albino giraffe," "nine she-camel-hairs" from Persia, a Maltese cross, and Versailles, becomes exotic. Williams' poem is self-sufficient and objective, making neither comment nor comparison (except for "hornlike," which makes one suspect Moore had Williams' poem in mind when she perceived her tree as a giraffe[54]). Moore's poem makes many comparisons as well as comments: the "albino giraffe" one may not recognize until the second reading is a comparison (actually, an "optical pun" as Hugh Kenner would call it[55]); the comments are both explicit—"there's more than just one kind of grace"—and implicit in words like "glamor" and "worthy." And whereas Williams' simple diction and syntax never interrupt the flow of the poem, Moore constantly makes the reader look back—to find that "chamois-white as/said" was "said" in "albino"—and startles with the unfamiliar—what is a "living lucky-stone"? "nine/she-camel-hairs aid memory"!

54. I agree with Slatin, *The Savage's Romance,* that Moore regularly included veiled allusions in her poems; Moore alludes to Williams' "Young Sycamore" at least twice in her prose (*Prose,* 144, 327).
55. Kenner, *A Homemade World,* 101.

Indeed, it is the interruptions that ultimately distinguish Moore's poem from Williams', just as her stream has "a chain of/stepping-stones" while in Williams' gutter "water/is trickling." Though one could hardly call Williams' poem narrative, it does take place in time, in the time it takes for the eye to follow the tree from the "wet//pavement and the gutter" upward to "the top," and conversely to read the poem from the top of the page to the bottom. The two main verbs of the poem's one sentence, "rises" and "thins," make the tree seem to grow with the poet's description of it, and the participles, "dividing and waning/sending out" and "bending," complement that growth. Moore's tree, in contrast, "tower[s]." Though technically an action verb, "tower" expresses size, not movement, and a rather immobile size at that. Nor do the other main verbs of the poem express movement: "saw," " lay," "[i]s," "like," "wilt," "die," "aid," "was," and "was." Instead of a fluid movement in time, Moore's poem creates a juxtaposition in space and, for once, a rather symmetrical juxtaposition. At the center of the central stanza is a couplet, an audibly rhymed epigram: "A commonplace:/there's more than just one kind of grace." On either side of the couplet are the two major images illustrating its principle, the tree itself and the unnamed "little dry/thing from the grass," each with various subordinate images attached by means of comparison.

Moore's poem presents not so much the tree itself as its abstract spatial qualities, especially size, shape, and pattern. (By "abstract," I mean that Moore does not use the spatial qualities to draw a mental picture of her subject as Williams does. Such abstraction is one of her most characteristic devices, as when she calls a swan's foot "maple-leaf like," and the top of a fir tree "an emerald turkey-foot." In "The Sycamore" the abstractions virtually bury their tenors.) It juxtaposes the size of the towering sycamore against the "retiringly formal" "little dry/thing" and the giraffe against a pig, a lucky-stone, an all-white butterfly, and a field mouse. It reinforces the shape of the sycamore's trunk with images of gun-metal, a giraffe's neck, a tower, the "stiffer stalk" to which "the little dry/thing" clings, and Imami's paintbrush. Moore explains in a footnote: "Imami, the Iranian miniaturist, draws 'with a brush made of nine hairs from a newborn she camel'" (*CP*, 287). Even more intriguing than sizes and shapes is the interplay of patterns, such as the "chain of/stepping-stones," "anything in motley," and the "all-white butterfly." To imagine an albino giraffe, the reader sees at once the patterned markings of a normal giraffe, like the pied base of the tree, and the pure "chamois-white" of the albino, like the rest of the tree. The juxtaposition of the Hampshire pig (black except for a white saddle) with its appositive, the lucky-stone (a dark stone with a natural white granite stripe through it), emphasizes the similar patterns of pig and stone while contrasting their sizes. Some of the patterns—the Persian miniatures, the Maltese cross, the vast rococo ornamentation of Versailles—suggest not only spatial design but world geography and history as well. Although there is no action or movement within the poem itself, time is contained in these spatial patterns. They resemble the snail shell, which embodies the hidden principles, the energy, that made it. A sycamore holds chronology in its immensity; flowers contain wilting and death in their beauty; and "nine/she-camel-hairs," as a paintbrush, "aid memory."

Because it occurs over time, however briefly, Williams' "Young Sycamore" does not fit Pound's definition of the image as "an intellectual and emotional complex in an instant of time" as strictly as does Pound's poem "In a Station of the Metro," in which there are no verbs.

The apparition of these faces in the crowd;
Petals on a wet, black bough.[56]

But Pound's poem does occur in time. The flux out of which the image is seized is as important to that image as are the unseen bodies to the apparition of faces. This is a poem as much about the flux of time as it is about the flux of the city, the flux of the crowd, and flux of the subway train. The isolated, snapshot image gives meaning to that flux just as Eliot's still point gives meaning to a turning world. Pound's poem resembles Moore's "The Sycamore" in its spatial juxtaposition and in its visual rhyme, but not in its sense of time. Whereas Pound's image exists in the moment of the glimpse, a moment that, in a sense, is between verbs, and Williams' "Young Sycamore" exists in the active present where things happen as we read about them, Moore's images exist in the present tense of generic statements. The middle stanza of "The Sycamore," for instance, is typical: "there's more than just one kind of grace./We don't like flowers that do/ not wilt; they must die, and nine/she-camel-hairs aid memory." But even the past tense of the first and third stanzas is not a narrative past expressing a sequence of actions or even a single event located in time; rather, it expresses recollected images, at least two of which are from photographs.[57]

56. Ezra Pound, *Personae: The Collected Poems of Ezra Pound* (New York, 1926), 109.
57. These photographs of an albino giraffe and of Hampshire pigs are reproduced in

In her provocative analysis of Moore's style, Marie Borroff systematically compares Moore's syntax and diction with Robert Frost's and Wallace Stevens' and reaches the conclusion that Moore's imagination "sees more meaning in fixity than in flux." In Moore's "An Egyptian Pulled Glass Bottle in the Shape of a Fish," for instance, one finds "a wave held up for us to see/in its essential perpendicularity" (*CP*, 83), whereas in Stevens' "Peter Quince at the Clavier" one finds a "wave, interminably flowing." [58] By comparing the ratios of nouns, verbs, adjectives, and adverbs in the three poets, Borroff discovers that Moore has proportionally fewer finite verbs (gerunds, participles, and infinitives are not finite verbs) than either Frost, who has the most, or Stevens, and that Moore's finite verb count resembles that of feature articles and scientific articles. [59] Not only are finite verbs infrequent, but when they do appear, they are usually stative rather than dynamic. Dynamic verbs express action and process (as "rises" and "thins" do in "Young Sycamore"); stative verbs express states of being, or facts. Borroff says:

> When language attempts to hold its subject matter constant, its grammar inevitably takes on stative characteristics. We can expect such language to contain few finite verbs; of the verbs it does contain, many, if not most, will be stative, and among these, the forms of *to be*, which can link any subject with any attribute in logical definition or factual statement, will tend to appear with obtrusive frequency. So will the passive voice, which in English usually takes the form of *to be* as "linking verb" followed by a past participle (i.e., a verbal adjective) . . . .
>
> All the above statements hold true for the language of Marianne Moore. [60]

"To a Snail," for example, uses "is" five times, plus the passive "is hid"; even the other finite verbs, "have," "occurs" and "values," link their subjects with attributes, not actions. "Those Various Scalpels" contains six finite verbs: "are" four times, "is" once, and "dissect"; the poem's first sen-

[Patricia C. Willis], "Albino and Motley in 'The Sycamore,'" *Marianne Moore Newsletter*, III (Fall, 1979), 9–10; see also Willis, *Vision into Verse*, 72–73.

58. Marie Borroff, *Language and the Poet: Verbal Artistry in Frost, Stevens, and Moore* (Chicago, 1979), 101.

59. *Ibid.*, 92–96.

60. *Ibid.*, 97.

tence, which occupies nearly four-fifths of the poem, has *no* predicate. The lack of dynamic verbs in Moore's poetry contributes to its apparent spatiality, its porcelain gardenness. Her poems are not events but exhibitions.

One of the great lessons of modernism is that "realism" in art is an illusion: the most straightforward sentence depends on the artifice of syntax and diction; the most "realistic" painting depends on conventions of perspective and line. That Henry James acknowledged the artifice of the novel, that Cézanne acknowledged the artifice of painting is what makes them both modern. Distorting, or abstracting, conventional forms of representation in order to expose their artifice is above all else the lesson of cubism. I have shown already that when Moore abstracts form in her stanza, she makes it spatial: she holds the syllabism, rhyme, and typography still against the current of the prose. Though it would appear that Moore's turn to free verse in the twenties marks a departure from such abstraction, by this time, as I intend to show, her syntax itself has become spatial, and it would remain so. This coincides with an increased attention to spatial imagery, where the shapes and patterns, as in "The Sycamore," are abstracted from the poem's subject. In lieu of her stepping-stone stanzas, in her free verse poems Moore creates a syntax of discrete, "hard" units through which the meaning must find its way. As she shifts from the imperative voice of her earliest poems to a more descriptive one, she uses proportionally more stative verbs, more multisyllable words, more catalogs, more out-of-context quotations, more hyphenated sequences, longer and more complex noun phrases. Present to some extent even in the early poems, these would characterize Moore's mature style.

The prose Moore admires even from the beginning is not fluid. The examples she commends in "The Accented Syllable" (1916) are, like Henry James's prose, characterized by strong interruptions—qualifiers, elliptical phrases, appositives, parenthetical asides. She admires a balance of long and short rhythmic units, as in the following sentence: "It is true enough to say that everybody is selfish provided we add, and unselfish" (quoted in *Prose*, 31). And although the rhythmic units, or prose "feet," are often punctuated, as in Ezra Pound's statement, "say nothing—nothing—that you couldn't in some circumstances, under stress of emotion, actually say," she especially admires cadence that does not depend on punctuation. Praising and quoting Gertrude Stein, she writes: "It is a feat of writing to make the rhythm of a sentence unmistakable without punctuation: for example, 'When they said reading made easy reading without tears and someone sent me such a beautiful copy of that'" (*Prose*, 341). I have shown already how in Moore's most experimental poems the balance of long and short syllabic lines creates a pattern at odds with the cadence. Now note the discrete prose "feet"—as determined by accent, syntax, and punctuation—that begin "Those Various Scalpels": "Those various scalpels[,] those various sounds, consistently indistinct like intermingled echoes struck from thin glasses successively at random— the inflection disguised: your hair, the tails of two fighting-cocks head to head in stone—like sculptured scimitars repeating the curve of your ears in reverse order." The unmistakable rhythm that Moore requires of her sentences demands an ornate, even obstructive syntax.

What Moore's syntax lacks in verbs she makes up for with nouns, producing what Kenner calls a "rain of nouns" and Borroff rephrases as a "hail" of nouns.[61] Catalogs of nouns appear more and more often after the mid-teens; an early example is the cryptic beginning to "Pedantic Literalist" (1916): "Prince Rupert's drop, paper muslin ghost, / white torch" (*CP*, 37). They proliferate in the free verse poems and reach their most extreme in "People's Surroundings," which consists nearly altogether of catalogs. But even when she has no concrete nouns, Moore nominalizes her syntax. Kenner points out her frequent use of nouns as adjectives,[62] such as "paper muslin ghost." "To a Snail" gives the impression of being as "hard" as any imagist poem because of its compactness and clarity; however, one is surprised to discover upon rereading it only two concrete images in the entire poem—the snail in the title and the occipital horn at the end. Whereas another poet might use "contract" in its verb form to describe the action of a snail, Moore transforms it not only into a noun but into an abstract quality, "contractility"; within this noun, however, dwells the energy of a verb, an energy not to be underestimated.

Quotation marks compress whole groups of words into nominative units. Moore uses quotations in some of her earliest poems, but as her style matures in the late teens and twenties, the quotations become shorter and more enigmatic. The quotation marks around "compression is the first grace of style" in "To a Snail," for instance, not only give the statement authority but also allow the quoted words to maintain a grammatical integrity of their own while functioning within the syntax of another sen-

---

61. *Ibid.*, 99; Kenner, *A Homemade World*, 101.
62. Kenner, *A Homemade World*, 110.

tence. As Margaret Holley points out, readers should be aware that quotation *marks* do not necessarily indicate direct quotations[63]; often the phrase included within the marks has been revised; sometimes direct quotations are not marked; and occasionally marks appear around phrases, such as "imaginary gardens with real toads in them," that may not be quotations at all. While quotations characterize Moore's poetry at all stages, they are densest in her free verse poems, especially "Marriage" and "An Octopus."

Moore's liberal use of hyphens creates similarly impenetrable syntactic units, such as "all-white butterfly" and "nine she-camel-hairs." Though not as pervasive as quotations, they also appear early. In "Roses Only" (1917) one finds: "it / is not because your petals are the without-which-nothing of pre-eminence. You would, minus thorns, / look like a what-is-this"; in "The Labors of Hercules" (1921): "the patron-saints-to-atheists, the Coliseum / meet-me-alone-by-moonlight maudlin troubadour" (*Obs*, 41, 63). Several extreme cases occur in "Virginia Britannia": "gray-blue-Andalusian-cock-feather pale ones, ink-lined on the edge" and "French plum-and-turquoise-piped / chaise-longue" (*CP*, 108, 109). Her frequent use of multisyllable words—such as "perpendicularity" and "fastidiousness"—has a similar effect, especially when they occur in dense, alliterative sequences: "to question / the congruence of the complement"; "that charitive Euroclydon / of frightening disinterestedness"; "miniature cavalcades of chlorophylless fungi" (*CP*, 84, 69, 74).

By using the generic present tense, Moore also manufactures syntactically "hard" facts and epigrams: who can question "Contractility is a virtue / as modesty is a virtue"? In "The Sycamore" even "nine/she-camel hairs aid memory" assumes the authority of the fact that precedes it, that flowers must die. The fact is like a quotation minus the quotation marks; it has a syntactic integrity of its own within a larger syntax, such as in this early example: "Prone to observe the self-evident fact: One cannot sweep the / Ocean dry, even when it comes against one's own door, but one can withdraw from the occupancy/Of land which is not very high: a just observation."[64] Not only her use of the generic present tense but also her diction contribute to the factuality of Moore's style. In comparing Moore's diction with that of Frost and Stevens, Borroff finds that although both Moore and Stevens have a high density of Romance-Latinate derivatives

63. Holley, *The Poetry of Marianne Moore*, 66–69.
64. MM, "An Ardent Platonist," *Lantern*, XXVI (Spring, 1918), 22 (Bryn Mawr).

in contrast to Frost, Stevens' "high formal language" comes from philosophy, Christianity, and traditional English poetry while Moore's "technical" idiom comes from journalistic and scientific prose. Thus, Stevens' archaisms express solemnity and reverence for the past,[65] but Moore's idiom has greater authority. The authority of science in modern society is so great that it demands neither solemnity nor reverence. Moore's technically and visually precise diction—"Without / leaves to modify," "chamois-white," "Hampshire pig"—and her consequent tone of clinical detachment thus contribute to the irrefutable hardness of her facts.

One of the most pervasive "information-compacting device[s]" in Moore's poetry, which is also characteristic of technical writing, is the complex noun phrase.[66] Consider the information compacted into this noun phrase from "An Octopus": "dots of cyclamen-red and maroon on its clearly defined pseudo-podia / made of glass that will bend—a much needed invention—/ comprising twenty-eight ice-fields from fifty to five hundred feet thick, / of unimagined delicacy" (CP, 71). It is from such compacting that Moore's poetry achieves its "flies in amber" effect. For by linking noun phrases together with few or no verbs, Moore creates entire poems that have the hardness of a chain of nouns. This catalog of abstractions from "To a Snail," for instance, "the principle that is hid: / in the absence of feet, 'a method of conclusions'; / 'a knowledge of principles,'" has the syntactic hardness of this catalog of concrete images from "The Sycamore": "Hampshire pig, the living lucky-stone; or / all-white butterfly." Thus, Moore compacts information (and energy) into nouns, quotations, hyphenated sequences, facts, and noun phrases. Where subordination or punctuation cannot link them, she uses an occasional stative verb as a link in the armor of her nominalized prose—a surface nearly as hermetic as that of the cubists.

Glenway Wescott writes of Moore's style: "The impulse of the mind is to avoid paths so stony, steep, and winding,"[67] which is why journalists, students, and other authors of expository prose are advised to avoid virtually all of the techniques I have just described. Like illuminated manuscripts and Blake's engravings, Moore's poetry makes readers look "at" her words. Not only do her dense noun phrases and stative verbs defy current pedagogy about expository writing, they defy what some consider

65. Borroff, *Language and the Poet*, 85–89.
66. *Ibid.*, 103.
67. Glenway Wescott, "Miss Moore's Observations," *Manikin*, no. 3 (1923), 1.

the very essence of language itself. The essential difference between poetry and painting according to Lessing is that one is temporal, the other spatial. Moore, however, like other modernists challenged such boundaries: cubist works such as *Nude Descending a Staircase* introduce the temporal into painting, and modernist writers, according to Joseph Frank and others, achieve spatial form in literature. Wendy Steiner says of the modernists, "The attempt to overreach the boundaries between one art and another is thus an attempt to dispel (or at least mask) the boundary between art and life, between sign and thing, between writing and dialogue."[68] Moore does attempt to overreach the boundaries of language—but never to make a painting out of words. For the thrust of her meaning, language's essential temporality, propels the reader along her stony path.

If one uses Moore's phrase, "the wave held up for us to see / in its essential perpendicularity," to demonstrate that Moore's imagination "sees more in fixity than in flux," one must acknowledge that the wave however perpendicular is itself an image of flux. Waves occur too frequently in Moore's poetry for this to be overlooked. As in this instance, the sea sometimes has an impossible stasis imposed upon it: it becomes "black jade" or is "etched / with waves as formal as the scales / on a fish" (*CP*, 32, 5). More often, as in "Novices," there is a "drama of water against rocks." Here the complacent novices, "perfect and poisonous from the beginning," are overpowered by the tumultuous sea, which Moore equates with "the spontaneous unforced passion of the Hebrew language," an "ocean of hurrying consonants" (*CP*, 60–61). But in "A Grave" it is the horizontal motions of the sea surface that invite complacency as they beautifully conceal the rapacious grave "in which dropped things are bound to sink" (*CP*, 49–50). In some cases the flux wins; in others the stasis.[69] What interests Moore is the drama between them.

68. Gotthold Ephraim Lessing, *Laocoön: An Essay on the Limits of Painting and Poetry*, trans. Edward Allen McCormick (1766; trans. Baltimore, 1984), 78; Joseph Frank, *The Widening Gyre: Crisis and Mastery in Modern Literature* (New Brunswick, N.J., 1963), 3–62; Steiner, *The Colors of Rhetoric*, 5.

69. Also see "The Fish," "In the Days of Prismatic Color," "Sojourn in the Whale," and "What Are Years."

3

PORTRAITS AND MISCELLANIES

The concern with the object in modern art cannot be overestimated. William Carlos Williams illustrates this modernist obsession with the following story:

> Alanson Hartpence was employed at the Daniel Gallery. One day, the proprietor being out, Hartpence was in charge. In walked one of their most important customers, a woman in her fifties who was much interested in some picture whose identity I may at one time have known. She liked it, and seemed about to make the purchase, walked away from it, approached it and said, finally, "But Mr. Hartpence, what is all that down in this left hand lower corner?"
> Hartpence came up close and carefully inspected the area mentioned. Then, after further consideration, "That, Madam," said he, "is paint."[1]

Thus is the art work itself, the signifier, objectified. In painting Cézanne is credited with first exploiting the tension between what Ellen Johnson calls "the painted object (oil, watercolour) and the object painted (mountain, tree)."[2] As discussed in the previous chapter, the means of representing the external world becomes increasingly opaque after Cézanne, forcing one to look "at" the canvas (or page) as well as "through" it. Picasso's pasting a piece of oilcloth onto the canvas in 1912 marks a significant moment in this progression. But collage really only advances the reification of the artist's materials that Cézanne, Braque, and Picasso himself had already begun. "They can paint with whatever they wish," wrote Apollinaire, "pipes, postage stamps, postcards or playing cards, candelabras,

---

1. Williams, *Autobiography*, 240.
2. Ellen H. Johnson, *Modern Art and the Object: A Century of Changing Attitudes* (London, 1976), 12.

pieces of oilcloth, starched collars."[3] The difference between collage and painting is one of degree: when part of a still life, an actual postage stamp relinquishes its thingness less readily than does a stroke of paint.

Discussions of collage—or the more general term *assemblage*—often point to a threefold objectification.[4] The first characterizes all representational art; it is "the object painted (mountain, tree)." Although this object can be extraordinarily elusive in twentieth-century art, it remains important in Cézanne, the cubists, and indeed all modern paintings and collages except arguably the purely abstract ones. The second object is what Cézanne and the analytic cubists called to the viewer's attention; it is "the painted object (oil, watercolour)." It consists of the formal properties of the art work—line, color, shape—that are also conventionally the artist's means of expression. Conventional paintings have form, too, but Cézanne and his followers abstracted it, making it distinct from the mountain or tree. By pasting unexpected materials into their compositions, the synthetic cubists introduced a third objectification: the non-paint object (oilcloth, postage stamp). Thus, a newspaper clipping pasted into a still life has a threefold function: it represents a newspaper (or, depending on its shape, possibly a bottle) in the scene described by the painting; its shape and placement contribute to the overall composition; and even Mr. Hartpence's customer would see that it also remains itself a newspaper. Likewise, in Arthur Dove's *Portrait of Ralph Dusenberry*, the folding carpenter's rule suggests Dusenberry's job as an architect, it frames the composition, and it very much *is* a pocket rule.

Just as important as recognizing that Cézanne's and the cubists' accomplishment was heightenening the *tension* between the represented subject and the formal painting is recognizing the tension in collage between subject, form, and the assembled objects. The equilibrium between the three is not, however, necessarily balanced; rather, since some assemblages are closer to one or two poles than another, imagining a three-way continuum among the poles provides a means for distinguishing assem-

3. Guillaume Apollinaire, *Apollinaire on Art: Essays and Reviews, 1902–1918,* ed. Leroy C. Breunig, trans. Susan Suleiman (New York, 1972), 281.

4. See, for instance, Barbara Haskell, *Arthur Dove* (San Francisco, 1974), 52. Katherine Hoffman, "Collage in the Twentieth Century: An Overview," in *Collage: Critical Views,* ed. Katherine Hoffman (Ann Arbor, 1989), provides a useful clarification of terms: *collage,* though commonly applied to many genres including literature, technically refers only to pasted paper; thus, *assemblage,* which includes collage, is more appropriate to three-dimensional art works and literature (5). I use these terms accordingly.

Figure 15 Kurt Schwitters, *Picture with Light Center*

1919. Collage of cut-and-pasted papers and oil on cardboard. $33\,1/4 \times 25\,7/8$ in. The Museum of Modern Art, New York. Purchase.

blages. At one pole are abstract collages, such as those by German artist Kurt Schwitters; while the disunity of the many fragments pulls against the unified formal composition, still the latter dominates. At another extreme, assemblages of a few objects such as Man Ray's assisted readymades

Figure 16 Man Ray, *Indestructible Object*

1964. Replica of 1923 original *Object to be Destroyed*. Metronome with cutout photograph of eye on pendulum. $8\,^{7}/_{8} \times 4\,^{3}/_{8} \times 4\,^{5}/_{8}$ in. The Museum of Modern Art, New York. James Thrall Soby Fund.

(one has a picture of an eye glued to the staff of a metronome) call attention to the objects themselves and deemphasize—rather, ironically subvert—the form. Both Schwitters and Ray distance themselves from rational representation. They are among the European and American dadaists who were attracted to the irrationality of juxtaposed objects: in Isidore

Figure 17 Arthur Dove, *Portrait of Ralph Dusenberry*

Ducasse's famous phrase, the "chance encounter of a sewing machine and an umbrella on a dissecting table." [5]

Closer to the representational pole are the assemblages of Arthur Dove.

5. Isidore Ducasse, quoted in Haskell, *Arthur Dove,* 54.

While Dove's assemblage portraits, such as *Portrait of Ralph Dusenberry* and *Grandmother*, do not represent what the subject looks like, the objects assembled represent individually and cumulatively the essence or soul of the person. Dove himself explains the playful significance of the hymn "Shall We Gather at the River," a fragment of which is included in *Portrait of Ralph Dusenberry*.

> Apropos of the hymn in the "Ralph Dusenberry," the Dusenberrys lived on a boat near us in Lloyd's Harbor. He could dive like a Kingfish[er] and swim like a fish. Was a sort of foreman on the Marshall Field Place. His father was a minister. He and his brother were architects in Port Washington. He drove in to Huntington in a sleigh one winter and stayed so long in a café there they had to bring a wagon to take him home. He came home to his boat one day with two bottles, making his wife so mad that she threw them overboard. He dived in right after them and came up with one in each hand. When tight he always sang "Shall we gather at the river."[6]

Nor is it difficult to justify the presence of other objects in this portrait: "The carpenter's rule as a symbol of architecture makes a frame; the flag, [suggests] the patriotic nature of Dusenberry, and the arrow forms his diving and swimming ability; while the weather-worn wood shingles suggest water and sun-soaked piers."[7] (Not all of Dove's assemblages are so easily explained.) Dove's assemblages are even closer to the representational pole, I would argue, than the more literally representational collages of the synthetic cubists, for in the latter there is play between real and invented, as in the imitation wood-grained wallpaper and the trompe l'oeil nameplate, but Dove's portraits aim for a deeper, ineffable reality beyond surface appearances. Barbara Haskell classifies certain of Dove's assemblages as object portraits: instead of representing the literal appearance of the subject, an object portrait uses an object or combination of objects to suggest, often cryptically, aspects of the subject's character.[8] Though Dove's are the only assemblages, Charles Demuth, Marsden Hartley, Francis Picabia, and Marius de Zayas also composed object por-

6. Arthur Dove, quoted in Frederick S. Wight, *Arthur G. Dove* (Berkeley, 1958), 51.

7. Suzanne Mullett Smith, "Arthur G. Dove" (M.A. thesis, American University, 1944), quoted in Wight, *Arthur G. Dove*, 52.

8. Haskell, *Arthur Dove*, 54.

traits. Unlike the European synthetic cubists who preferred still life, these members of the Stieglitz circle were drawn to portraiture, the most elusive of subjects.[9] It should not be surprising that writers such as Gertrude Stein and Marianne Moore, whose medium is more incorrigibly representational, should likewise be drawn to portraiture and are with Dove closer to the representational pole than are the synthetic cubists or dadaists.

Moore's extensive use of quotations and especially the dailiness of their sources—newspapers, advertisements—have made her affinities with collage seem obvious. Other poets used assemblage techniques as well. But whereas the quotations in Pound and Eliot are primarily from privileged texts of literature, history, and religion, the sources of quotations in Moore and Williams (especially in *Paterson*) are more democratic, more transient, more random. And the effect is different. The fragmented quotations in Pound and Eliot emphasize the brokenness of the texts from which they derive, because the whole of the text is known, at least culturally. In Moore and Williams, on the other hand, the fragments seem rescued from the flux of modern life as they do in virtually all visual collages of the twentieth century. Instead of alluding to the lost meaningfulness of European culture, the preserved fragments in Moore and Williams suggest an American exuberance at discovery. Still, Moore's use of assemblage differs from Williams': not only is it more pervasive in her work and more central to her aesthetic, but also it is more difficult, more enigmatic.

There is little question of influence here. Moore used a quotation in 1907 in her first published poem ("Under a Patched Sail") and published a "found poem" ("Councell to a Bachelor") as early as 1913. Her use of quotation predates synthetic cubism by five years and *Paterson* by more than thirty years; her "found poem" predates Duchamp's *Fountain* by at least four years. The threefold tension of assemblage described above is not only fundamental to Moore's aesthetic virtually from its inception, but it also provides a paradigm for explaining the progression of Moore's poetry from the portraits of the mid-teens to the assemblages of the twenties and beyond—which, as I shall explain, become "unintentional" self-portraits. If the three poles are conceived graphically as a triangle—

9. Both Demuth and Picabia had strong ties to the Arensberg circle too, but at the time they created their object portraits—Picabia in 1915, Demuth in the twenties—they were closely associated with Stieglitz.

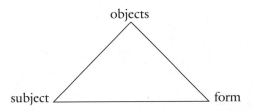

—then Moore's earliest poems exist in tension between the representational subject and the form, or stanza. The pull of the third pole becomes ever stronger throughout the late teens and early twenties, resulting in long, free verse assemblages in which as much as two-thirds of the poem is quoted material. From the thirties, when Moore returns to her formal stanzas and uses quotation more moderately, she moves back toward the center of the triangle, maintaining a greater equilibrium between the three poles.

To call Arthur Dove's portraits representational requires clarification, for they are not representational in the usual sense. Along with Kandinsky and Malevich, Dove is generally regarded as one of the earliest Western painters to use pure abstraction (around 1910) and repeatedly describes his own work as nonrepresentational. He refers to his own "search for a means of expression which did not depend upon representation. It should have order, size, intensity, spirit, nearer to the music of the eye." [10] Like other members of the Stieglitz circle, he believes in an invisible spirit underlying matter and tries to capture the essence, or spirit, of his subjects. His early abstractions, for instance, use "motifs" from nature—color and line—to capture the essence of a plant or cow or windy hillside without relying upon recognizable images. One of these he describes: "Then one day I made a drawing of a hillside. The wind was blowing. I chose three forms from the planes on the sides of the trees, and three colors, and black and white. From these was made a rhythmic painting which expressed the spirit of the whole thing." [11] So Dove does not really abandon representation even in his abstractions—but rather replaces the expected visible subject with an invisible one. When he turns to portraiture a decade later, his purpose does not change. In a poem (from which Moore

10. Arthur Dove to Samuel Kootz, 1910s, quoted in Haskell, *Arthur Dove*, 134.
11. *Ibid.*

103

Figure 18 Marius de Zayas, *Abstract Caricature of Alfred Stieglitz*

c. 1913. Charcoal.

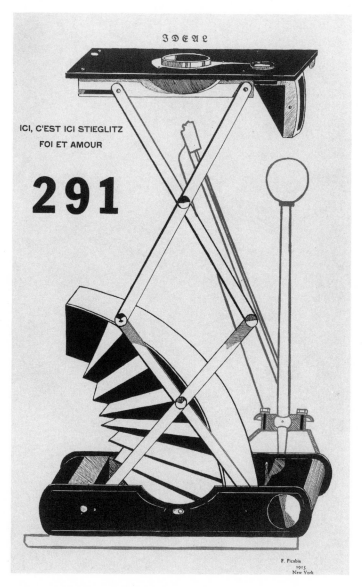

Figure 19 Francis Picabia, *Ici, c'est ici Stieglitz*

Lithograph. Cover for *291*, nos. 5–6 (July–August 1915). Philadelphia Museum of Art.
Louise and Walter Arensberg Collection.

Figure 20 Marsden Hartley, *Portrait of a German Officer*

1914. Oil on canvas. 68 ¼ x 41 ⅜ in. All rights reserved, The Metropolitan Museum of Art. The Alfred Stieglitz Collection. 1949. (49.70.42).

quotes approvingly, *Prose*, 150–51), Dove writes: "I'd rather have truth than beauty/I'd rather have a soul than a shape/ . . . I'd rather have the impossible than the possible."[12] Conventional representation works fine to convey "the possible," but to convey "truth," "a soul," and "the impossible" requires unconvention and indirection.

The elusiveness of a soul as a subject may account for the various experiments with portraits that engaged members of the Stieglitz circle, especially from 1915 through the twenties. The Mexican immigrant Marius de Zayas was well known as a newspaper caricaturist at the time he became associated with 291 and had his first exhibition there in January, 1909. Influenced by Apollinaire's *ideogrammes,* in the mid-teens de Zayas created experimental caricatures he called "psychotypes": instead of accentuating the appearance of the subject, these drawings use abstraction, words, and even mathematical equations to capture the spirit of the personality. During an extended stay in New York in 1915, Francis Picabia became closely associated with de Zayas and *291*, a magazine de Zayas had conceived and convinced Stieglitz to publish. Picabia at that time began creating "machine portraits," which resemble de Zayas' psychotypes in their use of words but which use a commercial-looking image of a machine to symbolize a personality. One of these drawings depicts Stieglitz as a broken camera.[13] The camera is an obvious symbol for Stieglitz, but how to explain its brokenness? Not only must the verbal phrases be read and understood, but also the visual images must be interpreted. For the symbolism is enigmatic to say the least and was often inaccessible even to Picabia's closest associates.[14]

Around the same time but in Berlin, Marsden Hartley was working on a series of abstract portraits commemorating the death of his intimate friend Karl von Freyburg. The most famous of these, *Portrait of a German Officer,* uses letters, numerals, and military emblems to symbolize not only his friend but also "all that is inspiring in young life."[15] These portraits are the fulfillment of an idea conceived several years earlier in Paris as a result of Hartley's readings in mysticism and his friend-

12. Arthur Dove, "What Photography Means to Me," *MSS.* (June 19, 1922), quoted in Haskell, *Arthur Dove,* 135.

13. Many of de Zayas' and Picabia's portraits appeared in *291* during the summer and fall of 1915; Moore likely saw these issues when she visited de Zayas' Modern Gallery in December of that year.

14. William A. Camfield, *Francis Picabia* (New York, 1970), 24.

15. Marsden Hartley to Adelaide Kuntz, May 30, 1929, quoted in Gail R. Scott, *Marsden Hartley* (New York, 1988), 53.

ship with Gertrude Stein, whose experimental prose portraits Hartley would have read in *Camera Work*. Hartley wrote Stieglitz from Paris that Stein "thinks I have gone miles beyond them all—Picasso included because I have succeeded in leaving out the physical element and giving for the first time the pure spiritual." [16] Also influenced by a friendship with Stein are Charles Demuth's poster portraits of the twenties. These portraits of avant-garde celebrities such as Georgia O'Keeffe, Eugene O'Neill, and William Carlos Williams use letters, numerals, and objects to evoke enigmatically the personality and artistic style of the subject; some also include private symbols of Demuth's relationship with the person. As with Dove's and Picabia's especially, the symbolism of Demuth's portraits invites a virtually literary reading. [17]

Besides Stein, another obvious influence on all of these artists is Stieglitz himself. His portraits are among his greatest photographic achievements, notably his serial portrait of Georgia O'Keeffe taken over many years. Though unlike the portraits just described they depict the subject's face (or hands or torso), they also aim, as do Stieglitz's other photographs, for something beyond appearances. Hartley praises Stieglitz's portraits above all in existence either in painting or photography for "so definitely present[ing], and in many instances with an almost haunting clairvoyance, the actualities existing in the sitter's mind and body and soul." [18]

When Marianne Moore arrived in New York in December, 1915, she had published nearly twenty poems in the past year, more than half of which are portraits. Her scrapbook of this time shows that she shared with de Zayas and Stieglitz an interest in caricature. And her letters as early as Bryn Mawr contain detailed prose portraits of persons who strongly impress her, such as C. R. Ashbee, an architect whom she heard lecture, and Paul Haviland's cousin, who introduced her to *Camera Work*. Her December, 1915, letters to her brother contain similarly detailed portraits of Stieglitz and the Kreymborgs. One of the more memorable and concise portraits from her letters (though a later one) recalls H.D. at Bryn Mawr.

My first impression of Hilda is very clear. There is a big forsythia bush

16. Marsden Hartley to Alfred Stieglitz, October 22, 1913 (Beinecke).

17. See Abraham A. Davidson, "Demuth's Poster Portraits," *Artforum*, XVII (November, 1978), 54–57; and Timothy Anglin Burgard, "Charles Demuth's *Longhi on Broadway: Homage to Eugene O'Neill*," *Arts Magazine*, LVIII (January, 1984), 110–13. Demuth's poster portraits of O'Keeffe and Dove appeared in the *Dial* during Moore's editorship.

18. Marsden Hartley, *Adventures in the Arts* (New York, 1921), 105.

on the campus at Bryn Mawr near Taylor Hall, the central building on the campus (an office building and lecture-hall combined) and a main campus path passes along the side of each side of the building. I remember Hilda passing this bush in a great hurry on the path leading from Rockefeller Hall—and the Bryn Mawr village—to Dalton Hall, the science building. She struck me as being extremely humanitarian and detached, as if she would not insult you by coldness in the necessary and at longest, brief moment of mutual inspection but I felt that she was not interested in the life of the moment. I remember her eyes which glittered and gave an impression of great acuteness and were, as I said, sunny and genial at the same time. I remember her seeming to lean forward as if resisting a high wind and have the impression of the toe of one foot turning in a little and giving an effect of positiveness and willfulness. I thought of her as an athlete, I believe. Hilda's being a nonresident was very much to the loss of the resident members of the class. Katherine Ecob a classmate of ours, who has no interest whatever in art and never thought of Hilda's having any, has a great affection for her and has chiefly the impression of her social charm and bed-rock reliability.[19]

Moore's early portrait poems indicate that she is well aware of what Wendy Steiner calls "the paradox of the co-presence in portraiture of two different and normally antagonistic sets of norms—the aesthetic and the specifically referential." A mug shot is not a portrait because, being entirely referential, it does not include an artist's interpretation; yet a portrait must refer to a specific thing external to the artist's imagination, an individual person.[20] If the viewer (or reader) shares the artist's perception—that looks just like so and so!—she takes pleasure in the referential; if there is little immediate recognition, as in the experimental object portraits described above, her attention is diverted from the referential to the artist's interpretation. (To jump ahead of myself, thus does the portrait become simultaneously something of a *self*-portrait of the artist.) While the aesthetic and referential are not unique to portraiture, their necessary copresence in the genre makes the portrait a vivid test case of the modernist dualism between what Cézanne calls "the eye and the brain": "The

---

19. MM to Winifred Ellerman [Bryher], July 7, 1921 (Rosenbach V:08:06).
20. Wendy Steiner, *Exact Resemblance to Exact Resemblance: The Literary Portraiture of Gertrude Stein* (New Haven, 1978), 4–5.

two must co-operate; one must work for the development of both, but as a painter: of the eye through the outlook on nature, of the brain through the logic of organized sensations which provide the means of expression."[21]

In most of Moore's portrait poems of 1915 the artist persona *I* addresses the subject of the portrait as *you*. This shows her interest not in merely representing her subject but in seizing the interaction between artist and subject, between the aesthetic and referential. Sometimes the reader will share the persona's response: "To Bernard Shaw: A Prize Bird" begins, "You suit me well for you can make me laugh."[22] But often the response is so personal that the reader is helplessly excluded: not until 1924, when the footnotes appeared in *Observations,* would readers learn that the stimulus for "To Browning" is a brief exchange about yellow roses in the letters of Robert and Elizabeth Browning. The inaccessibility of the reference deemphasizes Browning, the *you*, and highlights instead the unique subjectivity, even idiosyncrasy, of the artist's imagination. That Moore sometimes addresses abstract qualities ("To the Soul of 'Progress'") instead of persons indicates her interest at this time not just in portraiture but in the larger interplay of imagination and reality. That she was simultaneously developing her spatial stanza reinforces this interest, for the stanza is itself an imaginative construct opposed to the referentiality of the sentences. Thus do these early poems exist in tension between the referential subject and the poetic form (recall the triangle), between reality and the imagination, between the *you* and the *I*.

Any portrait that uses metaphor could be called an "object portrait." What is remarkable about Dove's and the other object portraits I mentioned is that they overcome the usual boundaries of visual art by using metaphor, a literary device. Metaphor's essential literariness is indicated even in these portraits by their reliance on words, at least in the form of a title, to convey the metaphor's tenor. The central metaphor in many of Moore's early portraits—Shaw is "a prize bird," Disraeli a chameleon—makes them, in a sense, object portraits, too, but this is hardly unusual for poetry. What happens in Moore's poetry after 1915 is that the two halves of the metaphor reverse their conventional hierarchy. The vehicle (the object) begins to dominate the tenor (the subject). The most obvious indication of this is the disappearance of proper names. Whereas ten of the

21. Paul Cézanne, quoted in Johnson, *Modern Art and the Object,* 11, from Joachim Gasquet, *Cézanne* (Paris, 1926), 205.

22. MM, "To Bernard Shaw: A Prize Bird," *Egoist,* II (August 2, 1915), 126.

1915 portraits had addressed famous persons by name, "Is Your Town Nineveh?" (1916) and "French Peacock" (1917) would be the last to name their subjects (Jonah and Moliére, respectively) for several decades. Moore also removed the proper names from some 1915 portraits as she republished them: "To Bernard Shaw: A Prize Bird" becomes "To a Prize Bird"; "To Browning" becomes "Injudicious Gardening." As some of these titles indicate, this shift away from the tenor would evolve toward the famous animal poems of the thirties and forties.

If the vehicle usurps the tenor completely, the metaphor ceases to be. There is little doubt, for instance, that "To a Steam Roller" (published October, 1915) is a metaphor even though the unimaginative critic who is the tenor of that metaphor is not named.[23] But in "You Are Like the Realistic Product of an Idealistic Search for Gold at the Foot of the Rainbow," published seven months later, it is not as clear that a person is being addressed rather than an actual chameleon. The tenor, if there is one, is well hidden.

Hid by the august foliage and fruit of the grape vine,
Twine
    Your anatomy
       Round the pruned and polished stem,
          Chameleon.
          Fire laid upon
       An emerald as long as
    The Dark King's massy
One,
Could not snap the spectrum up for food as you have done.[24]

Whether literally or figuratively, the subject of this poem is a chameleon, one of Moore's favorite animals, a master of disguise taunting the reader to discover its true identity. Though the reader may embark on "an ide-

23. MM, "To a Steam Roller," *Egoist*, II (October 1, 1915), 158. The lines "As for butterflies, I can hardly conceive / Of one's attending upon you" suggest the poem may be directed to the type of critic James McNeill Whistler quotes in *The Gentle Art of Making Enemies* (New York, 1890), one of Moore's favorite books at the time she wrote the poem. Whistler's signature was a butterfly, and above a collection of derisive comments from Whistler's critics included in this volume is his own remark: "Who breaks a butterfly upon a wheel?" (93).

24. MM, "You Are Like the Realistic Product of an Idealistic Search for Gold at the Foot of the Rainbow," *Egoist*, III (May 1, 1916), 71. The title later becomes "To a Chameleon."

alistic search" for a tenor to this metaphor, she cannot get past "the realistic product." The poet persona is taunting her reader, too, with an apparently unidentifiable allusion to the Dark King.[25] As in Picabia's single-object portraits, Moore's chameleon so dominates this portrait that both artist and subject recede into mysteriousness.

Thus, as Moore moves away from metaphor, the third pole of the triangle, the object, tugs against the other two, the aesthetic and the referential. But while the chameleon has much of the ironic ambiguity of objects in assemblages, still this poem is no assemblage. For the chameleon is not yet "assembled" with other objects and, more importantly, it has not been extracted from another existence. Over the next few years Moore would begin coalescing such enigmatic images, as in her most experimental object portrait, "Those Various Scalpels," and she had already begun to use quotations—which, though not as concrete as the chameleon, have a more direct claim to an external reality, their original text.

An admirer of Browning, Moore wrote most of her poems at Bryn Mawr as short dramatic monologues (a form of portrait). Apart from a dramatic monologue being itself an extended quotation, several of these poems and a few subsequent ones also contain quotations composed by Moore and attributed to her fictional characters. Two poems published in the *Egoist* in October, 1915, are the first to appropriate quotations from other sources: "To a Steam Roller" quotes Lawrence Gilman; "Diligence Is to Magic as Progress Is to Flight" quotes a nursery rhyme. Once started, Moore seems to have taken to this practice readily. "*So far as the future is concerned* . . ." (later titled "The Past Is the Present") typifies the quotations of late 1915 and early 1916 because the context of the original quotation relates to the subject of the poem; in this case the context is given within the poem: "This man said—I think that I repeat / His identical words: 'Hebrew poetry is / Prose with a sort of heightened consciousness. "Ecstasy affords / The occasion and expediency determines the form."'" Moore's poem is about Hebrew poetry, the man quoted (Moore's minister) is speaking about Hebrew poetry, and the source he quotes is presumably about Hebrew poetry.[26]

With "Pedantic Literalist" (June, 1916), the effect is quite differ-

25. See "Queries," *Marianne Moore Newsletter,* I (Spring, 1977), 20.

26. MM, "*So far as the future is concerned . . . ,*" *Others,* I (December, 1915), 106. Moore later closed the quotation after *consciousness* and did not use quotation marks at all around the final sentence.

ent, for here the context of the several quotations, all from Richard Baxter's *The Saints' Everlasting Rest*, has at best an ironic relationship to the subject of the poem. Moore demonstrates the foibles of pedantic literalism herself by showing how a change of context can distort the meaning of even literal quotations—yet another development in her exploration of the relationship between imagination and reality. The quotations are even more perplexing in "In This Age of Hard Trying Nonchalance Is Good, And" published the following month.

"Really, it is not the
Business of the gods to bake clay pots." They did not
Do it in this instance. A few
Revolved upon the axes of their worth,
As if excessive popularity might be a pot.

They did not venture the
Profession of humility. The polished wedge
That might have split the firmament
Was dumb. At last it threw itself away
And falling down, conferred on some poor fool a privilege.

"Taller by the length of
A conversation of five hundred years than all
The others," there was one, whose tales
Of what could never have been actual—
Were better than the haggish, uncompanionable drawl

Of certitude; his by-
Play was "more terrible in its effectiveness
Than the fiercest frontal attack."
The staff, the bag, the feigned inconsequence
Of manner, best bespeak that weapon—self-protectiveness.[27]

The first two quotations especially are so bizarre that one strains to imagine how they could have made sense in any context, but the quotation marks seem to assure that they have. Apparently when Moore wrote this poem, preserving the verification of her quotations was not as important

27. MM, "In This Age of Hard Trying Nonchalance Is Good, And," *Chimaera*, I (July, 1916), 52–55.

as it became later, for when she appended notes to it eight years later she misattributed the first quotation to Dostoyevsky (later she switched to Turgenev) and never cited sources for the other two. Not only the quotations tease readers with the possibility of reference just beyond their grasp, but "this instance," "The polished wedge," and "there was one" all seem to point to a specific "poor fool" who received a divine privilege—Christ? a saint? an inspired artist? The metaphor eludes. Though the author of the first quotation seems concerned with "the/Business of the gods," what interests Moore is the clay pots. Their lack of pretentiousness makes them an ideal guise for true divinity. She thus equates them with humility as opposed to excessive popularity, with nonchalance as opposed to hard trying, and with "The staff, the bag, the feigned inconsequence / of manner." Like the quotations, this concluding catalog seems to refer to a specific image (Laurence Stapleton suggests a Dürer painting of a disguised St. Christopher[28]), and Moore makes explicit here what had been perhaps implicit in "To a Chameleon": her hiding the referentiality of her metaphors and the workings of her imagination (including inspiration) behind nonchalant things—clay pots, staff, bag, quotations—is her own weapon of self-protectiveness.

Self-protection is a puzzling but enduring concern for Moore and partially explains her attraction to assemblage. Since Moore is sometimes accused of repressing her self, especially her feminine self, it is important to recognize that what she means to protect is not an autobiographical, confessional self. Indeed, any conventional means of representation, any "haggish, uncompanionable drawl//Of certitude," would itself be reductive and repressive. Nor is it an egocentric, godlike self "revolv[ing] upon the ax[is] of [its] worth" above earthly concerns. Rather, hers is like the self of the "poor fool," an elusive soul not opposed to the world but virtually indistinguishable from it. As in the object portraits of Arthur Dove, the true essence of this self, its spirit, can only be revealed through enigmatic disguise. Moore clearly recognizes this paradox in her description of Dove's *Portrait of Ralph Dusenberry* (emphasis added): "Arthur Dove, always the unexpected proof that something no one ever saw before is the only right thing, *affects homeliness and literalness as disguises for the exact opposite.* In the *Portrait of Ralph Dusenberry* for example—a wedge-shaped head with the speed of a comet, a fragment of 'Shall We Gather at the River?' taken from a hymn-book, a piece of American flag,

28. Stapleton, *The Poet's Advance,* 19.

etc., framed by sections of mustard yellow folding pocket-rule—he is *as accurate as the chameleon or cuttlefish in its adaptation of pigment to background.*"[29]

It may be useful to return to Bachelard, whose mind, like Moore's, looks for organic analogies for art. In *The Poetics of Space* he devotes a chapter each to shells and nests. Both are "primal images" of protection and refuge, both are enclosed spaces, and both conform uniquely to the creatures that make and inhabit them. But whereas a shell's mystery is its geometric construction and its protection its hardness, a nest's mystery is its intimacy and its protection its hiddenness within the environment to which it conforms. One cannot easily discover a nest in a tree during summer because the nest is the colors of the tree and is, in fact, made of the twigs and leaves of the tree. Whereas a shell grows from the organism itself, indeed, is the organism itself, a bird chooses for its nest bits of the environment—leaves, blades of grass, sticks, debris, dirt—which have served a purpose other than the one to which it now puts them to use. Likewise does Marianne Moore collect bits of her environment—newspaper clippings, magazine photos, snatches of conversation, postcards, artifacts—which simultaneously both reveal the shape of her imagination and camouflage it.

In his discussion of nests, Bachelard explores the idea that "values alter facts," meaning, "The moment we love an image, it cannot remain the copy of a fact." He cites Michelet: "In reality . . . a bird's tool is its own body, that is, its breast, with which it presses and tightens its materials until they have become absolutely pliant, well-blended and adapted to the general plan."[30] This is a key aspect of assemblage, that each thing taken from another context sacrifices some of its integrity to the art work, to the artist's general plan. Thus does a quotation in a Moore poem relinquish at least some of its original (for example, Turgenev's) meaning at the same time it accepts a new meaning (Moore's). Such nest-building, "the marriage," Bachelard calls it, "in the dry air and summer sunlight, of moss and down"[31] is analogous to Moore's famous definition of poems as "imaginary gardens with real toads in them." This is the challenge of the assemblage artist, to achieve "a marriage . . . of moss and down." As Arthur Dove writes: "Actuality! At that point where mind and matter meet. That

29. MM, "Concerning the Marvelous" (Rosenbach II:01:30).
30. Bachelard, *The Poetics of Space*, 100.
31. *Ibid.*, 102.

is at present where I should like to paint. The spirit is always there."[32]

To return to my triangle. Despite the difference of medium, painted portraits and written ones are alike in maintaining a dualism between the aesthetic form and the referential subject, but how can a poem achieve the third kind of objectivity that a collage has? The greater difficulty for the poet is not how to create imaginary gardens but how to preserve the reality of the toads. Because it is in the nature of language that all words are reused, it is more difficult for words than for newspaper clippings or twigs to maintain their integrity as things; like paint, they become transparent. Quoting is one way to preserve the thingness of words. For quotation marks at least appear to verify the existence of the words in another reality. The two contexts are thus, as in collage, brought into tension with one another.

Moore's assemblage techniques are not, however, limited to quotations. The quotations in "In This Age of Hard Trying" are more collagelike than those in "The Past Is the Present" because they seem more foreign to the poem; this is so regardless of the footnotes or whether the quotations in either poem are real. The more enigmatic the thing, the more alien it seems, the more it remains a thing independent of its context; this holds true even for things that are not quotations—the staff, the bag, the polished wedge. The same holds true in visual assemblages. It is not hard to recognize the art critic in Dove's *The Critic* because his torso is cut from a newspaper art review, but why the vacuum cleaner? Why the roller skates? Both Moore and Dove delight in the enigma of their private allusions. When an allusion or metaphor is lucid, one looks "through" it to what it refers or represents; when it seems out of place, one looks "at" it wondering where it belongs and why the artist selected it. Moore says, "the most difficult thing for me is to be satisfactorily lucid, yet have enough implication in [the poem] to suit myself" (*MMR*, 261). Though Moore often disclaims her use of enigma, as she does just after this comment, she defends its use in Elizabeth Bishop: "the enigma must be clear to the author, not necessarily to us" (*Prose*, 328). As long as the enigma is an honest expression of the self, it works *for* Moore's purposes rather than against them. This cannot be overemphasized. Enigma insures autonomy—both for the artist's elusive self and for her materials. For to be

---

32. Arthur Dove, unpublished notes, quoted in Haskell, *Arthur Dove*, 136. Dove is using *actuality* in the Hegelian sense. As I show in Chapter 5, Moore uses the term similarly in "Granite and Steel."

understood "is to be no longer mysterious; it is to be no/ Longer privileged." [33] By resisting the unifying powers of form, of the syntax and stanzas, enigma preserves the rawness of the materials, "the raw material of poetry in / all its rawness" (*CP*, 267).

Moore understood well the subversiveness, the "byplay," of assemblage, which threatens not only art's traditional role of representation but also its dignity. By using the materials of daily life, assemblage gives up art's privileged remove from usefulness and draws closer to life itself. Donald Kuspit says that collage exists in the limbo between art and life, hence that it is hard to take collage seriously as art. [34] It is this seriousness, of course, that modernist collage undermines. The arts and crafts movement raised similar questions, but with less wit, about the conventional separation between art and life, specifically between the fine arts such as sculpture and painting that are removed from life and the applied arts such as weaving and pottery that are absorbed into it. Moore's early exposure to arts and crafts ideology made such questions enduring concerns for her, and she repeatedly insisted that poetry be useful: "these things are important not because a // high-sounding interpretation can be put upon them but because they are / useful" (*CP*, 266–67). Closely tied to the arts and crafts movement, feminism both then and now likewise raises questions about the historical hierarchy between predominantly male fine arts and predominantly female crafts. In recognition of the affinities between twentieth-century collage and historically feminine crafts, Miriam Schapiro recently coined the term *femmage* to refer to "work by women of history who sewed, pieced, hooked, cut, appliquéd, quilted, tatted, wrote, painted, and combined materials using traditional women's techniques to achieve their art-activities." [35] The witty subversiveness of collage would have appealed to Moore as a modernist, as a feminist (she was feminist at least in this concern), and as an American—for the impulse of collage is antihierarchical and democratic. When Moore quotes, "Really, it is not the business of the gods to bake clay pots," it is the hierarchy implicit in the statement that her poem ironically undermines, both in message and method. [36]

33. MM, "An Ardent Platonist," *Lantern*, XXVI (Spring, 1918), 22 (Bryn Mawr).

34. Donald B. Kuspit, "Collage: The Organizing Principle of Art in the Age of the Relativity of Art," in *Relativism in the Arts*, ed. Betty Craig (Athens, Ga., 1983), reprinted in *Collage*, ed. Hoffman, 40–41. This provocative essay has informed my thinking throughout this chapter.

35. Miriam Schapiro, "Femmage," in *Collage*, ed. Hoffman, 296.

36. It is an unfortunate paradox of modernism that in drawing closer to "life," art be-

Barbara Haskell points to "the national mania for the literal" as a possible reason for Dove's assemblages of 1924 to 1930.[37] A surge of postwar nationalism in the twenties caused American artists to turn away from abstraction toward what they perceived as an American realism and literalism (I explain this at greater length in Chapter 5). And the search for a distinctly American tradition in art led mainstream artists and collectors to look seriously at American folk art, which like folk art in other cultures uses assemblage; a piece of dried plant may be pasted into a painting, for example, to represent a tree. Though Moore's "mania for the literal" long precedes the war and the folk art exhibitions she saw during the twenties, her assemblage techniques reach greater extremes in this decade. The poems of 1923 and 1924—"Novices," "Marriage," "An Octopus," "Sea Unicorns and Land Unicorns"—contain the highest density of quotations of any of her poems. And in 1924 with the publication of *Observations* Moore first appends footnotes to her poems, which offer even further verification than do the quotation marks that the words are extracted from another reality. The footnotes also verify the dailiness of the sources, the newspapers, advertisements, overheard conversations. Possibly the footnotes to Eliot's *The Waste Land*, published in 1922, gave Moore the idea, but if so, Moore uses her notes to opposite effect. Instead of encouraging readers to look up the references, Moore's notes virtually dare her readers to do so. To adapt Moore's own phrase, they are "satire[s] upon curiosity" (*CP*, 48). Not only are many of her sources unavailable in libraries, but the more likely the source is to be found on a library shelf, the more likely Moore will have stripped the quotation of its original meaning. Subversiveness at work again—this time against the authority of the canonized text.

Moore was well aware of the "national mania for the literal" during the twenties, of a delight in untranscendent things. This is the decade of Williams' red wheelbarrow and of Jay Gatsby's "soft rich heap" of shirts. It is also the decade of Moore's association with the *Dial*. When asked years later about any deliberate policy of the *Dial*, Moore responds: "As George Grosz [himself a collage artist] said, at that last meeting he at-

---

came increasingly less accessible. Moore's poetry is a prime example of this, which probably explains her tortured struggle between using life's raw enigma and being "satisfactorily lucid."

37. Haskell, *Arthur Dove*, 49.

tended at the National Institute, 'How did I come to be an artist? Endless curiosity, observation, research—and a great amount of joy in the thing.' It was a matter of taking a liking to things. Things that were in accordance with your taste. I think that was it. And we didn't care how unhomogeneous they might seem. Didn't Aristotle say that it is the mark of a poet to see resemblances between apparently incongruous things?" (*MMR*, 266). At the same time Moore shared her generation's "great amount of joy in the thing," she also felt a moral ambivalence about the postwar materialism that engendered it. Two poems published together in the *Dial* in July, 1921, "When I Buy Pictures" and "A Graveyard" (later "A Grave"), reveal this ambivalence.[38] As discussed above, an essential quality of assemblage is that "values alter facts," that the selected thing relinquish some of its individuality to the collector's purpose. Picasso said: "I put all the things I like into my pictures. The things—so much the worse for them; they just have to put up with it."[39] This is a form of tyranny. Removing tribal artifacts to a museum or even to an artist's canvas, for example, is an imperialist gesture denying those artifacts the use and context for which they were intended. In "When I Buy Pictures," Moore distances herself from the tyranny of possessiveness by qualifying the title, "or what is closer to the truth, / when I look at that of which I may regard myself as the imaginary possessor," but she recognizes that even imaginary possessions, or perhaps especially imaginary possessions, become reflections of herself; the original poem concludes: "then I 'take it in hand as a savage would take a looking-glass.'" "A Grave" is harsher: "the sea is a collector, quick to return a rapacious look." There is no "joy in the thing" here, for in the sea "dropped things are bound to sink" and eventually to decompose. Perhaps it is the sea's indifference (reflecting humans' indifferent greed) that destroys the things it collects, whereas an "imaginary [and imaginative] possessor" can look "with piercing glances into the life of things." Moore's longest assemblage, "Marriage," also explores this theme—whether it is possible to possess something (or someone) and still allow it the freedom to be itself. Preserving the reality of the toads is, then, for Moore not merely an aesthetic challenge but a moral imperative.

This moral imperative must nevertheless continually be violated, for one cannot appropriate things without distorting them. In the same month

---

38. MM, "When I Buy Pictures" and "A Graveyard," *Dial*, LXXVII (1921), 33–34.

39. Pablo Picasso, remark to Christian Zervos, 1935, quoted in Johnson, *Modern Art and the Object*, 97.

that "A Graveyard" and "When I Buy Pictures" appeared in the *Dial*, Moore wrote to Bryher: "I think in a work of art, one must get at the individuality of a thing one is describing literally. . . . I do not mean of course, that things cannot be distorted for the sake of art for they can so long as you don't do violence to the essence of a thing."[40] Moore does distort her appropriations for the sake of art again and again by taking them out of context, by misquoting them. Here, however, she means the "thing one is describing," the represented subject. Hartley, Dove, and other members of the Stieglitz circle would heartily concur with her sentiment; this is what the object portrait is after, the elusive "essence of a thing."

Unless one reads Moore's animal poems as portraits, Moore moves away from portraiture in the late teens and begins experimenting with what would become an equally important genre for her, landscape. "The Fish" (1918) is her first seascape; "England" (1920), ironically, would be the first of several ambitious American landscapes. Getting at the "essence of a thing" is as important and perhaps as difficult for the landscapist as for the portraitist. Marsden Hartley wrote Stieglitz that it takes a "long time and much patience 'to see over the surface of a place and find the key.'"[41] Dove's assemblages include seascapes and landscapes as well as portraits. Moore's landscapes are less private than her portraits (unlike in some of the portraits the subject is always named) and arguably more accessible. In the twenties she would sometimes spell out "the essence of a thing" in the poem and even signal that she was doing so: "It comes to this: . . . ," "the essence of the matter: . . . ," ". . . is the nature of this octopus" (*CP*, 48, 70, 76). Nevertheless, the centripetal essence is usually no match for the centrifugal diversity and mystery of the assembled images.

One of Moore's twenties landscapes, "New York," exemplifies not only the assemblage techniques I have discussed so far but also Moore's love of visual pattern and texture. Five months before "New York" appeared in the *Dial*, Moore wrote to H.D. about an exhibition she had seen that included "a wool map of New York in minute stitches by Marguerite Zorach; the color is lovely; blue, lavender and champagne color, green and much orange."[42] Marguerite and William Zorach were among

---

40. MM to Winifred Ellerman [Bryher], July 27, 1921 (Rosenbach V:08:06).

41. Marsden Hartley to Alfred Stieglitz, February 2, 1926, quoted in Scott, *Marsden Hartley*, 76.

42. MM to Hilda Doolittle [H.D.], July 26, 1921 (Rosenbach V:23:32).

the earliest modernists to take an interest in American folk art, and through her embroidered tapestries Marguerite acknowledges the tradition Miriam Schapiro has since called "femmage." For Zorach sometimes includes words in her tapestries that recall embroidered samplers and other folk works.[43] Zorach's attraction to embroidery was both aesthetic—she loved the colors of wool yarns—and practical—when she turned from painting to needlework, she was rearing small children. Moore composed her own "New York" not of wool but, appropriately, of furs.

> the savage's romance,
> accreted where we need the space for commerce—
> the centre of the wholesale fur trade,
> starred with tepees of ermine and peopled with foxes,
> the long guard-hairs waving two inches beyond the body of the
> > > pelt;
> the ground dotted with deer-skins—white with white spots
> "as satin needle-work in a single colour may carry a varied pattern,"
> and blankets of eagles' down—
> submarine forest upon submarine forest of tropical seaweed.
> It is a far cry from the "queen full of jewels"
> and the beau with the muff,
> from the gilt coach shaped like a perfume bottle,
> to the conjunction of the Monongahela and the Allegheny
> and the scholastic philosophy of the wilderness,
> to combat which one must stand outside and laugh
> since to go in is to be lost.
> It is not the dime-novel exterior,
> Niagara Falls, the calico horses, and the war canoe;
> it is not that "if the fur is not finer than such as one sees others wear,
> one would rather be without it—"
> that estimated in raw meat and berries, we could feed the universe;
> it is not the atmosphere of ingenuity,
> the otter, the beaver, the puma skins
> without shooting-irons or dogs;
> it is not the plunder,
> it is the "accessibility to experience." [44]

43. Marguerite Zorach discusses needlework as a woman's tradition in "Embroidery as Art," *Art in America*, XLIV (Fall, 1956), 48–51.

44. MM, "New York," *Dial*, LXXI (1921), 637.

Figure 21 Marguerite Zorach, *The City of New York*

1920. Embroidered tapestry. Collection of Mr. and Mrs. Peter Rosenbaum.

Her depicting the city of steel and skyscrapers in a patchwork of ermine, fox, deer, otter, beaver, and puma skins reminds one of the humorous illogic in Meret Oppenheim's 1936 fur-covered teacup. Though equally humorous, Moore's fur has the logical explanation that "in 1921 New York succeeded St. Louis as the center of the wholesale fur trade" (*CP*, 269). And in addition to the various colors and textures of the furs, she brings into her landscape satin needlework, gilt, eagles' down, and calico.

The most striking similarity between Zorach's *The City of New York* and Moore's "New York" is the multiple juxtaposed images and their varied perspectives. Though not a map in the usual sense, the flatness of Zorach's surface gives a maplike effect. The sizes are grossly disproportional: two figures in derby hats are the same height as the length of a city block. In some cases the viewer sees the images from eye level (near or distant), in others from an aerial or maplike vantage. Similarly, in Moore's poem, "starred" and "dotted" (lines 4 and 6) move the reader to a great height above the skins, but "spots" (line 6) zooms in close enough for the reader to discern white on white. A similar jolt occurs with "the gilt coach shaped like a perfume bottle." In line 5, "pelt," though apparently referring to furs worn in the city, oddly suggests the shape of New York State as well. Indeed, the entire poem shifts from New York City to New York State, from "the centre of the wholesale fur trade" to Niagara Falls and "raw meat and berries." There are other kinds of shifts too, line 3 indicating a commercial perspective, line 4 a fanciful one. By taking advantage of assemblage's ability to present multiple perspectives, both Moore and Zorach undermine the nineteenth-century assumption that one can see an entire landscape from a single, dominant perspective.

Moore's poem is full of the enigmatic facts, images, and quotations that characterize her mature assemblage style. Nearly every line mystifies: Why the reference to Pittsburgh, where the Monongahela and Allegheny rivers converge, in a poem about New York? What can "queen full of jewels" mean? What is "the scholastic philosophy of the wilderness"? Patricia Willis shows that several of the places named or implied in the poem have personal significance for Moore: St. Louis, the former "centre of the wholesale fur trade," is her birthplace; she lived in Pittsburgh briefly after moving from St. Louis; and New York is her current home. Willis also suggests that Moore may have had in mind an anonymous oil landscape that was in her family; typifying the high vantage point of nineteenth-century landscape, it depicts a tranquil river scene a few miles from the convergence of the Monongahela and Allegheny.[45] Also, needlework could allude to Zorach's tapestry, and the beaver and fawn could allude to family nicknames for Mary Norcross (who also did needlework) and Moore's mother, respectively. Moore surely did not expect her contemporaries to uncover these private allusions—yet the very enigma of the images, as in Dove's portraits, paradoxically both reveals the elusive persona and hides her.

While each image in the poem resists an altogether rational explanation, patterns and relationships emerge which Moore surely did intend her readers to see. Fur is a paradigm of the assembled object both aesthetically and morally, for it serves two purposes, first in the life of the animal and second in the life of the city, as a valuable commodity. This is the paradox of New York that Moore's poem repeatedly describes, the accretion of the wild and the seemingly civilized: "ermine teepees," "peopled with foxes," guard-hairs measured in inches. The second sentence contrasts romantic images of civilization—the queen, a beau with (fur) muff, a gilt coach—with a wilderness where rivers with lilting Indian names converge, which happens also to be Pittsburgh, a place famous for industry. "Ingenuity" describes both the animals—otter, beaver, puma—and the methods of trapping them "without shooting-irons or dogs." "The savage's romance" presents a similar but more complex paradox: on one hand is America's idealized, noble "savage" suggested by teepees (New York Indians never lived in teepees), war canoes, and Indian geographical names; on the other hand is the savagery of commerce plundering the state's bountiful resources. This plunder takes various forms, including the idealizing "dime-novel exterior." This is, then, the paradoxical "savage's romance": to romanticize the "savage" is itself savage.

In the final sentence of the poem Moore uses an effective assemblage device that is unavailable to the visual artist. She catalogs what her subject is not. Again paradoxically, she both invokes images in the reader's mind and at the same time denies them. This positive/negative catalog builds rhythmically and rhetorically to the essence of New York, what "it" is, in the final line. With "not" Moore has it both ways: she can condemn the plunder that is the essence of commercial New York at the same time she guides the reader down from a romanticizing, nineteenth-century distance into the direct "experience" of the wilderness, where paradox and enigma prevail, where "to go in is to be lost." Once again Moore describes her

45. Willis, *Vision into Verse*, 36–37.

method as well as her subject, for assemblage itself is such a wilderness, its essence "accessibility to experience."

One conventional aspect of art that assemblage calls into question is the artist's role as maker. The assembler must, of course, still make a design from found objects, but a great part of the process is selecting the objects from the environment. To some extent this is so in conventional art—any artist must choose a subject and possibly pose or arrange it—but traditionally only the making is valued as art. An art teacher's arranging a still life, for example, does not seem to violate the students' art as would adding brush strokes to their canvases. The simultaneous rise of assemblage and of straight photography as legitimate art forms is no coincidence. For whereas pictorial photography was an art of making, of posing the subject and manipulating the negative and print, straight photography, by minimizing these variables, is fundamentally an art of selection—selecting where to crop the subject in a viewfinder, selecting the moment to release the shutter, and, in many cases, selecting one negative from perhaps hundreds of the same subject. Stieglitz regarded the selection of a print as no less important.[46] What is probably more important than the processes and materials these art forms introduced is their reconception of art generally. In an article about Stieglitz that Moore saved, she marked the following passage and underlined two sentences: "*The esthetic basis of all art is selection.* Selection implies a standard for which selection is made and the sensibility to distinguish according to this standard. *The exercise of sensibility in keeping with a standard is an elementary definition of art.*"[47] Assemblage and straight photography revolutionize art by shifting the conventional relationship between the imagination and the world of things and facts: instead of taking rational dominion over that world, the imagination submits itself to a world that is ordinary, arbitrary, and mysterious.

46. Stieglitz wrote: "You seem to assume that a photograph is one of a dozen or a hundred or maybe a million,—all prints from one negative necessarily being alike and so replaceable. But then along comes one print that really embodies something that you have to say that is subtle and elusive, something that is still a straight print, but when shown with a thousand mechanically made prints has something that the others don't have. What is it that this print has? It is certainly something not based on a trick. It is something born out of spirit,—and spirit is an intangible while the mechanical is tangible." Alfred Stieglitz to James T. Soby, January 19, 1942, in *Alfred Stieglitz,* by Greenough and Hamilton, 216.

47. James Johnson Sweeney, "Rebel with a Camera," *New York Times Magazine,* June 8, 1947, p. 21 (Rosenbach vertical files).

Margaret Holley, who traces the use of the first-person pronoun throughout Moore's career, observes an inverse correlation between the number of *I*'s in Moore's poems and the number of appended notes.[48] The recession of the first-person pronoun and the proliferation of appropriated things in Moore's poems of the mid-twenties are both symptoms of her move on my triangular continuum away from the formal pole (where the artist's presence seems strongest) toward greater autonomy for the assembled objects. That Moore composes her poems of the mid-twenties exclusively in free verse is a further symptom of this shift. The aesthetic force seems weak in comparison to the tension between the other two. I do not mean to suggest that Moore abandoned formal considerations in her free verse poems, but for a poet with as intricate a stanzaic form as Moore had developed, the poems of 1923 and 1924 relinquish considerable artistic authority. Making gives way to selecting.

Rather than disappearing, however, the self assumes a different form. Donald Kuspit says, "The collage seems unwilled, and yet it is willful," and further, "By its seeming indifference to the fragments that constitute it—conveyed by the seemingly random way in which those fragments are gathered together—the collage forces us to turn from the fragments to the attention that selected them, the individuality they acquire by being brought together by a particular kind of attention."[49] If "the esthetic basis of all art is selection," what distinguishes assemblage is the way in which the selecting consciousness asserts itself. Moore considers assemblage a disguise for the self. Kuspit agrees: "The fragments that find their way into the field are only superficially found by chance. Chance is a disguise for the uncertain yet highly personal significance they are felt to have. They are fascinating because they are the objects of a belief that only half knows itself, and so experiences the world in a chance way. The fragments are experienced as profoundly meaningful, but the meaning cannot be spelled out completely and never seems to truly surface."[50] Thus do Moore's cryptic early portraits evolve into a kind of disguised self-portrait, what she calls an "unintentional portrait" or "psychic map of the creative mind."

The many private allusions in Moore's poems, such as those in "New York," and her interest in disguise suggest that the self-portraiture in her assemblages is deliberate. She had already published less disguised self-

48. Holley, *The Poetry of Marianne Moore*, 122–23.
49. Kuspit, "Collage," in *Collage*, ed. Hoffman, 43, 45.
50. *Ibid.*, 46.

portraits such as "Radical" and several poems about rats. She also directly addresses this issue in her prose. A 1927 "Comment" begins: "Academic feeling, or prejudice possibly, in favor of continuity and completeness is opposed to miscellany—to music programs, composite picture exhibitions, newspapers, magazines, and anthologies. Any zoo, aquarium, library, garden, or volume of letters, however, is an anthology and certain of these selected findings are highly satisfactory. The science of assorting and the art of investing an assortment with dignity are obviously not being neglected, as is manifest in 'exhibitions and sales of artistic property,' and in that sometimes disparaged, most powerful phase of the anthology, the museum" (*Prose*, 182). Moore's appreciation for zoos, museums, exhibitions, and libraries is legendary; such miscellanies extend well beyond recognized art forms. Like Kuspit, Moore recognizes an inherent tension in miscellanies; her essay concludes: "However expressive the content of an anthology, one notes that a yet more distinct unity is afforded in the unintentional portrait given, of the mind which brought the assembled integers together" (183). In an unpublished review of the Museum of Modern Art's "Fantastic Art, Dada, Surrealism" exhibition (in which collage is a major motif) she writes similarly, "The exhibition of the marvelous . . . is educational as a kind of psychic map of the creative mind; also as a portrait of the mind of an organizer . . . Alfred H. Barr, Jr." And she can not resist adding to this review mention of "a corresponding study in imaginative organizing . . . The Mariner's Museum at Newport News, Virginia, founded by Mr. Archer M. Huntingdon. . . . This museum is a Shakespeare's or Sidney's or Dürer's or Hogarth's paradise,—its groupings no more accidental than a work of art is accidental." [51] Moore's readers who regret her lack of poems from the late twenties should recognize that her editing a "miscellany" such as the *Dial* is no departure from her art but rather a culmination of it.

The idea of the "unintentional portrait" forms the subject of Moore's 1922 poem that begins with title as first line, "People's Surroundings / they answer one's questions." [52] The first sentence of the poem moves through six free-verse stanzas, each describing the surroundings of a different personality. The first three are interiors: one of modest yet stylish simplicity, one of old-fashioned opulence, and one of modern efficiency.

51. Both quotations are from "Art and Interpretation," a draft of "Concerning the Marvelous" (Rosenbach II:01:30).

52. MM, "People's Surroundings," *Dial*, LXXII (1922), 588–90.

The exteriors that follow progress from a densely ornate garden, through the "straight lines" and "common sense" of the American West, to the most alluring of all the settings, "Bluebeard's tower above the coral reefs." This brilliantly colored tropical paradise is really a "magic mousetrap," a "dungeon with odd notions of hospitality"; the descriptions proceed through dazzling surfaces—"lizards glittering and without thickness / like splashes of fire and silver on the pierced turquoise of the lattices"—inward to the "mind of this establishment [which] has come to the conclusion / that it would be impossible to revolve about one's self too much." According to legend, Bluebeard gave his seventh wife the keys to his tower with the warning that she not open one door. Unable to restrain her curiosity, the disobedient wife opens the door to discover the corpses of the six previous wives, each of whom Bluebeard had murdered for disobeying him. The "acacia-like lady" in Moore's poem recalls Bluebeard's wives as well as other women in paradisial settings, Eve and Pandora, for whom "answer[ing] one's questions" has grim consequences.

The poem's seventh stanza and second sentence begins with a relatively lucid statement about finding the "unintentional portrait."

> In these noncommittal, personal-impersonal expressions of
> appearance,
> the eye knows what to skip;
> the physiognomy of conduct must not reveal the skeleton;
> "a setting must not have the air of being one"
> yet with x-raylike inquisitive intensity upon it, the surfaces go back;
> the interfering fringes of expression are but a stain on what stands out,
> there is neither up nor down to it;
> we see the exterior and the fundamental structure—

Furnishings good or bad, cheap or opulent, are "noncommittal, personal-impersonal expressions," and the perceptive "eye" is the same one that in "When I Buy Pictures" can look "with piercing glances into the life of things." On a more subtle level, Moore is playing with the skeleton-in-the-closet idea of the Bluebeard story. In the first stanza, she refers to "this dried bone of arrangement" as an instance where "one's style is not lost"; the bone is visible. But in the seventh stanza "skeleton" and "x-ray" both suggest hidden danger as well as figuratively the "fundamental structure" behind the exterior.

Lest the reader become too confident of her own x-raylike vision,

Moore concludes the poem with an impenetrable barrage of people and settings that challenges the reader to discover Moore's own mind.

> captains of armies, cooks, carpenters,
> cutlers, gamesters, surgeons, and armourers,
> lapidaries, silkmen, glovers, fiddlers, and ballad-singers,
> sextons of churches, dyers of black cloth, hostlers, and chimney-sweeps,
> queens, countesses, ladies, emperors, travellers, and mariners,
> dukes, princes, and gentlemen
> in their respective places—
> camps, forges, and battlefields,
> conventions, oratories, and wardrobes,
> dens, deserts, railway stations, asylums, and places where engines
> > are made,
> shops, prisons, brickyards, and altars of churches—
> in magnificent places clean and decent,
> castles, palaces, dining-halls, theatres, and imperial
> > audience-chambers.

Each of the persons is a variation of the artist, transforming things, presenting appearances. The poem that begins with "a deal table" revealing "one's style" ends with "magnificent places" (literally "made grand") designed to impress and deceive. Though the impersonal persona of the poem, "one," seems to prefer the deal table to other forms of "bad furniture," in fact the artist most resembles Bluebeard, presenting dazzling exteriors, "imperial audience-chambers," and tantalizing readers with multiple locked doors.

Despite its potential hazards, Moore encourages "x-raylike inquisitive intensity" in the reader and thereby reverses the misogynist moral of the Bluebeard, Pandora, and Eden stories. To punish curiosity is to "cut the nerve of progress." Indeed, the poem celebrates a particularly, though not exclusively, feminine inquisitiveness. By aestheticizing the selection of home furnishings, the arts and crafts movement had validated a language women traditionally know well, an understated and potentially subversive language of "personal-impersonal expression." (Moore's contemporary Susan Glaspell based her play *Trifles* on this language.) Moore's letters continually describe in elaborate detail the surroundings of persons who strongly impress her. That Moore studied and valued the language of "people's surroundings" from her adolescence to the end of her life is

Figure 22 Marianne Moore Room at the Rosenbach Museum and Library
Marianne Moore Papers.

indicated by her agreement with the Rosenbach Museum and Library to preserve not only her papers but also the furnishings of her living room. According to Moore's wishes, the Rosenbach has duplicated the arrangement of her furniture, pictures, and many curios in a room of the exact dimensions of Moore's own living room. Visitors may regard this room, then, as Moore's final "unintentional portrait."

In writing on the poetics of houses, Bachelard says that it is possible to "write a room," "read a room," or "read a house."[53] Bachelard conceives of poetry as a space that draws the imagination into revery. What he means by "reading" here resembles what Moore means by "People's Surroundings / they answer one's questions." But it is not only the possibility of finding the "unintentional portrait" in the arrangement of things that attracts the reader but also the power in each thing individually. Bachelard describes housework as a potentially creative activity because

53. Bachelard, *The Poetics of Space*, 14.

130

"consciousness rejuvenates everything": "when a poet rubs a piece of furniture—even vicariously—when he puts a little fragrant wax on his table with the woolen cloth that lends warmth to everything it touches, he creates a new object; he increases the object's human dignity; he registers this object officially as a member of the human household." [54] In discussing Moore's assemblages, I have emphasized the composite meanings suggested by her images, but no reader is likely to enjoy Moore who does not share her delight in each polished curio: "the municipal bat-roost of mosquito warfare," "black butterflies with blue half circles on their wings," "a small collision of the orchids." Like Bachelard's housewife, Moore "awakens furniture that was asleep." [55]

If "the esthetic basis for all art is selection," what is the standard that distinguishes a work of genuine art? Selection is merely the process whereby the artist exercises what Stieglitz and his associates continually call *seeing*. Susan Sontag says: "Photographic seeing meant an aptitude for discovering beauty in what everybody sees but neglects as too ordinary. Photographers were supposed to do more than just see the world as it is, including its already acclaimed marvels; they were to create interest, by new visual decisions." [56] But *seeing* for Stieglitz means more than "discovering beauty." He says: "I refuse to identify *seeing* with *knowing*. Seeing signifies awareness resulting from inner experience." [57] When he tries to explain the quality that makes one print a work of art in comparison to other merely mechanical prints from the same negative, he describes the quality as "subtle and elusive . . . something born out of spirit." [58]

For Moore the criteria of selection is similarly intuitive. In "Picking and Choosing," " 'A right good salvo of barks,' a few strong wrinkles puck-

54. *Ibid.*, 67.

55. *Ibid.*, 68. Moore may have shared Bachelard's esteem for housework. In MM, March 7, 1925, Notebook 1250/25 (Rosenbach VII:11:01), she records a conversation with Scofield Thayer in which she said: "I feel that Mme. Lachaise's cleaning house and not permitting a wrinkle in the tablecloth or a book out of its place is innate not a pretense. One day when I arrived she was cleaning house and had on a little canary yellow silk cap." At this Thayer laughed, and Moore retorted: "I see you are unworthy of my confidence. Mme. Lachaise's dignity is in our keeping."

56. Susan Sontag, *On Photography* (New York, 1977), 89.

57. Alfred Stieglitz, quoted in Dorothy Norman, *Alfred Stieglitz: Introduction to an American Seer* (New York, 1960), 52.

58. Stieglitz to Soby, January 19, 1942, in *Alfred Stieglitz*, by Greenough and Hamilton, 216.

ering/the skin between the ears, is all we ask" (*CP*, 45). In "The Labors of Hercules," among the Herculean tasks she enumerates is

to teach the bard with too elastic a selectiveness
that one detects creative power by its capacity to eliminate
detachment;
that while it may have more elasticity than logic,
it knows where it is going;
it flies along in a straight line like electricity
and devastates those areas that boast of their remoteness.[59]

"To eliminate detachment" is to make selectivity personal rather than rational; while it cannot logically be explained, "it knows where it is going." It sees beyond the obvious to the remote. Like Stieglitz, Moore continually emphasizes the importance of seeing and for her also seeing is spiritual. Yet another poem of this period about selectiveness, "When I Buy Pictures," asserts most clearly her own criteria.

it must be "lit with piercing glances into the life of things";
it must acknowledge the spiritual forces which have made it. (*CP*, 48)

"When I Buy Pictures" begins, "or what is closer to the truth, / when I look at that of which I may regard myself as the imaginary possessor." Anything a person really sees becomes her own. Seeing is possessing. Leo Steinberg uses Picasso's own phrase when he writes that Picasso draws "as if to possess." He means that Picasso, in drawing the female nude, wants to possess all aspects of her and shows that both before and after his cubist phase, Picasso tried various methods of containing the three-dimensional nude within the two dimensions of the canvas or paper.[60] Moore also observes her subject "as if to possess." To look at a picture or at a poem, or at a nude or an object or an animal, and really to see it is to "buy" it, to display it in the house that is the imagination. Each of Moore's poems is a room that contains the things she *sees*, the things of which she is "the imaginary possessor."

Bachelard says that when the poet-housewife waxes a piece of furniture, "he creates a new object." If seeing is possessing, seeing is also making. Earlier I said that assemblage calls into question the artist's role as

59. MM, "The Labours of Hercules," *Dial*, LXXI (1921), 638.
60. Leo Steinberg, *Other Criteria: Confrontations with Twentieth-Century Art* (London, 1972), 174–92.

maker. Once an artist has seen an object with "x-raylike inquisitive intensity," that object becomes part of the artist's imaginary furnishings; it becomes an "unintentional portrait," a new object. Moore explores the paradox of "making" such an object in her 1944 poem "A Carriage from Sweden" (*CP*, 131–33). The concluding lines, "a surface that says/ Made in Sweden: carts are my trade," refer to not only the cart made in Sweden but also the cart made in Brooklyn by Marianne Moore. In the first three stanzas she contrasts the cart's two geographical homes (note the reiteration of "made").

> They say there is a sweeter air
>   where it was made, than we have here;
>   a Hamlet's castle atmosphere.
> At all events there is in Brooklyn
> something that makes me feel at home.
>
> No one may see this put-away
>   museum-piece, this country cart
>   that inner happiness made art;
> and yet, in this city of freckled
> integrity it is a vein
>
> of resined straightness from north-wind
>   hardened Sweden's once-opposed-to-
>   compromise archipelago
> of rocks.

The carriage provides an occasion for the Brooklyn poet to imagine the Sweden that she describes in the rest of the poem. She assembles facts and images from her reading in order to create an imagined, if not imaginary, country. Though the cart she describes does exist and was made elsewhere, the persona imaginatively creates the cart as well as its native country, since "No one may see this put-away / museum-piece." To see is to imagine; to imagine is to make.

This is an unsolvable dilemma, that as much as Moore wants to grant a thing its autonomy, she cannot, for by selecting it she inevitably remakes it. This dilemma intrigued Moore early in her career, and as "A Carriage from Sweden" and her persistent use of assemblage indicate, it continued to do so long after her experiments of the twenties. Perhaps none of her experiments challenged her as much as did editing the *Dial*. Why does one not question her poetic license to alter a quotation, to add "clay" to Turgenev's "Really, it is not the business of the gods to bake pots," but condemns her asking Hart Crane to alter his words? Moore's shortcoming as an editor is what she advocated for the artist: "to eliminate detachment." The poems Moore wrote before and after her tenure as editor show her at the height of her creative powers. That she bestowed all of these on the *Dial* shows her willingness to relinquish making to the humbler art of selecting. Her conviction that aesthetic selectiveness has "more elasticity than logic" is consistent with the *Dial*'s policy of high but ineffable standards. Each issue is a miscellany—therefore, by her own direction, an "unintentional portrait." Such a miscellany demands an irresolvable paradox: on the one hand, the consciousness necessarily distorts what it sees and "possesses"; on the other hand, indifferent collectors like "A Grave" are worse: "that ocean in which dropped things are bound to sink— / in which if they turn and twist, it is neither with volition nor consciousness" (*CP*, 50). It is a low insult to the steam-roller critic to declare: "Were not 'impersonal judgment in aesthetic / matters, a metaphysical impossibility,' you // might fairly achieve / it" (*CP*, 84). Moore's aesthetic of the miscellany undermines not only the conventional hierarchy between art and life but also that between artist and connoisseur. For as much imagination is demanded of the editor, the critic, the collector, as of the artist—all must *see* "with piercing glances into the life of things."

4

INNER NECESSITY

Selecting is a humbler art than making. Although it is certainly more a difference of degree than of kind, Marianne Moore's inclination toward the former distinguishes her from other modernist poets. For her the poet is not "the single artificer of the world" nor poetry the "supreme fiction." Eliot recommends the poet surrender himself, but that to which he surrenders (and contributes) is "the mind of Europe," a tradition made by poets. Moore's surrender, on the other hand, is to enigmatic experience, "the raw material of poetry in all its rawness." While Moore values individual artists from the past, she does not share Pound's and Eliot's reverence for "the past." She regards tradition not as a creator, but as an obscurer, of truth.[1] For Moore the challenge of the artist is not to create truth but to *see* it.

Of course Stevens, Eliot, and Pound all questioned their European heritage, too, and sought alternatives beyond it. But because of the long-standing domination of the Academy over European painting, rebellion against the visual-arts tradition took greater extremes. The Academy prescribed not only conventions for executing art but also those for evaluating it. By the nineteenth century, there was even a hierarchy of subject matter, scenes from mythology and history being preferable to portraits, for instance, and portraits being preferable to genre paintings and landscapes. The overthrow of such criteria went hand in hand with the overthrow of academic conventions. A simultaneous awareness of, and growing appreciation for, such non-Western works as Japanese prints and African masks made academic criteria seem all the more provincial.

1. Moore does not necessarily conceive of tradition as "white male," yet her skepticism toward it anticipates that of recent feminists. Jeanne Heuving, *Omissions Are Not Accidents: Gender in the Art of Marianne Moore* (Detroit, 1992), reaches similar conclusions about Moore's difference from her literary peers but does so from a feminist perspective (esp. 30–48).

Many modernists found a freshness of vision and a spirituality in such works that had been missing for centuries from mainstream Western art. For certain Americans, including Moore, this diversity presented an ethical challenge as well as an aesthetic one.

To understand Moore's aesthetic judgments is to understand her moral ones. This has long been recognized and assumed. Many readers feel a sharp moral presence in her poems. And yet the nature of her moral judgments is the greatest point of controversy among her readers, whether she is, in Margaret Holley's words, a modernist in spirit as well as in style.[2] Some critics argue that Moore acknowledges only "irresolvable multiplicity"; others, that she "knew and truly loved the old pieties" and that she "strives to apprehend permanent truths."[3] Generally, those who argue for Moore's modernist and even postmodernist vision deny her belief in permanent truths, while those who acknowledge her adherence to truth seem reconciled to her quaintness. Both sides equate modernism with relativism; they assume that the modernist, in despair over the loss of truth, must create some kind of "mythical method" or "supreme fiction." Stieglitz, however, and many of the artists he supported believed unabashedly in spiritual truth. Whereas Williams was uncomfortable with Stieglitz's mysticism, Moore was not.[4] She too believed in "spiritual forces" underlying the visible world. She called Stieglitz "not exactly a theologian but a godly man" (*Prose*, 646). Nor despite her Presbyterianism was her own vision specifically Christian, as was the later Eliot's. What has stumped Moore's critics is that her beliefs are pluralist, but not relativist. Rather than lamenting the loss of traditional values in an increasingly diverse world, Moore witnesses truth in the diversity itself. The "old pieties" to which she does adhere—humility, sincerity, hard work, courage—support a radically pluralist view. Moore shared with the visual artists she knew an appreciation for art from diverse cultural origins; underlying that, a moral resistance not only to conventions in art but to conventional, hierarchical standards

2. Holley, *The Poetry of Marianne Moore,* 19–20.

3. Taffy Martin, *Marianne Moore: Subversive Modernist* (Austin, 1986), xiii; Holley, *The Poetry of Marianne Moore,* ix; Schulman, *The Poetry of Engagement,* 27.

4. See Dickran Tashjian, *William Carlos Williams and the American Scene, 1920–1940* (New York, 1978), 90. Also, note that Williams tries to explain away the mysticism in Moore's poetry, whereas another friend, Kenneth Burke, perceives Moore's difference from Williams in this regard; Burke calls her "visionary." See Williams, *Selected Essays,* 124; and Kenneth Burke, "Motives and Motifs in the Poetry of Marianne Moore," *Accent,* II (1942), reprinted in *Marianne Moore,* ed. Tomlinson, 87.

of any kind; and ultimately the belief that such standards obstruct one's ability to see the "spiritual forces."

Modern artists' appreciation for art that is untainted by Western convention can perhaps most easily, if imprecisely, be called "primitivism." In the catalog for the exhibit "'Primitivism' in 20th Century Art," William Rubin says that in the late nineteenth century, artists used "savage" and "primitivism" "admiringly . . . to describe virtually any art alien to the Greco-Roman line of Western realism that had been reaffirmed and systematized in the Renaissance," and that even well into the twentieth century "primitivism" included not only tribal art—that of Africa, the Pacific islands, and North American Indians—but also "Japanese, Egyptian, Persian, Cambodian, and most other non-Western court styles" as well as pre-Columbian art. It could also loosely include folk art, children's art, and naive art such as that of Henri Rousseau. Acknowledging the unsuitability of the word *primitivism* to define the art from any, or certainly all, of these origins, Rubin uses "primitivism" (in quotation marks) to describe the tastes and interests of modern Western artists, which often could be indiscriminate and ill-informed.[5] Certainly, like the ethnocentric term *primitive,* primitivism is imperialistic, since Europeans attained knowledge of non-Western artifacts literally through imperialist exploits. But even though the writings of early modernists are often clouded by imperialist and racist attitudes, primitivism as a phenomenon of modern Western art represented above all else a challenge to aesthetic provincialism and particularly to the conventionalized, academic paintings of the nineteenth century.

This was a challenge Marianne Moore wholeheartedly endorsed. As editor of the *Dial* she protested Teddy Roosevelt's remark that the modern imitation of primitive art is "only a smirking pose of retrogression and is not praiseworthy." Defending the painters and writers the *Dial* supported, she responds, "Our attachment is to the art of Egypt and the Primitives rather than to the later Renaissance and to Impressionism." Clearly she perceives modern art as breaking free from a strictly European tradition; however, she adds, "One has . . . a feeling for being one's self" (*Prose*, 191). This phrase more aptly describes Moore's own eclectic but highly discriminating taste in art than does "primitivism." For if she seems

5. William Rubin, "Modernist Primitivism: An Introduction," in *"Primitivism" in 20th Century Art: Affinity of the Tribal and the Modern,* ed. William Rubin (2 vols.; New York, 1984) I, 2–3.

not to care much for Greek sculpture, she can be found admiring the manes of the Parthenon horses; if she generally has little use for the Italian Renaissance, she has great admiration for Botticelli and for Leonardo's drawings; and if she has a strong taste for non-Western art, she has a stronger love for such Western artists as Dürer, El Greco, Blake, and Rousseau. "A feeling for being one's self" can arise in any era and from any culture. Moore would agree with one of the major assertions of *Der Blaue Reiter*, the influential almanac of art work and essays edited by Wassily Kandinsky and Franz Marc: "In all the arts . . . every method that arises from an inner necessity is right."[6]

Moore's own appreciation for art from outside the Western realist tradition developed early. By exalting crafts such as pottery, weaving, and jewelry-making, the arts and crafts movement called attention to works from various cultures that had previously been dismissed as mere crafts. Japanism—the fascination with Japanese prints, textiles, and ceramics that swept Europe and America in the late nineteenth century—contributed greatly to arts and crafts taste, but in addition, the American arts and crafts movement aroused interest, for instance, in the crafts of American Indians. During her senior year at Bryn Mawr, Moore wrote home detailed notes from a lecture on the Pre-Raphaelite Brotherhood given by C. R. Ashbee, an English architect and important liaison between the English and American arts and crafts movements. She notes with special interest the link between aesthetics, spirituality, and morality that evolved out of pre-Raphaelitism into arts and crafts ideology: "The subject first had to be felt strongly. Details next had to be handled with greatest care with regard to nature and truth. There is nothing sentimental or gross in any of [the pre-Raphaelite] pictures. We find in the PR.B. *the canon of fundamental purity of mind and heart* nothing to do with conventional morals. This is *very* important I think. Mr. Ashbee said if you're going through a gallery and judging the pictures you will find in the pictures you consider best, this fundamental purity."[7] Although Moore never adhered to anti-industrialism, the most urgent message of the arts and crafts movement, which Ashbee also addressed in his lecture, she would continue to uphold the pre-Raphaelite ideal of moral and aesthetic "purity" as well

6. Thomas van Hartmann, "On Anarchy in Music," in *The "Blaue Reiter" Almanac*, ed. Wassily Kandinsky and Franz Marc, trans. Henning Falkenstein and ed. Klaus Lankheit (1912; new documentary ed., New York, 1974), 113.

7. MM to her family, November 15, 1908 (Rosenbach VI:14:10).

as the arts and crafts morality of hard work. She would also maintain a democratic appreciation for decorative arts.

Moore's Oriental history teacher at Bryn Mawr no doubt influenced her predilection for pre-Renaissance art. George A. Barton, whose specialty then was Assyria, was a rising scholar of biblical history and archaeology. In her senior year she took a trip with Dr. Barton's class to the archaeological museum at the University of Pennsylvania, where she saw Egyptian, Babylonian, and Assyrian artifacts; despite the apathy of her classmates, the trip was not lost on Moore, who in her letter home describes the artifacts in detail and adds, "I lost my head completely."[8] The letters she wrote about her trip to England and Paris two years later in 1911 reveal her continued enthusiasm for "antiquities." She reports drawing in the British Museum an Assyrian leopard, a battle scene from an Etruscan vase, and the head of an Assyrian lion. But especially revealing is her account of the Louvre: "The Louvre is full of 'rotten Rubens.' I have never seen such atrocities. Mary de Medici's and Henry IV's floating in Elysian 'deshabile' amidst cherubs and fat homeric porters. But if you could see the 'antiquities,' the Victory Samothrace and some Assyrian things they have. The Assyrian Gallery could put the British Museum in its pocket."[9]

When Moore visited New York City in December, 1915, she found that members of the avant-garde shared her enthusiasm for art from diverse cultural origins. Stieglitz's 291 gallery played a central role in educating American artists not only about the innovations of European modernists but also about "primitive" art. By the time Moore visited 291, Stieglitz had exhibited African sculpture, Mexican pottery and carvings, three shows of children's work, and the first one-man show anywhere of Henri Rousseau. *Camera Work* regularly contained articles that called attention to tribal, folk, and Oriental art. During this visit Kreymborg offered to show Moore his collection of Japanese prints and told her to ask Stieglitz to see "his Congo things." In the issue of *Camera Work* that Stieglitz gave Moore to look at upon her second visit to 291 (he did not have any "Congo things" at the time to show her), she noted that one of the articles in the special number, "What is 291?," had been written by "Hodge Kirnon the elevator man (colored)" and was "considered one of the best in the book."[10] The interest in Japanese prints, African sculp-

8. MM to her family, March 28, 1909 (Rosenbach VI:15a:04).

9. MM to JWM, August 13, 1911, in *Marianne Moore Newsletter*, VI (1982), 26.

10. MM to JWM, December 19, 1915 (Rosenbach VI:21:13).

ture, and an elevator man's prose that Moore encountered in New York was central to the mission of 291—its resistance to conventional hierarchies and its openness to diverse forms of expression.

Edward Abrahams has linked 291's emphasis on individual expression and cultural pluralism to the social and political ideology of certain Greenwich Village radicals, sometimes called "the Lyrical Left."[11] While some intellectuals were advocating strict regulation of America's rapidly growing immigrant population and subsequent education (*i.e.*, Americanization) programs, the lyrical left opposed this "melting pot" concept and pushed for a multinational America that preserved its diverse ethnic origins. This respect for individual differences applied not only to European immigrants but also to African Americans and women. Stieglitz, himself Jewish and the son of German immigrants, supported many artists who were first- and second-generation immigrants. And throughout his career he published and exhibited the work of women, notably Gertrude Stein and Georgia O'Keeffe. Stieglitz defined the "spirit" of 291 as "honesty of aim, honesty of self-expression, honesty of revolt against the autocracy of convention."[12] The "autocracy of convention," as Abrahams shows, included social as well as aesthetic cultural standards.

Moore wholly sympathized with the lyrical left's advocacy of individual expression and cultural pluralism and repeatedly praised artists who "refuse to compromise." Her close association with the *Dial* throughout the twenties attests to these convictions. For like Stieglitz, the *Dial* avoided aligning itself with movements or defining its aesthetic standards except by example. Asked later if the *Dial* had any deliberate policy, Moore recalls: "I think that individuality was the great thing. We were not conforming to anything" (*MMR*, 266).

Correlative to their appreciation for diversity was a longing among both American and European artists to find a single aesthetic uniting various cultures and eras. Using "primitive" to describe all art which seems alien to Western conventions demonstrates this assumption. Arthur Wesley Dow, for instance, the influential teacher of 291 artists Max Weber and

11. Edward Abrahams, *The Lyrical Left: Randolph Bourne, Alfred Stieglitz, and the Origins of Cultural Radicalism in America* (Charlottesville, 1986), esp. 11–20, 64–78, 148–51. I had reached most of my conclusions before reading Abrahams, who does not mention Moore, but was gratified to find him so extensively confirm my own findings about Moore's milieu.

12. [Alfred Stieglitz], "The Editors' Page," *Camera Work*, XVIII (April, 1907), reprinted in *Camera Work*, ed. Green, 118.

Georgia O'Keeffe, encouraged his students to "bring into play the primitive springs of thought, impulse and action that exist in every human being," to be thus "*en rapport* with the primitive state of mind." The "natural method" Dow taught was indebted to the Japanese-inspired aesthetics of his mentor Ernest Fenollosa, to the arts and crafts teachings of Sylvester Baxter, and to the findings of Frank Hamilton Cushing, an ethnologist who had lived for five years among the Zuni Indians of New Mexico.[13] All of them found a universal impulse linking Asian, European, and tribal arts.

One of the boldest assertions of what Franz Marc called the "secret connection of all new artistic production" was *Der Blaue Reiter*, the single publication "almanac" that he edited with Kandinsky in Munich; as stated in Marc's subscription prospectus and as exemplified in the art works and articles in the almanac, *Der Blaue Reiter* "includes the latest movements in French, German, and Russian painting. It reveals subtle connections with Gothic and primitive art, with Africa and the vast Orient, with the highly expressive, spontaneous folk and children's art, and especially with the most recent musical movements in Europe and the new ideas for the theater of our time."[14] The illustrations include the work of modern artists—such as Picasso, Matisse, Delaunay, Cézanne, Rousseau, Gauguin, Arp, Klee, Van Gogh, Kandinsky, Marc—juxtaposed with glass paintings by Bavarian folk artists; masks from Brazil, New Caledonia, Ceylon, and Gabon; Russian folk art; an Eskimo cape from Alaska; children's drawings; work by Delacroix and El Greco; an Italian mosaic; sculpture from Borneo, Easter Island, the Cameroons, Mexico, and Malay; medieval woodcuts and sculpture; and various drawings and paintings from Egypt, China, Arabia, and Japan. This juxtaposition of artists and works certainly impressed Moore, for the front and back covers of her copy of *Der Blaue Reiter* became bowed by her own eclectic collection—she accumulated some 150 drawings and newspaper clippings there over five decades.[15]

13. Gail Levin, "American Art," in *"Primitivism" in 20th Century Art,* ed. Rubin, II, 453; the quotations are from Sylvester Baxter, "Handicraft and Its Extension at Ipswich," *Handicraft,* I (1903), 253–54.

14. Franz Marc, Subscription prospectus for *Der Blaue Reiter,* in *The "Blaue Reiter" Almanac,* ed. Kandinsky and Marc, 252.

15. Wassily Kandinsky and Franz Marc, eds., *Der Blaue Reiter* (Munich: R. Piper & Co., 1912). Moore's copy of *Der Blaue Reiter* [*The "Blaue Reiter" Almanac*] and its clippings are at the Rosenbach; I am grateful to Patricia C. Willis for calling them to my attention. These clippings are so diverse that it is impossible to generalize about them; they include

For members of the Blaue Reiter, the group of painters associated with Kandinsky and Marc, and for the Stieglitz circle, the factor which unified genuine works of art, honest expressions of self, was spirit. As Gail Levin has explained, Kandinsky's painting and especially his theories found an enthusiastic reception among American avant-garde artists not so much because of their novelty but because Kandinsky articulated ideas which the Americans already believed.[16] Stieglitz purchased the only Kandinsky painting exhibited in the Armory Show, and in 1912 *Camera Work* published an English translation of an excerpt from Kandinsky's *Concerning the Spiritual in Art* (*Über das Geistige in der Kunst*) shortly after it was published in Germany. Both Kandinsky and Stieglitz read and were influenced by the German romantics and the French symbolists, but Kandinsky's ideas probably appealed more broadly to Americans because they echoed familiar ideals of transcendentalism and self-reliance.[17] Levin emphasizes two aspects of Kandinsky's theories that attracted American interest: his belief in an invisible spiritual presence behind matter and his notion that painting could, through abstract composition, attain the purely emotional effect of music. But also Kandinsky's concept of "inner necessity"—related to these other concepts by the interchangeable terms "spiritual necessity" and "inner sound"—had special appeal to artists who

---

works by Europeans such as Botticelli (his *Birth of Venus* cut from a magazine ad), Dürer, Holbein, Picasso, Toulouse-Lautrec, Léger, and de Chirico; works by Americans such as Thomas Eakins, Frank Stella, Charles Sheeler, and Loren MacIver; works by folk artists; artifacts from Greece and Assyria; an original woodcut Christmas card from the Zorachs; some of Moore's own tracings of American Indian drawings; and articles about Shostakovich, Stravinsky, and Frank Lloyd Wright among others.

16. Sandra Gail Levin, "Wassily Kandinsky and the American Avant-Garde, 1912–1950" (Ph.D. dissertation, Rutgers University, 1976), esp. 1–17.

17. Sixten Ringbom, "Transcending the Visible: The Generation of the Abstract Pioneers," and Harriett Watts, "Arp, Kandinsky, and the Legacy of Jakob Böhme," trace the roots of Kandinsky's mysticism to theosophy, symbolism, and German romanticism; Charles C. Eldredge, "Nature Symbolized: American Painting from Ryder to Hartley," points out connections between European symbolism and American transcendentalism. All three essays are in Maurice Tuchman *et al., The Spiritual in Art: Abstract Painting, 1890–1985* (Los Angeles and New York, 1986), 134–39, 244, 115–16. Neither this excellent catalog nor the *"Primitivism" in 20th Century Art* catalog explores the connection between primitivism and spirituality for Kandinsky and his American enthusiasts, though the connection is evident in the writings of the artists both catalogs discuss, especially Max Weber, Marsden Hartley, and Arthur Dove.

revered individual expression. Variations of these terms recur frequently in the writings of the Stieglitz circle. Perhaps Kandinsky's most important contribution to American avant-garde artists was theoretically linking the beliefs they already held: the sanctity of individual expression, the resistance to cultural and aesthetic conventions (and hence an appreciation for abstract as well as so-called "primitive" art), and, underlying both of these, the belief that art which eschews conventions and which expresses the uniqueness of the individual is also an expression of the invisible "spirit."

Except for the concern specifically with abstract painting, these are all beliefs that Moore shared with members of the Stieglitz circle. That Moore even owned a copy of *Der Blaue Reiter* is significant, since it was an expensive, lavishly illustrated book published in Germany. She purchased her copy in January, 1916, a few weeks after first visiting 291. While Kandinsky's effusive prose may seem an unlikely source of inspiration for a poet as unfanatical as Moore is, there is much in Kandinsky that would appeal to her.[18] The collection of clippings she saved in her copy of *Der Blaue Reiter* indicates that she found especially appealing the juxtaposition of diverse art works and its underlying assumption: art that comes from "inner necessity" is spiritual. Kandinsky's notion of "inner necessity," which he introduces in *Concerning the Spiritual in Art* but develops more cogently in his *Blaue Reiter* essay "On the Question of Form," resembles Moore's notion of "the genuine." For both Kandinsky and Moore, art that arises from "inner necessity," or "a feeling for being one's self," is good, morally and aesthetically; art that conforms to external pressures and conventions is false and even evil.

And although Moore probably did not share Kandinsky's enthusiasm for theosophy, she was not averse to mysticism. To Moore, "A reverence for mystery is not a vague, invertebrate thing" (*Prose*, 74). In her poetry she refers to "the fact that spirit creates form" (*SP*, 42) and states, "The power of the visible / is the invisible" (*CP*, 100); her prose reveals that she admired certain mystics such as Jacopone da Todi, William Blake, and the theosophist Annie Besant (*Prose*, 47, 184–85, 259); and throughout her

---

18. Since *Der Blaue Reiter* was not translated into English until after Moore's death, she would have had to read it in German; she was modest about her German because of the difficulty she had passing her German oral examination in college, but she passed the German translation exam with honors. In any case, I am not arguing that Kandinsky necessarily influenced Moore but that *Der Blaue Reiter* appealed to her and certain of her contemporaries for similar reasons.

life the artists she admired most and who often became her friends—including Alfeo Faggi, E. McKnight Kauffer, Robert Andrew Parker, Malvina Hoffman, and Joseph Cornell—were those who acknowledged the "spiritual forces." Her criteria for choosing a work of art—"it must be 'lit with piercing glances into the life of things'; / it must acknowledge the spiritual forces which have made it" (*CP*, 48)—shows that she agrees with Kandinsky both that an artist must create out of spiritual necessity and that he must be able to see "the creative spirit" hidden in matter.[19] Her remarks on Jean de Bosschére best describe her own views on the spiritual in art: "This Frenchman . . . sees the characteristics, as of individual life, which lurk in inanimate objects and even in situations, as well as in living beings. He feels what might be called the soul of these. This form of vision is perhaps mysticism, but it is entirely apart from, though not contradictory to, theological mysticism. To one with a developed sensitiveness this form of individuality is a thing as real—in this world of illusions—as material appearances are" (*Prose*, 36). Likewise, the "spiritual forces" Moore acknowledges in art are "entirely apart from, though not contradictory to," her Christian beliefs.[20] Like Stieglitz and Kandinsky, Moore believed that art can make the power of the invisible visible.

The 291 artist most directly affected by Kandinsky is Marsden Hartley, who even exhibited with the Blaue Reiter group in Berlin. Hartley's exposure to their almanac and *Concerning the Spiritual in Art* while in Paris precipitated his interest in tribal art. He wrote to Stieglitz regarding the Trocadero, Paris's natural history museum: "Yes—one can always find the real thing at the Trocadero. These people . . . created out of spiritual necessity."[21] Hartley became especially intrigued by American Indian art. He incorporated Indian artifacts into a 1912 still life, and in 1914, after returning to Berlin from America, began an important series of paintings called "Amerika," which abstractly renders Indian motifs. Hartley

19. Wassily Kandinsky, "On the Question of Form," in *The "Blaue Reiter" Almanac,* ed. Kandinsky and Marc, 147.

20. For discussion of Moore's religious beliefs, see Eileen G. Moran, "Portrait of the Artist: Marianne Moore's Letters to Hildegarde Watson," in *A Celebration of H.D. and Marianne Moore,* special issue of *Poesis,* VI, nos. 3/4 (1985), 133–36; and Andrew J. Kappel, "Notes on the Presbyterian Poetry of Marianne Moore," in *Woman and Poet,* ed. Willis, 39–51.

21. Marsden Hartley to Alfred Stieglitz, October 9, 1912 (Beinecke). For more thorough discussion of Hartley's and other American artists' interest in tribal art, see Levin, "American Art," in *"Primitivism" in 20th Century Art,* ed. Rubin, II, 453–73.

also published a number of essays praising Indian life and calling for its recognition as a vital aesthetic and cultural resource.

Moore shared Hartley's appreciation for American Indians, for after teaching at the Carlisle Indian School for four years, she maintained an interest in the Indians' work and welfare that was more than theoretical. The Eskimo crafts she saw while visiting her brother in Seattle in 1923 greatly impressed her, as did the Field Museum exhibit of North American Indian art she saw on her return trip through Chicago.[22] She convinced Scofield Thayer to publish her own tracing of an Indian drawing in the *Dial*.[23] As editor she made more explicit the views she had expressed earlier in "New York": "It is impossible not to be ashamed of our civilized ignorance in moving-picture and other representations of the Indian, for Chief Standing Bear finds that we prefer a pseudo-Indian life to the actual one and are indifferent when reasoned with" (*Prose*, 206).

Moore approved her contemporaries' experimentation with "primitive" art. She wrote Robert McAlmon: "A painting of Marsden Hartley's—the Virgin of Guadalupe—is reproduced in The Studio this month, a kind of modern primitive, very definite and impressive."[24] Primitivism is especially evident in the work of the sculptors Moore knew and admired—Alfeo Faggi, Elie Nadelman, William Zorach, and Gaston Lachaise. According to his friend and patron Lincoln Kirstein, Lachaise reacted against the "Renaissance imitation of Greek ideals" and turned instead for inspiration to African sculpture and European cave paintings of "beasts with shaggy mountainous bodies delicately balanced on small, careful hoofs."[25] Monroe Wheeler, who probably understood Moore's taste in art better than anyone else, regularly gave her copies of the books he published for the Museum of Modern Art, including catalogs for exhibits of Mexican art, art of the South Seas, American Indian art, and for exhibits of such modern primitives as Henri Rousseau, Paul Klee, and Georges Rouault.[26]

22. MM to JWM, October 28, 1923 (Rosenbach VI:26:11).

23. MM to JWM, April 4, 1921 (Rosenbach VI:24:05). *Rain-in-the-Face* appeared in the *Dial*, LXXI (November 1921), after p. 550.

24. MM to Robert McAlmon, June 18, 1921 (Rosenbach V:40:06).

25. Lincoln Kirstein, catalog essay for Gaston Lachaise Retrospective Exhibition, Museum of Modern Art, January, 1935, quoted in *The Sculpture of Gaston Lachaise* (New York, 1967), 32, 31.

26. These catalogs with inscriptions from Wheeler are at the Rosenbach. Mr. Wheeler told me he concurred with my assessment that Moore valued art which comes from "inner necessity" (Wheeler to the author, August 7, 1988).

Figure 23 Marsden Hartley, *Virgin of Guadalupe*

1919. Oil on composition board. 31 x 23 7/8 in. All rights reserved, The Metropolitan Museum of Art. The Alfred Stieglitz Collection. 1949. (49.70.44).

Figure 24 Gaston Lachaise, *Standing Woman (Elevation)*

1912–27. Bronze. Philadelphia Museum of Art. Given by R. Sturgis and Marion B. F. Ingersoll.

Other friends who shared Moore's interest in primitivism were William and Marguerite Zorach. In his autobiography, William tells of his early fascination as an art student in Paris with Japanese prints and with Gauguin, who he says "took me into the mysterious inner world of the spirit." And he says that after he returned to New York, in order to free himself from the "academic way of seeing the world about me," he tried drawing with his left hand instead of his trained right hand: "The left hand had no habits to overcome; it was clumsy but free." Like Moore, Zorach frequented the Museum of Natural History, where he studied Eskimo, Aztec, and Mayan sculpture; these "fundamentals" he felt were "an expression

147

of life directly spiritual in the sense of being of a spirit unhampered by external values."[27] Zorach's own sculptures show affinities with African and ancient Egyptian sculpture.

Moore's acquaintance with the Zorachs and their work inspired her poem "In the Days of Prismatic Color," which began as an observation, her own or someone else's, that she recorded in her notebook: "The Zorachs. Their fineness of early civilization art I have never seen such primeval color. It is color of the sort that existed when Adam was there alone and there was no smoke when there was nothing to modify it but mist that went up. May there be a veil before our eyes that we may not see but which would harrow up our souls and may that veil be love not insensibility."[28] The appearance of Adam and Eve in Moore's poem is appropriate, for this mythic couple and their idyllic garden were favorite subjects of the Zorachs. They would often exhibit their work in their own uniquely decorated studio. The "floors were red lead" and "the walls lemon yellow"; the hall was made "into a garden of Eden with a life-sized Adam and Eve and a red and white snake draped around the trunk of a decorative tree, with tropical foliage surrounding it all."[29] In the vestibule of their apartment hung Marguerite's painting of Adam and Eve (she also made a rug titled *Eden* after this painting),[30] and William executed several sculptures of Adam and Eve over the course of his career. But Moore's Adam seems to be more than a personal allusion to her friends. "In the Days of Prismatic Color" not only captures the Zorachs' use of brilliant color (they had been influenced by fauvism) and their predilection for Edenic scenes and figures but also expresses succinctly the mystical and primitivist beliefs Moore shared with them and other artists in their circle.

IN THE DAYS OF PRISMATIC COLOR

not in the days of Adam and Eve, but when Adam
    was alone; when there was no smoke and color was
fine, not with the refinement

27. Zorach, *Art Is My Life,* 65, 33, 34.
28. MM, Spring, 1919, Notebook 1250/24, (Rosenbach VII:10:07), 32–33. MM, "In the Days of Prismatic Color" first appeared in the *Lantern,* XXVII (1919), 35 (Bryn Mawr).
29. Zorach, *Art Is My Life,* 37.
30. Tarbell, *Marguerite Zorach,* 47. In addition to those in Tarbell, see also the reproductions in Marilyn Friedman Hoffman, *William and Marguerite Zorach: The Cubist Years, 1915–1918* (Manchester, N.H., and Hanover, N.H., 1987).

Figure 25. Marguerite Zorach, *Eden*

Hooked rug. 78 x 30 in. Collection of Pamela C. Grossman.

Figure 26 William Zorach, *Man with a Scythe*

1917. Oil on canvas. Collection of Mr. and Mrs. Peter Cardone.

of early civilization art, but because
of its originality; with nothing to modify it but the

mist that went up, obliqueness was a variation
    of the perpendicular, plain to see and
to account for: it is no
    longer that; nor did the blue-red-yellow band
of incandescence that was color keep its stripe: it also is one of

those things into which much that is peculiar can be
    read; complexity is not a crime, but carry
it to the point of murkiness
    and nothing is plain. Complexity,
moreover, that has been committed to darkness, instead of

granting itself to be the pestilence that it is, moves all a-
    bout as if to bewilder us with the dismal
fallacy that insistence
    is the measure of achievement and that all
truth must be dark. Principally throat, sophistication is as it al-

ways has been—at the antipodes from the init-
    ial great truths. "Part of it was crawling, part of it
was about to crawl, the rest
    was torpid in its lair." In the short-legged, fit-
ful advance, the gurgling and all the minutiae—we have the classic

multitude of feet. To what purpose! Truth is no Apollo
    Belvedere, no formal thing. The wave may go over it if it likes.
Know that it will be there when it says,
    "I shall be there when the wave has gone by." (*CP,* 41–42)

The "Days of Prismatic Color // . . . when Adam/was alone" are for
Moore the days of spiritual oneness, the days before society, even a society of two, could create civilization, language, art, and the other "refinement[s]" that make truth murky.[31] The distinction between mist and smoke
is significant. There was no smoke in the days of prismatic color (partly

31. Slatin, *The Savage's Romance,* expresses bafflement at Moore's blaming Eve for the
fall (265), but that is not, I believe, her intention. Her point is that before Eve "Adam was
alone"; it is society and civilization that bring an end to "the days of prismatic color," not
Eve's temptation.

because Adam did not yet have the fire necessary for civilized life), and there was nothing to modify the "fine" color, the color not yet "refined" by early civilization art, except the mist. Although in the poem Moore does not call the veil of mist "love" and the smoke "insensibility," as she implies in her notebook, she makes it clear that the mist is necessary to reveal the prismatic color whereas smoke blurs that vision. The subject of the first sentence emphasizes this distinction: "obliqueness" is both mistlike and smokelike, for in its original sense it describes the light rays refracted by the prism, but in its present sense it means not "plain to see." Moore seems to justify the complexity of her own poems by distinguishing between, on one hand, an undesirable "obliqueness" that obscures the truth and, on the other hand, an "obliqueness" that is difficult because its truth threatens familiar, easy misconceptions. Although "not a crime" unless carried "to the point of murkiness," complexity "that has been committed to darkness" instead of to incandescent truth becomes a "pestilence," a disease of civilization.

Of the two prevailing images of "In the Days of Prismatic Color" the first, which governs the first four stanzas, is light—the incandescence that the mist, perhaps Adam's God, reveals in prismatic color. Prismatic color is both a spiritual and an aesthetic vision. The "incandescence" and "darkness" seem to recall Kandinsky's distinction between "*The white, fertilizing ray*" that is creative and good and "*The black, fatal hand*" of convention that is destructive and evil.[32] But Adam does not see Kandinsky's white ray, nor does Moore concur with Shelley that life is "like a dome of many-coloured glass" that "Stains the white radiance of Eternity" (*Adonais*, lines 462–63). The eternal radiance here is not a single white light but rather its components, the prismatic colors. According to Annie Besant, this is a vision witnessed by mystics of various faiths: "These vibrations . . . give rise . . . to the most exquisite and constantly changing colours, waves of varying shades like the rainbow hues in mother-of-pearl, etherealised and brightened to an indescribable extent, sweeping over and through every form, so that each presents a harmony of rippling, living, luminous, delicate, colours, including many not ever known to earth. . . . Every seer who has witnessed [this subtle matter], Hindu, Buddhist, Christian, speaks in rapturous terms of its glorious beauty."[33]

32. Kandinsky, "On the Question of Form," in *The "Blaue Reiter" Almanac*, ed. Kandinsky and Marc, 147–48.

33. Annie Besant, *The Ancient Wisdom: An Outline of Theosophical Teachings* (1897; rpr. Adyar, India, 1949), 128.

The second prevailing image of the poem is a many-footed primeval creature, perhaps the evolutionary counterpart to Adam. First hinted at with the word "pestilence" in the fourth stanza, the beast becomes vivid in the quotation from Nestor, "Part of it was crawling, part of it/was about to crawl, the rest/was torpid in its lair." Moore seems to enjoy this creature's feet a great deal; "classic//multitude of feet" suggests first the creature's "short-legged, fit-/ful advance," but then "classic" brings to mind the "multitude of feet" in Greek friezes as well as the "multitude of feet" in classical verse. Thus, the "short-legged, fit-/ful advance, the gurgling and all the minutiae" is the advance of civilization and its art, and with this advance away from "the init-/ial great truths" comes "sophistication" and the "formal" conventions of art such as those evident in the Apollo Belvedere. The Apollo Belvedere at the Vatican is a Roman copy in marble of a now lost Greek bronze; during the Renaissance, and especially during the eighteenth century, it came to epitomize the perfection of Greek sculpture, but when artists in the nineteenth century began to question the conventions that had so dominated Western art since the Renaissance, the Apollo Belvedere came to epitomize the sterility of academic art. Thus, for Moore the Apollo Belvedere signifies "sophistication" and the smoky conventions of art that prevent spiritual vision.

Nor is it only "early civilization art" and the conventions of the Renaissance that Moore is protesting in this poem. Her present tense is emphatic when she says, "sophistication is as it al-//ways has been." When she complains of "the dismal/fallacy that insistence/is the measure of achievement and that all/truth must be dark," she criticizes the modern assumption that truth is unknowable and that through insistence one must try to create meaning. Although Moore's unabashed truth that will be there "when the wave has gone by" may raise a few modernist eyebrows, it is not hard to see that a poet who envisions truth in "prismatic color" would have little use for Stevens' "supreme fiction" or Eliot's "mythical method."

Some critics interpret truth's statement in the final line of the poem ironically because they cannot reconcile Moore's delight in difference and multiplicity with a vision of permanent truth.[34] But I find the last two lines are as emphatic as Moore ever gets. The final stanza departs abruptly from the pattern of the earlier stanzas (in which even in its final version Moore preserved four divided words), so that line breaks and syntax epi-

34. See Costello, *Imaginary Possessions,* 28–29, and Martin, *Subversive Modernist,* 102.

grammatically coincide. Moore does delight in multiplicity, and Bonnie Costello correctly asserts that Moore's "poems do not seek a still center in the turning world."[35] The spiritual truth that will "be there when the wave has gone by" is certainly permanent, however. But it is also uncentered and pluralist. For the vision Adam sees (and Moore envies) is neither a god nor a single white ray of truth, but rather "prismatic color": "the blue-red-yellow band / of incandescence."

While Marianne Moore embraced the primitivism of her contemporaries, she was more sensitive than most to the problems of romanticizing the "savage." Stieglitz's statement to Arthur Dove, for example, typifies the unconscious racism that often accompanied Westerners' enthusiasm over tribal art: "There is a wonderful show on now by Negro savages. . . . It is possibly the most important show we have ever had [at 291]."[36] The offensiveness of such epithets was probably not as obvious to Moore as to readers today (she wrote enthusiastically to her brother about certain "darky shows" playing in New York during the twenties[37]), but her *Dial* "Comment" on Indians and especially "New York" show her realization that preferring a "pseudo-Indian life to the actual one" is itself a form of savagery. In her poem lamenting the obfuscating effects of civilization, Moore avoids a noble savage stereotype by choosing Adam as her hypothetical primitive. Increasingly in the twenties and afterward, Moore avoids the ethnocentrism endemic to much modernist literature by extolling animal virtues instead of human ones.

Her family's whimsical fictions taught Moore the subversive fun of characterizing people as animals. Often in the Moores' letters the animal personae are more impudent than their human counterparts can afford to be. When Warner and Marianne were students, Baby Fawn (Mrs. Moore) had to defer to the protection and sage guidance of her two adoptive uncles, Fangs (Marianne) and Biter (Warner). Even much later, the animals have no obligation, for instance, to Mrs. Moore's strictures about proper English usage and therefore often speak in a candid vernacular. It may be that all of Moore's animals are masks for people. "Fish," "Basilisk,"

35. Costello, *Imaginary Possessions,* 3.
36. Alfred Stieglitz to Arthur Dove, November 5, 1914 (Beinecke).
37. MM to JWM, November 9, 1923 (Rosenbach VI:26:12). For a thorough and sensitive analysis of Moore and race, see Cristanne Miller, "Marianne Moore's Black Maternal Hero: A Study in Categorization," *American Literary History,* I (1989), 786–815.

and "Pangolin" were family nicknames long before they became poems. Henry McBride, who knew Moore well, wrote her upon receiving *The Pangolin and Other Verse*: "I thought at first The Pangolin was going to be a self-portrait—the creature was so well armoured—but then I read on and found myself included and practically all of my acquaintance." [38] Although even during her portrait phase Moore avoided naming the persons she censured (the pedantic literalist, the steam roller), her move away from proper names after 1915 may indicate her awareness that, as Hugh Kenner says, "To be crisp even in praise of people's excellence is to make oneself a little the proprietor of their virtue." [39] The usefulness of poetry was too important to her, however, to give up its didactic function. By adopting animals as subjects instead of persons, the moral critic could go disguised as animal lover.

"Black Earth," first published in 1918, marks an important transition in Moore's animal poems. [40] The earlier animals had been either metaphors for named individuals ("To a Prize Bird," "To the Peacock of France") or for unnamed persons or types ("Critics and Connoisseurs," "The Monkeys"). The later animals ("Peter," "The Jerboa") drop their human tenors, or seem to do so, altogether. Like "To a Chameleon," "Black Earth" may be read either way. In 1951 Moore changed the title to "Melanchthon" (Greek for "black earth"), indicating that the poem may well be about Philip Melanchthon, the Reformation leader who adopted the hellenization of his family name, Schwarzerd. [41] Moore and her mother both admired Melanchthon, who was Martin Luther's collaborator, friend, and humbler, more diplomatic complement. Besides the title and the poem's spiritual theme, the specific mention of the "Renaissance" also suggests Melanchthon's role in "the history of power."

Nevertheless, "Black Earth" works just as well as a literal elephant, and its virtues anticipate those of the later animals. (With "Black Earth" and "Dock Rats" Moore experimented with making the animal the speaker of the poem, a practice she then discontinued.) The reader learns first that the elephant acts out of inner necessity.

---

38. Henry McBride to MM, February 4, 1939 (Rosenbach V:40:07).
39. Kenner, *A Homemade World*, 117.
40. MM, "Black Earth," *Egoist*, IV (April, 1918), 55–56.
41. MM, *Collected Poems* (New York, 1951), 45.

Openly, yes
With the naturalness
   Of the hippopotamus or the alligator
   When it climbs out on the bank to experience the

Sun, I do these
Things which I do, which please
   No one but myself.

And though here this seems only a pleasure-seeking impulse, as the poem progresses it becomes clearly a spiritual necessity, too: the impenetrable "soul," the elusive center of "spiritual poise," and by the end of the poem, the "Beautiful element of unreason" behind the thick skin.

Philip Melanchthon's father was an armorer by trade, and appropriately Black Earth is the first of Moore's many armored creatures. She makes much of the "elephant skin / . . . fibred over like the shell of / The coconut, this piece of black glass through which no light // Can filter—cut / Into checkers by rut / Upon rut of unpreventable experience." The thick skin is the elephant's most distinctive feature in this poem, for it symbolically unifies spirit and earth: "The sediment of the river" is one with the elephant who lies in it; "do away /With it," he says, "and I am myself done away with." Although the elephant's experience is "unpreventable" rather than chosen, the relationship between spirit and earth resembles the paradoxical one between imagination and things in Moore's assemblages. Earth forms a cryptic shield that simultaneously both reveals and protects the self; the rutted skin is "a manual for the peanut-tongued and the // Hairy toed"—accessible only to those who can "see" and "hear."

"Black Earth" also anticipates later poems by contrasting animal virtues against human foibles.

   . . . I see
And I hear, unlike the
   Wandlike body of which one hears so much, which was made
   To see and not to see; to hear and not to hear.

The "tree trunk without/Roots" lacks both the elephant's "spiritual poise" and its connectedness to the earth. This prevents it from seeing, from seeing the spiritual presence, the "Beautiful element of unreason" under the elephant's thick skin. Being defenseless themselves, "Translucent like the atmosphere—a cortex merely," humans have no understanding of thickness or depth, the elephant seeming to their ignorance merely "That on which darts cannot strike decisively the first/Time." Their dart attacks are futile, however, for not even a wooden spear can cut into the elephant's soul.

An essential feature of Moore's spirituality and one that distinguishes hers from that of, say, her mother is that there is no opposition between a single, external spirit and earth's material diversity, but rather that a pluralist spirit requires matter, the "patina of circumstance," to reveal itself. In "In This Age of Hard Trying . . ." "the polished wedge" of genuine spirituality seeks the earthly "poor fool" rather than the egocentric gods "revolv[ing] upon the axes of their worth." In "In the Days of Prismatic Color" mist is necessary to reveal the spiritual vision. But in "Black Earth" the interdependence of spirit and earth is more emphatic. It is the thick skin, the gray earth, the unpreventable experience that makes the elephant spiritually superior to one who is "Spiritual / Brother to the coral / Plant." To have skin like "black glass through which no light // Can filter" is preferable to humans' translucence, which absorbs the "equable sapphire light" and turns it "a nebulous green." Decades later Moore found an analogue for her spiritual and aesthetic views in Mai-Mai Sze's *The Tao of Painting*, which she explains at some length in an unpublished essay and paraphrases: "Painting should be a fusion of that which pertains to Heaven— the spirit—and of matter, which pertains to Earth." [42]

According to one scholar, primitive existence forces upon human beings the recognition that animals are "stronger, fiercer, cleverer than themselves, and certainly more beautiful." Tribal artists often regard animals as mankind's ancestors, and dancers may wear animal masks to reenact the ancestors' deeds or to impersonate "animals, or animal-like heroes, who taught humanity essential skills." [43] Before "Black Earth," Moore often complimented her human subjects by comparing them to animals, but thereafter she exalts the animals' beauty and purity as a heroic ideal to which erring humans can only aspire. To explain to one interviewer her admiration for animals she even calls them "Our ancestors!" [44] The poems

42. MM, "The Tao of Painting" ["Tedium and Integrity"] (Rosenbach II:06:12). This may have been one of Moore's most important essays along with "Feeling and Precision" and "Humility, Concentration, and Gusto" had she not lost the first four pages (see *Prose*, 550).

43. Douglas Newton, *The Nelson A. Rockefeller Collection: Masterpieces of Primitive Art* (New York, 1978), 198.

44. Winthrop Sargeant, "Humility, Concentration, and Gusto," *New Yorker*, February 16, 1957, p. 44.

themselves become a kind of animal dance, often with reminders of the animal's totemic importance: in "Black Earth" "through-/Out childhood to the present time, the unity of /Life and death has been expressed by the circumference//Described by my/Trunk"; in "The Plumet Basilisk," "the basilisk portrays / mythology's wish / to be interchangeably man and fish" (*CP*, 23). In one *Dial* "Comment" Moore acknowledges the dangers of animal deification but calls for a renewed awe before animals, serpents in particular: "A certain ritual of awe—animistic and animalistic—need not, however, be effaced from our literary consciousness. The serpent as a motive in art, as an idea, as beauty, is surely not beneath us, as we see it in the stone and the gold hamadryads of Egypt; in the turtle zoomorphs, feathered serpent columns, and coiled rattlesnakes of Yucatan; in the silver-white snakes, 'chameleon lizards,' and stone dragons of Northern Siam" (*Prose*, 187). (Even a quick comparison of "Black Earth" with D. H. Lawrence's "The Elephant Is Slow to Mate" reveals that Moore's primitivism is considerably more "animistic" than "animalistic.") Other modernists shared Moore's "ritual of awe." Horses are a favorite subject of Franz Marc, whom Marsden Hartley calls "psychic in his rendering of the soul life of animals." [45] And while animals are not Gaston Lachaise's most frequent subjects, he writes: "On certain occasions I have made use of animals, sea-gulls, sea-lions, dolphins, peacocks, penguins, to translate spiritual forces." [46] Many more, of course—Hartley, Dove, O'Keeffe, the Zorachs—continually turned to nature for inspiration. Moore's knowledge of animals was hardly ever unmitigated by a photographer, zoo keeper, or natural historian; nevertheless, the creatures of nature were her favorite subjects. [47]

45. Marsden Hartley to Alfred Stieglitz, February, 1913 (Beinecke).

46. Gaston Lachaise, "A Comment on My Sculpture," *Creative Art*, III (August, 1928), xxiii.

47. When Moore was in college, her mother advised her to find "relaxation in the outside air—in country scenes, in the antics of animals, in anything that's clean and wholesome, and outside yourself" (MWM to MM, January 14, 1907, Rosenbach VI:13a:02). Yet oddly, this family of animal lovers did not as a rule keep pets (except for imaginary ones, such as "Porker," Warner's sassy pig, and "Willow," Marianne's rat). Both Moore and her mother enjoyed watching their neighbors' cat, the immortalized Peter. Yet a few weeks after adopting a stray kitten of their own, and naming it Buffalo, Mrs. Moore chloroformed it. She felt remorse at this, especially for the grief it caused Marianne, but her lengthy explanation to Warner offers little beyond: "*We* cannot have animals. That is not for us" (MWM to JWM, April 30, 1923, Rosenbach VI:26:05).

"Peter" (first published in *Observations* in 1924) is the earliest poem in which the animal itself seems more important than what it signifies. Even the animals in "To a Chameleon" and "Black Earth" are more hypothetical than actual. As Moore's animals after the twenties become more metonymic and her diction more scientific (I discuss this in the next chapter), her attention turns simultaneously to the exotic animals she knows through natural history magazines and films: "The Jerboa," "The Plumet Basilisk," "The Frigate-Pelican," "The Pangolin," to name a few. While Moore's interest in these animals must be to a large extent uncalculated, exotic animals do demonstrate, perhaps more clearly than anything else could, her aesthetic and moral principles. Animals cannot be hypocritical or false; they cannot act other than out of inner necessity. And since it is a "fact that spirit creates form" (*SP*, 42), the animals' peculiar physical attributes reveal their spiritual necessity, too. Moore would agree with Kandinsky that "*Form is the outer expression of the inner content.*"

Since form is only an expression of content, and content is different with different artists, it is clear that there may be *many different forms at the same time* that are *equally good.*

Necessity creates form. Fish that live at great depths have no eyes. The elephant has a trunk. The chameleon changes its color, etc., etc.

Form reflects the spirit of the individual artist. Form bears the stamp of the *personality.*[48]

This explains why Moore comes to prefer animals as subjects more than people and why she prefers exotic animals to the everyday ones, for animals are more apparently various than people are and therefore illustrate more clearly the aesthetic principle that "*necessity creates form*" and the aesthetic and moral principle that "there may be *many different forms at the same time* that are *equally good.*" Although all animals must, for example, protect themselves, each animal does so in a different way according to its own inner necessity—some with speed, some with color, some with armor (few of Moore's animals fight); the wide variations in physical appearance—the stripes, spots, shells, wings, and tails—demonstrate vividly that "there's more than just one kind of grace" (*CP*, 167).

For both Moore and Kandinsky aesthetic principles are also moral

48. Kandinsky, "On the Question of Form," in *The "Blaue Reiter" Almanac*, ed. Kandinsky and Marc, 149–50.

ones. In Kandinsky this becomes clear in a footnote: "One should not make a uniform out of the form. Works of art are not soldiers. One and the same form can therefore, even with the same artist, be at one time the best, at another the worst. In the first case it grew in the soil of inner necessity, in the second in the soil of outer necessity: out of ambition and greed." [49] But whereas this morality remains an implication in Kandinsky, it is Moore's overriding concern. The moral aspects of Moore's aesthetic are evident throughout her work but are especially evident in those poems, such as "Peter," "The Jerboa," and "He 'Digesteth Harde Yron,'" that contrast the moral purity of the animal with the often impure motives of human beings. Moore sees beauty and moral good in animals that act, as they must, out of inner necessity and evil in those human beings who act out of outer necessity, especially those who act "out of ambition and greed." Often her language echoes Kandinsky's inner/outer distinction, as in the contrast of "external poise" (based on pride) and "spiritual poise" in "Black Earth," and in her calling "externalists" those who are insensitive to exploitation in "He 'Digesteth Harde Yron.'"

In "Peter" the human beings with which the domestic cat must put up are not immoral, only "unprofitable" as compared to the cat. Watching Peter's indifference to human society, Moore observes:

> to sit caged by the rungs of a domestic chair
> would be unprofitable—human. What is the good of hypocrisy?
> It is permissible to choose one's employment,
> to abandon the nail, or roly-poly,
> when it shows signs of being no longer a pleasure,
> to score the nearby magazine with a double line of strokes. (*CP*, 43–44)

Throughout the poem she contrasts the inner necessity of the cat with the hypocrisy of polite human society. But in "He 'Digesteth Harde Yron'" (1941) the heroic ostrich must put up with not only hypocrisy but also something much worse—the near extinction of his species.

> ... How
> could he, prized for plumes and eggs and young,
> used even as a riding-beast, respect men
> hiding actor-like in ostrich skins, with the right hand
> making the neck move as if alive

49. *Ibid.*, 153.

and from a bag the left hand strewing grain, that ostriches

might be decoyed and killed! (*CP*, 99)

The close connection between Moore's moral and aesthetic judgments becomes evident in "The Jerboa" (*CP*, 10–15), in which the two parts of the poem called "*Too Much*" and "*Abundance*" juxtapose the immorality of false art with the humble beauty of the jerboa. "*Too Much*" begins with an art work created according to "outer necessity": "A Roman had an / artist, a freedman, / contrive a cone." The work is *contrived* by a "freedman," who artistically is not at all free. This horrendous cone-shaped fountain "passed / for art"; "it looks like a work of art made to give / to a Pompey, or native // of Thebes," not like one that arose from the artist's inner necessity. Most of the rest of the first section of the poem describes the morally decadent Egyptians, whose art (after its early period of inventiveness) became as academic as Roman art. But it is not the academic aspect of their art that Moore emphasizes; rather it is their exploitation of animals and people: they "put goose-grease / paint in round bone boxes," "kept in a buck / or rhinoceros horn, / the ground horn; and locust oil in stone locusts"; the dwarfs they kept provided "a fantasy / and a verisimilitude that were / right to those with, everywhere, // power over the poor," and "Those who tended flower- / beds and stables were like the king's cane in the / form of a hand."

In contrast to the "tamed // Pharaoh's rat" is the jerboa, "a small desert rat, / and not famous, that / lives without water," and "has a shining silver house // of sand." Though he has no things, no water even, he has "happiness." And in contrast to the decadent Romans and Egyptians are the blacks of Africa, described at the beginning of the second section of the poem: "that choice race with an elegance / ignored by one's ignorance." In its freedom both from possessors and from possessions, the jerboa exhibits moral and aesthetic wholeness, conforming to nature both in its behavior and in its physical appearance.

> . . . The fine hairs on the tail,
>   repeating the other pale
>
> markings, lengthen until
> at the tip they fill
>   out in a tuft—black and

white; strange detail of the simplified creature,
fish-shaped and silvered to steel by the force
of the large desert moon.

And the jerboa's rhythmic leaps "By fifths and sevenths" are like "the uneven notes / of the Bedouin flute," the Bedouins being, like the jerboa,
self-sufficient desert wanderers.

The poem's indictment of exploitation and of racial ignorance demonstrates, on one hand, Moore's commitment to rectifying social wrongs
(not just describing animals) but, on the other hand, the inherent difficulty of addressing racial injustice without substituting one form of ignorance for another, an idealization of blacks. As Cristanne Miller observes
about the treatment of Africans in this poem: " 'The blacks,' like other un-
materialistic and unimperialistic poor, provide models for those who live
in middle- and upper-class decadence—that is, for those who keep them
poor." [50] Thus, here Moore virtually succumbs to the noble savage stereotype she had decried a decade earlier in "New York." Writing about animals instead of peoples enables Moore to challenge "one's ignorance"
without making racial generalizations, but it also allows readers to dismiss
her poetry as quaint, removed from the serious social and political issues
of her day.

Though less frequently than animals in Moore's oeuvre, plants also
demonstrate moral and spiritual perfection. In "Roses Only" Moore praises
the rose for surpassing "anything an // ambitious civilization might pro-
duce" (SP, 42). And "Nevertheless" applauds the "fortitude" of various
plants, such as "a strawberry / that's had a struggle," that follow their inner drives to idiosyncratic extremes in order to survive (CP, 125–26). With
objects in Moore's poems it is sometimes more difficult to distinguish her
approval from her disapproval. Like the toys the Egyptians made for themselves in "The Jerboa," which seem to be at once fascinating and morally
repugnant to Moore, the "chintz china" swan in the "Louis Fifteenth /
candelabrum-tree" of "No Swan So Fine" is both beautiful, "at ease and
tall," and a reminder of a decadent king, now dead (CP, 19). Human motives are more complex than those of animals and plants—hence the greater
difficulty of distinguishing in human behavior and in art objects the
genuine from the hypocritical.

Moore rejects a relativist morality. She believes in enduring principles

50. Miller, "Marianne Moore's Black Maternal Hero," 788.

of good and evil. And yet the great amount of tolerance that her pluralist ethic (and aesthetic) demands makes her reluctant to pass judgment on
what she does not fully comprehend. In one version of "Poetry" she asserts: "enigmas are not poetry" (*Obs*, 31). Yet when she backs away from
this definiteness, realizing perhaps that the "raw material of poetry" is often enigmatic, and returns to an earlier version of the poem, she makes a
significant punctuation change. In the first published version of "Poetry,"
Moore says of things that are "genuine" and "useful": "when they become
so derivative as to become unintelligible, the / same thing may be said
for all of us—that we / do not admire what / we cannot understand." [51] The
reader assumes that "what / we cannot understand" is murky and derivative (like academic art) and that Moore concurs with the statement. In
1935 she changed the period after "understand" to a colon. While the
original meaning still holds, that derivative art is unintelligible and
hence undesirable, the catalog following the colon ironically undermines the assertion that "we / do not admire what / we cannot understand."

> the same thing may be said for all of us, that we
>   do not admire what
>   we cannot understand: the bat
>   holding on upside down or in quest of something to
>
> eat, elephants pushing, a wild horse taking a roll, a tireless wolf under
> a tree, the immovable critic twitching his skin like a horse that feels
>   a flea, the base-
>   ball fan, the statistician—
>   nor is it valid
>   to discriminate against 'business documents and
>
> school-books'; all these phenomena are important. (*SP*, 36)

Moore's famous predilection for animals and sports suggests she might
very well admire what she cannot understand; moreover, she calls for the
recognition of such phenomena as *important*. "Complexity is not a crime,"
Moore says in "In the Days of Prismatic Color," unless it has been carried
"to the point of murkiness." Although some complexities are derivative
and unintelligible since they arise from outer necessity, some, like "the

51. MM, "Poetry," *Others*, V (July, 1919), 5.

bat / holding on upside down," "the statistician," and the "base- / ball fan," though not easily explained, warrant observation and even admiration because they are "genuine." Just as in her assemblages Moore allows "the raw material" to retain its mysterious autonomy, so here she allows "genuine" behavior the same freedom.

"Snakes, Mongooses, Snake-Charmers, and the Like" (*CP*, 58) presents the same principle in more obviously ethical terms. Without naming India, she calls it "the country in which everything is hard work, the country of the grass-getter, / the torch-bearer, the dog-servant, the messenger-bearer, the holy-man." Like the catalog in "Poetry," these are all individuals engaged in perplexing activities; none are as perplexing to her, however, as the snake-charmer. Contrary to Moore's own immense curiosity and predilection for diversity, the snake-charmer has admiration for one thing only, the snake. Nevertheless, the poem concludes: "The passion for setting people right is in itself an afflictive disease. / Distaste which takes no credit to itself is best." In this case Moore's propriety instructs her to refrain from judgment even though she finds snake-charming to be distasteful. The ability to refrain from judging what one does not understand and at the same time to recognize that an apparently unproductive "train of thought" may after all be "genuine" is the highest good in Moore's pluralist ethic. This is the essence of what elsewhere she calls "humility."

The perplexing and at least potentially genuine forms of behavior in "Snakes, Mongooses, Snake-Charmers, and the Like" are called merely "hard work." Moore repeatedly insists upon the importance of hard work to the artist (*Prose*, 203, 208, 362), of "the sense of artistic difficulty" (*Prose*, 427), of the artist's willingness to "waste effort" (*MMR*, 273).[52] But because of the negative connotations of the word, it is easy to overlook the greater precision of "fastidiousness" in describing the inexplicable inner necessity that drives the artist. Besides the famous opening line of "Critics and Connoisseurs," Moore also wrote a *Dial* "Comment" in praise of literary fastidiousness (*Prose*, 165–67). "Fastidiousness" is hard work that is inexplicable to others; "unconscious fastidiousness" is hard work that is inexplicable to oneself. Both are, in Moore's lexicon, manifestations of inner necessity.

---

52. Members of the Stieglitz circle continually insisted on the importance of hard work, which was also essential to arts and crafts ideology. Arthur Dove, for instance, wrote in his notes: "To search and find, that is God as we call it. In other words *work*. It is the only thing that gives happiness" (quoted in Haskell, *Arthur Dove,* 136).

For as restrained a writer as Moore is, the opening statement of "Critics and Connoisseurs" (*CP*, 38–39) is strong indeed: "There is a great amount of poetry in unconscious/fastidiousness." Most critics do themselves an injustice when they give it the negative interpretation, "There is *no* poetry in the *conscious* fastidiousness of critics and connoisseurs." If one assumes that Moore fits the cliché that poets hate and distrust critics, she will miss the point, for in "Poetry" Moore ranks the "critic twitching his skin" with "the bat/holding on upside down" and the "base-/ball fan," not with the despicable "half poets." And in "Picking and Choosing" unadulterated admiration prompts her saying, "Gordon Craig so inclinational and unashamed—a critic" (*CP*, 267, 45).[53] So when she describes the fastidiousness of the swan and ant in "Critics and Connoisseurs," she also speaks with admiration, qualified only by the fact that she likes unconscious fastidiousness better. In "Profit Is a Dead Weight" she says similarly, "Overinitiative has something to be said for it. . . . Humility is yet mightier" (*Prose*, 568). (Of course, Moore does not admire all critics; "To a Steam Roller" satirizes the critic who cannot appreciate diversity, who "crush[es] all the particles down/into close conformity.")

The first stanza of "Critics and Connoisseurs" presents two extremes of fastidiousness: "Certain Ming/products" at one extreme and what the persona prefers, "a/mere childish attempt to make an imperfectly bal-/lasted animal stand up," at the other—in other words, fastidiousness in its most sophisticated form versus fastidiousness in its most primitive impulse. Conscious fastidiousness, the necessary choice usually of artists as well as critics, differs only in degree from the unconscious fastidiousness of the child. Rather than ridicule the critic and connoisseur, Moore watches them with awe and curiosity just as she watches a swan refuse to follow a bit of food in the stream and an ant carry a stick "north, south,/east, west, till it turned on/itself, struck out from the flower-bed into the lawn,/and returned to the point// from which it had started."

"I have seen," she says, "ambition without/understanding in a variety of forms." Most readers take Moore's contempt here for granted, but "ambition without/understanding" paraphrases "unconscious/fastidiousness," in which "There is a great amount of poetry." Attempting "to make an imperfectly bal-/lasted animal stand up" or "to make a pup/eat

53. Celeste Goodridge, *Hints and Disguises*, supports this point at greater length, contrasting Moore's view of criticism as a creative activity with Eliot's view that criticism is always secondary to the work it describes (18–20).

his meat from the plate" *is* "ambition without / understanding"; it is giving in to one's inner necessity without analyzing it. Equally interesting to Moore is the "variety of forms" that inner necessity can take. As in her exotic menagerie, the forms reveal one's true individuality at the same time they subvert the observer's categorical expectations. The observer does not expect the swan to refuse food or the industrious ant to waste effort carrying a particle of whitewash; nor does the reader expect to find poetry in the fastidiousness of the critic and connoisseur.

In this poem Moore directly addresses the reader, connoisseur if not critic, as "you": "I have seen this swan and / I have seen you." The reader may be like the swan, a critic, eager to defend his own standards (at Oxford, no less) but finally pursuing those bits of food that the poet proffers. Or the reader may be like the ant, a connoisseur, carrying a poem or an interpretation that strikes his fancy north, south, east, west, finally returning to the point from which he started and then carrying another poem through the same procedure. Nor are poetry readers unlike the child trying "to make an imperfectly bal- / lasted animal stand up," similarly determined "to make a pup / eat his meat from the plate"; when faced with a poem, however imperfect or willfully complex, readers try to make it conform to their own sense of rightness. At the end of "Critics and Connoisseurs" Moore's question is not merely rhetorical.

> What is
> there in being able
> to say that one has dominated the stream in an attitude of self-
> defense;
> in proving that one has had the experience
> of carrying a stick?

"What is there," she could ask, "in being able to say that one has written four fastidiously duplicated stanzas; in proving that one has read a poem with understanding?" As in her aesthetic of the miscellany, Moore refuses to acknowledge a hierarchical difference between artist and audience, between poet and connoisseur.

The oxymoron in "unconscious fastidiousness" describes the artist's activity—the paradoxical blend of the deliberate and the inexplicable. While Moore believes, like Lachaise, "in a large amount of work," she also insists that her best work is spontaneous if not unconscious. She tells Donald Hall: "I never knew anyone who had a passion for words who had as

166

much difficulty in saying things as I do and I very seldom say them in a manner I like. If I do it's because I don't know I'm trying" and "Spontaneous initial originality—say, impetus—seems difficult to reproduce consciously later" (*MMR*, 259, 263). She expresses bewilderment at her own inner necessity but respects it nevertheless. To respect the inner necessity of another requires "humility"; to respect it in oneself requires "courage." When Moore praises artists such as Lachaise and Cornell for refusing to compromise, she is acknowledging their courage to follow their unique inner forces rather than bending to external categories and expectations. Praising the cartoonist David Low, Moore says: "he has never compromised; he goes right on doing what idiosyncrasy tells him to do. The thing is to see the vision and not deny it; to care and admit that we do" (*Prose*, 426).

"Unconscious fastidiousness" also describes the paradoxical nature of Moore's stanza that she was just perfecting at the time she wrote "Critics and Connoisseurs." This is the dualism between what Margaret Holley calls "organic" and "mechanical" forms.[54] The organic, or unconscious, pattern of the first stanza is duplicated mechanically, or fastidiously, throughout the rest of the poem. Even before Moore conceives her proto-stanza as organic in the thirties, she sees its origins as mysterious, as "a matter of expediency," [55] "expediency" being one of Moore's own terms for inner necessity. And Moore seems to agree with Kandinsky that "one and the same form can . . . even with the same artist, be at one time the best, at another the worst"; thus each poem must express a unique poetic impulse, for if a stanzaic form were repeated in a second poem, it would already be derivative. At a time when other poets were experimenting with free verse as an alternative to conventional verse forms, one may wonder why an artist following her "spontaneous initial originality" would duplicate stanzas at all, even within the same poem. Moore's observation of nature—and of Oriental, tribal, and modern art, too—taught her that inner necessity manifests itself in mathematical rhythms, in both behavioral and physical patterns, such as the jerboa's leaps "By fifths and sevenths" and the basilisk's tail that has "eight green/bands . . . painted on" it (*CP*, 14, 22). "As rhythmical as a zebra" is how she describes the Zorachs' tapestry that she admired.[56]

54. Holley, "The Model Stanza," in *Marianne Moore*, ed. Kappel, special issue of *Twentieth Century Literature*, 185–88.
55. MM to Pound, January 9, 1919, in *Marianne Moore*, ed. Tomlinson, 17.
56. MM to JWM, December 19, 1916 (Rosenbach VI:21:13).

Moore's terms for what Kandinsky calls inner necessity vary: "expediency," "unconscious fastidiousness," "a feeling for being one's self," "spontaneous initial originality—say, impetus." But they are all variations of a primal, or primitive, impulse. Like Arthur Dove, Georgia O'Keeffe, Gaston Lachaise, and other contemporaries, Moore perceived this force—actually forces—both in art and in nature. Sherrye Cohn finds analogues for Dove's early abstractions in contemporary concepts of organic form. According to such concepts, which pervaded Western thought after the turn of the century, "organic form is that in which the inner structure is propelled outward by internal force and in which outer form must adapt to the exigencies of the environment. Its visual and intellectual appeal lies in its inherent regularity and manifest variety," in its "glorious array of patterns, textures, colors, and shapes."[57] Such concepts appealed to artists not only because they matched popular aesthetic theories, such as Kandinsky's and Dow's, but also because they seemed to validate such theories scientifically.

Not all of Moore's contemporaries would have concurred with so orderly a vision of the primitive. The dadaists embraced a chaotic, "animalistic" primitivism in reaction against the idea that art should be harmonious. In her provocative analysis of primitivism in modern Western thought, Marianna Torgovnick finds that society uses variations of the primitive to define itself, both to confront its deepest fears and to envision its own primal essence.[58] For Moore the primitive is never evil; rather, it is a utopian "days of prismatic color" or else, more often, the mysterious forces that manifest themselves in an infinitely various but rhythmic world. Evil is that which denies variety—egotism, bigotry, hypocrisy, greed, tyranny. Moore's ethic demands radical humility toward the idiosyncrasies and mysteries in the world—in order to *see* "the spiritual forces which have made it."

57. Sherrye Cohn, "Arthur Dove and the Organic Analogy: A Rapprochement Between Art and Nature," *Arts Magazine,* LIX (Summer, 1985), 87.

58. Marianna Torgovnick, *Gone Primitive: Savage Intellects, Modern Lives* (Chicago, 1990), 18 and *passim.*

5

A DISTINCTLY NATIONAL PRODUCT

In 1923 Marianne Moore applies an unprecedented and hence tempting label to herself when she says in her poem "Bowls": "I learn that we are precisionists"[1]—unprecedented for a poet who resisted the many -*ism*'s of her generation; tempting since *precisionist* now refers to an indigenous style of American painting that emerged after World War I. Adding to the temptation are the links already drawn between writers and precisionist painters, particularly between William Carlos Williams and his friends Charles Sheeler and Charles Demuth. Also, Moore's poetry has a precisionist aura to it—what Williams calls her "porcelain garden" style and Pound calls her "arid clarity."[2] But although Moore sometimes does link writers and painters when she uses the first-person plural, "Bowls" seems rather distinctly literary, referring to "playwrights and poets and novelists," the etymology of words, and letters. That the precisionist painters never identified themselves with each other and resisted critics' attempts to do so further complicates the matter. Nor do the critics themselves concur in their use of the term.[3] But however inadequate "precisionism" may be to describe painting, much less poetry, both

1. Moore originally used the term *precisians* in this poem (*Obs,* 70); she changed it to *precisionists* shortly after critics began applying *precisionism* to painting (adding further to the temptation); see MM, *Collected Poems* (New York, 1951), 66; and Rick Stewart, "Charles Sheeler, William Carlos Williams, and Precisionism: A Redefinition," *Arts Magazine,* LVIII (November, 1983), 100, 113.

2. Williams, *Selected Essays,* 124; Pound, "Marianne Moore and Mina Loy," from "A List of Books," *Little Review,* X (March, 1918), reprinted in *Marianne Moore,* ed. Tomlinson, 46. In the same essay Pound says Moore and Loy have written "a distinctly national product" (47).

3. See Martin L. Friedman, *The Precisionist View in American Art* (Minneapolis, 1960); Karen Tsujimoto, *Images of America: Precisionist Painting and Modern Photography* (San Francisco and Seattle, 1982); and Stewart, "Sheeler, Williams, and Precisionism," 100–14.

Marianne Moore and the precisionist painters, among other artists of the twenties, respond to some common problems: how to define America and how to reconcile artistic expression with the increasing domination of the machine. For many intellectuals of the time, these questions were inextricable.

Until World War I the American avant-garde had been largely followers of the European avant-garde, but for a number of reasons including a surge of postwar nationalism and an enthusiasm for America among certain European artists, after the war American artists sought to claim their cultural independence from Europe. When Francis Picabia and Marcel Duchamp crossed the Atlantic in 1913 and 1915 respectively, they were met at the dock by reporters and treated as celebrities. Both artists would have a lasting influence on American art, and their much publicized remarks gave American artists a new perspective on themselves. Picabia told an interviewer: "I see much, much more, perhaps, than you who are used to it see. I see your stupendous skyscrapers, your mammoth buildings and marvellous subways, a thousand evidences of your great wealth on all sides." He called New York "the cubist, the futurist city. It expresses in its architecture, its life, its spirit, the modern thought."[4] Duchamp told a reporter, "If only America would realize that the art of Europe is finished—dead—and that America is the country of the art of the future, instead of trying to base everything she does on European traditions!"[5] and his famous *Fountain* seemed to celebrate plumbing as an indigenous American art. Following the spirit of Picabia and Duchamp, certain artists of the twenties, especially those associated with New York dadaism, defended American plumbing and skyscrapers as valid and refreshing expressions of a new age.[6]

Many artists, however, opposed such a view. They perceived the rampant materialism of New York City to be hostile to art and artists. More

4. Francis Picabia in a 1913 interview with the New York *Tribune,* quoted in Arthur Jerome Eddy, *Cubists and Post-Impressionism* (Chicago, 1914), 96.

5. Marcel Duchamp in a 1915 interview with the New York *Tribune,* quoted in "The Iconoclastic Opinions of M. Marcel Duchamps [*sic*] Concerning Art and America," *Current Opinion,* LIX (November, 1915), 346.

6. Extensive discussions of America's self-image and its attitude toward technology can be found in Lisa M. Steinman, *Made in America: Science, Technology, and American Modernist Poets* (New Haven, 1987); Dickran Tashjian, *Skyscraper Primitives: Dada and the American Avant-Garde, 1910–1925* (Middletown, Conn., 1975); and Tashjian, "Engineering a New Art," in *The Machine Age in America, 1918–1941* (New York, 1986), 205–69.

Figure 27 Alfred Stieglitz, *The Flatiron*

1902. Photogravure, 1910. 12 7/8 x 6 1/2 in. (32.7 x 16.7 cm.). Alfred Stieglitz Collection.
© 1994 Board of Trustees, National Gallery of Art, Washington.

than a decade before Picabia and Duchamp arrived in New York, Stieglitz's photographs of the city's trains, boats, and skyscrapers had been among the first art works to celebrate the industrial American city. But by 1916 Stieglitz's enthusiasm was waning; he wrote O'Keeffe: "Hartley hates the place [New York] because the 'people have no soul.'—It fascinated me for years because of the lack—I thought that the huge machine would eventually discover its soul—Will it?"[7] By 1920 he was calling New York a "blood-sucker" and praising Waldo Frank's *Our America*, which urged Americans to overcome their identification with industrialism.[8]

By the end of the first World War the Arensberg circle had dissolved and 291 had closed. But the more or less friendly differences that had existed between the two groups became openly competitive and even hostile. Dadaism evolved out of the Arensberg circle in direct opposition to the more idealistic values held by Stieglitz and the artists he continued to exhibit and support. At one extreme were artists such as Man Ray, Duchamp, and their friend and spokesman Matthew Josephson, all three of whom moved to Paris in the early twenties and aligned themselves with European dadaists; at the other extreme were writers such as Waldo Frank, Sherwood Anderson, and Paul Rosenfeld, and at a lesser extreme Stieglitz, their friend and admirer. *Broom*, which began as anti-dadaist, became the leading publication of the American dadaists under the editorship of Josephson. Also, *Secession* and the *Little Review* were sympathetic to dadaism. The *Dial*, which did not take sides, was more closely identified with the anti-dadaists because of Paul Rosenfeld's regular contributions and also its support of other writers and painters associated with Stieglitz. The controversy centered on what American artists' attitude toward technology should be: whether to celebrate the newness, power, and utility of the machine—the machine aesthetic—or to defend traditional values that technology threatened to destroy.[9]

7. Alfred Stieglitz to Georgia O'Keeffe, October 7, 1916, in *Alfred Stieglitz*, by Greenough and Hamilton, 201. Stieglitz's attitude toward New York and the machine was ambivalent at this time but became increasingly more negative; see William Innes Homer, *Alfred Stieglitz and the American Avant-Garde* (Boston, 1977), 190–200.

8. Alfred Stieglitz to Paul Strand, September 16, 1920, and August 24, 1920, in Paul Strand Collection, Center for Creative Photography, University of Arizona, Tucson (photocopies in Beinecke).

9. See Edmund Wilson, "An Imaginary Conversation: Mr. Paul Rosenfeld and Mr. Matthew Josephson," *New Republic*, April 9, 1924, pp. 179–82; and Tashjian, *Skyscraper Primitives*, 116–42.

Creating a distinctly American tradition was not controversial. Both sides saw themselves as pioneers. An article in the first issue of *Broom* cautions against identifying America too narrowly with machines but approves the new self-consciousness among American artists: "America—made of the Puritan, by the Puritan, for the Puritan, remade of the Machine, by the Machine, for the Machine—is only passing through what is practically her first decade of a generation that deliberately, consciously, by means of concerted action and creation strikes out upon paths of cultural life." [10] In addition to frequent discussions in magazines, several books defining America emerged in these years, including Frank's *Our America* and Williams' *In the American Grain.*

In the spring of 1920 Marianne Moore wrote Lola Ridge regarding a recent conversation: "I am interested in Marsden Hartley's exposition of the American quality in poetry. I am not just ready myself to say what I think that quality is." [11] During the twenties, however, both in her poetry and in her prose, she turns to the subject of defining the American quality in art repeatedly. Her *Dial* "Comments" focus upon "action, business, adventure, discovery" and especially "speed" as distinctively American qualities (*Prose*, 150, 160), but at the same time Moore commends these attributes—praising the virtues of young American artists as "a corollary to momentum" and refuting the charge that "America's predilection for huge dimensions, for speed and success, is corrupting the world"—she also recognizes them as potentially dangerous, as indicated by her reference to "speed-ridden and to some extent coreless modern expertness" (*Prose*, 191, 174, 213).[12] In short, Moore does not take sides. Her association with the *Dial* during these years indicates her allegiances—both her resistance to movements and factions and also her stronger affinities with those artists supported by the *Dial*. She was, however, admired by both sides. Josephson asked her to edit *Broom*, and *Secession* exempted her from its criticism of the *Dial*.[13] For Moore's restraint and "arid clarity" ap-

10. Emmy Veronica Sanders, "America Invades Europe," *Broom*, I (November, 1921), 90–91. Moore saved this passage, quoted in a review of *Broom*, inside her copy of *Der Blaue Reiter.*

11. MM to Lola Ridge, May 25, 1920, in Sophia Smith Collection, Smith College, Northampton, Mass. (photocopy in Bryn Mawr).

12. In addition to these "Comments" on American artists, American undergraduates, Columbus, and American folk dancing and music, see also those on books about America and New York (*Prose*, 179–80), and on English, especially American, diction (*Prose*, 165–67). Also, see the discussion of this topic in Steinman, *Made in America*, 116–18.

13. "[The *Dial*] features a wallowing ox of a stylist who retails each month acres of vague

pealed to dadaist sensibilities. More than most writers of the time she seemed to synthesize what both sides valued. In the first issue of *Broom*, Emmy Veronica Sanders wrote: "If an ingeniously constructed, intricate little piece of machinery, a dainty little thing with cogs and wheels and flashes of iron and steel, should suddenly be given a human voice to pour its 'soul' into song—to transmute itself into a 'poem'—it would stand revealed as a bit of writing by Miss Moore." [14]

Some artists who were uncomfortable with the extremes of dadaism and its ties to Europe pursued a middle road through the controversy; they sought ways to synthesize new ideas about technology with traditional ideas about artistic expression. Prominent among these were Paul Strand, Charles Sheeler, Georgia O'Keeffe, and Charles Demuth. Often labeled as precisionist painters, straight photographers, or in Sheeler's case both, they never organized or labeled themselves and in some cases were not even friendly with one another. Nevertheless, certain of their works from the twenties bear resemblances: industrial subject matter, sharply focused realism, and cubist-inspired composition. These represent a synthesis of trends from the prewar decade: the "machine aesthetic" came from the Arensberg circle; the "straight photography" aesthetic from the Stieglitz group; the cubist influence from Europe had pervaded both groups.

Whereas the dadaists celebrated the freedom from tradition they found in American industrial products, the less radical artists sought an American tradition. Several artists, including Sheeler, Demuth, the Zorachs, and the sculptor Elie Nadelman, began collecting and exhibiting American folk art. The Whitney Studio Club (later the Whitney Museum of American Art) held the first exhibition of American folk art in 1924; it included works from the collections of Sheeler, Demuth, and other artists; a number of other exhibitions followed. In claiming their independence from European influences, many American artists turned away from African art, which they had come to appreciate via European modernists, to "American primitives," as they called folk art, and they turned from tribal abstraction to the clear-sighted realism they observed in American folk painting. The precisionists saw themselves as defining and participating in an

---

impressionistic excrement on music, painting, and books. [Paul Rosenfeld's name is not mentioned] . . . But this soft place next to Marianne Moore!" G[orham] B. M[unson], "Exposé No. 1," *Secession*, no. 1 (Spring, 1922), 22–23.

14. Sanders, "America Invades Europe," 92.

Figure 28 Charles Sheeler, *Skyscrapers*

1922. Oil on canvas. 20 x 13 in. © The Phillips Collection, Washington, D.C.

Figure 29 Charles Sheeler, *Bucks County Barn*

1923. Tempera and crayon on paper. sight: 19 1/4 x 25 1/2 in. (48.9 x 64.8 cm.). Collection of Whitney Museum of American Art. Gift of Gertrude Vanderbilt Whitney. 31.468. Photograph by Geoffrey Clements.

American realist tradition, a tradition defined neatly by Ellen Johnson as "emotive factualism"; describing American artists from the unknown seventeenth-century portraitists through the painters of the 1970s, she writes: "A quality of concentration, clarity and oneness, giving no harbour to the irrelevant, distinguishes the American tradition in art. It is a tradition not in the sense of an inherited method but of a shared attitude towards art and reality: an emotive factualism which uncovers the unknown in the familiar and a stubborn need on the part of the artist to wrest the image from his own personal experience." [15] Also appealing to the precisionists, Sheeler in particular, was the naive perspective in folk painting, which resembles the consciously flattened cubist perspective. In his interiors Sheeler often flattens the perspective of variously patterned American rugs and textiles in order to achieve a cubistlike composition that is nevertheless reminiscent of American folk paintings. Sheeler admired Cézanne for his ability to see "an underlying abstract structure" in nature more so than

15. Johnson, *Modern Art and the Object,* 125.

176

Figure 30 Charles Sheeler, *Interior*

1926. Oil on canvas. 33 x 22 in. (83.8 x 55.9 cm.). Collection of Whitney Museum of American Art. Gift of Gertrude Vanderbilt Whitney. 31.344. Photograph by Geoffrey Clements.

the cubists, who distorted reality.[16] But whereas Cézanne usually found abstract structure in landscapes, fruit, and human figures, Sheeler found it in American-made subjects: early American architecture and furniture and American cities and factories. Indeed, in Sheeler's work the cubist geometry and smooth surfaces of his Bucks County barns, Shaker furniture, skyscrapers, and factories seem to define "American."

Considering the readiness with which Moore is often linked with technology (as in the *Broom* quotation above), she shows remarkably little interest in the controversy over machines during the twenties. While Moore does not address technology directly until much later, she had an early and enduring interest in the relationship between science and art. Lisa Steinman observes a tendency among early twentieth-century artists to confuse science and technology [17]; Moore does not demonstrate this tendency, and neither should her readers. Her pre-1915 scrapbooks and notebooks demonstrate a keen interest in color theory, the application to painting of scientific analyses of color and optics, which had intrigued a number of European and American painters since the late nineteenth century. Throughout her career she drew analogies between the scientist and the artist. Defending the *Dial*'s editorial standards, she writes, "May we not assert confidently that oppositions of science are not oppositions to poetry but oppositions to falseness" (*Prose*, 157). In her interview with Donald Hall she asks: "Do the poet and scientist not work analogously? Both are willing to waste effort. To be hard on himself is one of the main strengths of each. Each is attentive to clues, each must narrow the choice, must strive for precision." And: "Did laboratory studies affect my poetry? I am sure they did. . . . Precision, economy of statement, logic employed to ends that are disinterested, drawing and identifying, liberate—at least have some bearing on—the imagination, it seems to me" (*MMR*, 273, 254–55). It is important to recognize that "precision" for Moore as an artist more closely resembles that of the laboratory scientist rather than that of the machine or engineer. Like the biologist, she is a classifier, "drawing and identifying," "narrow[ing] the choice." While she certainly admires mechanical precision—as her later work indicates—as an artist she aspires to the disinterested passion of the scientist. For a machine does not "waste effort" and need not be "attentive to clues." It is the scientist's "striv[ing] for precision" that for Moore "liberates" the imagination.

16. Charles Sheeler, Paper read at a Symposium on Photography, Museum of Modern Art, 1950, quoted in Martin L. Friedman *et al.*, *Charles Sheeler* (Washington, D.C., 1968), 96.

17. Steinman, *Made in America*, 2–3.

Both in her poetry and her prose of the twenties, Moore approaches
the problem of defining America as a classifier rather than as an advocate
for or against the machine. Most frequently she tests characteristics associated with other countries but not with America, or vice versa, against her
own observations. Her first two *Dial* "Comments" employ this method:
the first (July, 1925) describes American poetry; the second (August,
1925), American painting and photography. The second one, ostensibly
a review of Stieglitz's "Seven Americans" exhibition, is a treatise on American art generally (*Prose*, 150–51). She uses this important exhibit,
which had occurred five months previously, as evidence to prove her opening assertion: " 'Action, business, adventure, discovery,' are not preroga-
tives exclusively American; and obversely, creative power is not the pre-
rogative of every country other than America." In both "Comments" she
links American art to that of other nationalities and centuries. In the
July one she links H.D. to the Greeks, Wallace Stevens to the French, Ezra
Pound to medieval romance, E. E. Cummings to the courtly tradition,
T. S. Eliot to Donne, and Amy Lowell to Keats. In the August one she
links John Marin to Botticelli and Turner, Paul Strand to Canaletto and
seventeenth-century botanists, Charles Demuth's paintings to Chinese
silks, and Georgia O'Keeffe's paintings to "Central African, . . . Singhalese
and Javanese experienced adornment." She concludes by placing these
artists in an American tradition, one that includes Whistler and Sargent
but that begins with folk art: "the grasshopper weather-vane of gilded copper with glass eye, made by an American for Faneuil Hall in 1742 . . . the
silk embroidered lady in an empire dress, half kneeling under a willow tree
by George Washington's tomb . . . the early American kitten held by an
early American child." [18] What Moore emphasizes is not any defining characteristic of American art but rather its diversity and exoticism. Rather
than, for instance, praising Strand's photographs of machine parts as images of American industrialism, Moore evokes the Orient and exotic
wildlife: "We welcome the power-house in the drawing-room when we

18. Moore shared her contemporaries' interest in American folk art. Her library and
files at the Rosenbach include catalogs for the 1924 Whitney Studio Club exhibition,
Early American Art; the 1932 Museum of Modern Art exhibition, *American Folk Art:
The Art of the Common Man in America, 1750–1900;* and Mrs. John D. Rockefeller's collection of American folk art. This last collection, later housed in the Abby Aldrich Folk Art
Center, was displayed in various houses when Moore and her mother visited Williamsburg
in 1935. Moore likely saw the painting of the child and kitten at the Dudensing Gallery in
early 1925. The Faneuil Hall weather vane reappears in "In the Public Garden" (*CP,*
190).

examine his orientally perfect combining of discs, parabolas, and verticals—when we perceive the silver flexibility of skin or the depth of tone upon the anaconda-like curves of central bearings." Likewise by juxtaposing Sargent's sophisticated portraits with a grasshopper weather vane, Moore defies definition but nevertheless proves her thesis, which she restates: "Yet obviously, past and present, creative effort is here."

This recalls the technique employed in a poem about America that she published in the *Dial* five years earlier called, ironically, "England" (*CP*, 46–47) because the title serves as first line. Again she compares America with other countries, listed both at the beginning and end of the poem. "Plain American which cats and dogs can read," the language of her "languageless country," does not invite "proof-readers" or "digressions" but rather is a language of distinctions, a precise language capable of defying clichés and imprecise thinking, of demarcating mushrooms from toadstools.

> Does it follow that because there are poisonous toadstools
> which resemble mushrooms, both are dangerous?
> Of mettlesomeness which may be mistaken for appetite,
> of heat which may appear to be haste,
> no conclusions may be drawn.
>
> To have misapprehended the matter is to have confessed that one has
>   not looked far enough.

Looking far enough is the essence of America. Without the distractions of "digressions" or "echoing . . . criterion," the explorer who looks far enough might discover in this wilderness potentially any of the world's virtues.

> The sublimated wisdom of China, Egyptian discernment,
> the cataclysmic torrent of emotion
> compressed in the verbs of the Hebrew language,
> the books of the man who is able to say,
> "I envy nobody but him, and him only,
> who catches more fish than I do"—
> the flower and fruit of all that noted superiority—
> if not stumbled upon in America,
> must one imagine that it is not there?
> It has never been confined to one locality.

These superior virtues are all virtues of precision. Yet Moore does not claim precision as an exclusively American virtue, for even to do that would be imprecise. Similarly, in a 1926 "Comment" she writes: "Perfect diction is not particularly an attribute of America. We have it, however"; and she finds it in Henry James, Poe's criticism, Whistler, Stevens, Pound, and Cummings while acknowledging Americans' aptitude for slang (*Prose*, 165). She defines America by refusing to define it: "American" resists both inclusive and exclusive definitions.

America is the subject of Moore's two great landscape poems, "An Octopus" (1924) and "Virginia Britannia" (1935). "An Octopus" (*Obs*, 83–90), one of Moore's longest, most perplexing, and arguably greatest poems, is Moore's American myth. The most identifiable subject of the poem, the glacier atop Mount Rainier, is implicitly compared with the Greeks' mythic mountain, Olympus. (Neither Mount Rainier nor Olympus is named in the poem, however; Moore uses the Indian name Takoma, meaning "The Mountain who is God."[19]) The unexpected symmetry of "Octopus" with "Olympus" and the dissimilarity of their referents typifies the tone and subject of the poem. Instead of the remote single peak, which in many mythologies symbolizes divine truth, Moore's peak is composed of "twenty-eight ice fields" and remains "intact when it is cut." A map of the glacier system suggests "an octopus"; thus, instead of being regarded with awe from below—like Olympus or, for instance, Shelley's "Mont Blanc"—Moore's peak is viewed from above and in miniature. Furthermore, the all important central "peak" is missing: "an explosion blew it off." As in "In the Days of Prismatic Color," Moore's divine truth is decentered and "many legged."[20]

Here the culture against which she contrasts America is ancient Greece—like America, a new civilization. "An Octopus" may be read as a witty response to *The Waste Land*, which appeared two years earlier and which also juxtaposes the modern world against the ancient. "Big Snow Mountain" is, of course, a far cry from Eliot's postwar London and, with its vigorous plant and animal life, lakes and waterfalls, is hardly a waste

19. Patricia C. Willis, "The Road to Paradise: First Notes on Marianne Moore's 'An Octopus,'" in *Marianne Moore*, ed. Kappel, special issue of *Twentieth Century Literature*, 242. This essay discusses many actual and possible sources for the poem, including literary analogues in Genesis, Milton, and Dante. Despite her extensive discussion of Greeks in the poem and of the Moores' 1922 trip to Mount Rainier, Willis does not mention Mount Olympus even though, interestingly, there is a Mount Olympus (in what is now Olympic National Park) just west of Bremerton, Washington, where Warner was stationed at the time. Mount Olympus and Mount Rainier are thus, in a sense, also physically juxtaposed.

20. A line that Moore later omitted referred to truth as "many legged"; see MM, "In the Days of Prismatic Color," *Lantern*, XXVII (1919), 35 (Bryn Mawr).

land. It is also a far cry from Homer's Olympus, which is never "swept by the winds nor touched by snow; a purer air surrounds it, a white clarity envelops it and the gods there taste of a happiness which lasts as long as their eternal lives" (*Odyssey*, Book VI). Moore's mountain, in contrast, has "winds that 'tear the snow to bits / and hurl it like a sandblast'" as well as lightning, rain, and avalanches. The Greeks' idea of "happiness" receives several amused comments in the poem—the Greeks are first compared to "happy souls in Hell." Though certainly a paradise, "An Octopus" presents a distinctly (even ridiculously) American one, one dressed in a "cavalcade of calico" of red, white, and blue—"Larkspur, blue pincushions, blue peas, and lupin; / white flowers with white, and red with red"—and presided over by eagles.

Like Olympus and other mythic mountains, it is the origin of life: its fir trees are "austere specimens of our American royal families"; it is "Preempted by [the] ancestors" of elk, deer, wolves, goats, ducks, porcupines, beavers, and bears. The royal abodes, dens, are made of "calcium gems and alabaster pillars, / topaz, tourmaline crystals, and amethyst quartz." In the position of supreme omniscience—described in mythic regality as standing "on cliffs the color of the clouds, of petrified white vapor" and dressed in "ermine" no less—is the goat. The goat comically reverses the hierarchy of Greek mythology, where the goat symbolizes man's basest instincts, and of Christian mythology, where Satan is given goatlike features. This goat is a "special antelope" "acclimated to 'grottoes from which issue penetrating draughts.'" And again, unlike the draughts issuing from Greek mountains that were interpreted as divine oracles, this mountain issues "odd oracles of cool official sarcasm."

As in Moore's other definitions of America, the emphasis of "An Octopus" is diversity: "Maintaining many minds . . . Big Snow Mountain is the home of a diversity of creatures"; thus, we have catalog after catalog of flora, fauna, and gems. In contrast to the Greeks' yearning for "smoothness" and "benevolent conclusiveness," this American mountain and its diversity of creatures seem rustic indeed. But this rusticity and diversity, while providing a playful contrast to Olympus, constitutes a familiar American myth of the wilderness. It would be uncharacteristic of Moore to leave us with this easy distinction, and she does not; she compares her mountain to America's least "rustic" product, Henry James. Having just told us that the Greeks' "wisdom was remote," Moore now tells us that both Mount Takoma and Henry James are "damned for [their] sacrosanct remoteness." The American public, whose intelligence is "practised in adapting their intelligence / to eagle traps and snowshoes," is "out of sympathy with neatness." Thus, James's "love of doing hard things," which results in "restraint," rebuffs them; their own "love of doing hard things," reading James, "wore them out." While James shares with his countrymen "the love of doing hard things," is he not rather Greek in his enjoyment of "mental difficulties" and in his "Neatness of finish"? This diverse American wilderness includes James too; hence the elation of discovery: "Neatness of finish! Neatness of finish!" The mountain also is "concise without a shiver," "planed by ice and polished by the wind." Like Henry James's "decorum," which closer scrutiny reveals to be "restraint," the discovery of "Neatness of finish" demands a new definition of America, which Moore provides: "Relentless accuracy is the nature of this octopus / with its capacity for fact." "Relentless accuracy" will discover both Henry James and "the mountain guide evolving from the trapper."

Moore concludes her American myth by reminding readers of the inadequacy of preconceptions, of the need for redefinition.

> Is tree the word for these strange things
> "flat on the ground like vines";
> some "bent in a half circle with branches on one side
> suggesting dustbrushes, not trees;
> some finding strength in union, forming little stunted groves,
> their flattened mats of branches shrunk in trying to escape"
> from the hard mountain "planed by ice and polished by the wind"—

As the usual meaning of "tree" must be expanded to allow for "these strange things . . . suggesting dustbrushes," so must new facts be admitted into the American ideal of "strength in union." Moore concludes her poem in paradox: "with a sound like the crack of a rifle, / in a curtain of powdered snow launched like a waterfall"; this recalls the "unimagined delicacy" and "concentric crushing rigor of the python" with which the poem began. As the companion to this poem, "Marriage," dispels myths about that institution and the sexes, so does "An Octopus" dispel myths about America. Together the two poems suggest an intrinsic relationship between precision and freedom both in the personal and public realms, for the "essence" of marriage is a political principle: "Liberty and union, / Now and forever" (*Obs*, 81). Precision grants a thing the freedom to be unique. Only by allowing diversity through "relentless accuracy" and constant redefinition can one achieve the "strength in union" for which the institutions of marriage and America both stand.

A decade later Moore would use Henry James again to define America, or rather she used America to define Henry James. In an important essay, "Henry James as a Characteristic American" (*Prose*, 316–22), she catalogs a number of characteristics typically thought to be American but not necessarily Jamesian—including "an air of rurality," "idealism," an indebtedness to Emerson, "a good conscience," the ability "to make [one]self comfortable," an "affection for family and country"—and proves that they are true of James. She concludes the essay by applying to James his own definition of the American: " 'intrinsically and actively ample . . . reaching westward, southward, anywhere, everywhere,' with a mind 'incapable of the shut door in any direction.' " Perhaps she had this statement in mind when she said this essay contained her "outlook on life." [21] The one quality Moore repeatedly turns to as a virtue endemically but not exclusively American is precision. The plurality of America demands a "mind 'incapable of the shut door in any direction' " in order to discover what is there and "Relentless accuracy" in order to name it.

Rick Stewart argues "that the underlying aesthetic of Precisionism [in painting] was not industrialism but functionalism," [22] the architectural principle that "form follows function." By redefining precisionism, Stewart aims to include among Sheeler's precisionist works his paintings and drawings of Shaker buildings and his interiors of American furniture and textiles, all of which along with his factory landscapes were favorite subjects of Sheeler's during the twenties and thirties. Stewart's redefinition is, on one hand, useful because it acknowledges that the precisionists were not interested strictly in industrial forms; Georgia O'Keeffe, to name another example, began painting flowers during the same years she was painting cityscapes. It also acknowledges implicitly that the precisionist aesthetic is larger than it first appears and not confined to painting. But on the other hand, the definition itself raises problems, since *functionalism* is an even more controversial term than *precisionism*. The elasticity of both terms stems from the breadth of responses to a fundamental question of the industrial age: how to reconcile artistic expression with the impersonality of the machine.

The aesthetic of functionalism, rather than industrialism, also underlies much of Moore's postwar poetry. She would not turn to technology

21. MM to Dorothea Gray, November 5, 1935, in *Marianne Moore Newsletter,* II (Fall, 1978), 11.

22. Stewart, "Sheeler, Williams, and Precisionism," 110.

as an explicit subject for poetry until 1940 with "Four Quartz Crystal Clocks." (One possible exception, "To a Steam Roller," does not address technology.) And even though she remarks to Donald Hall regarding her 1955 Ford Motor Company correspondence, "I got deep in motors and turbines and recessed wheels. . . . I am interested in mechanisms, mechanics in general" (*MMR*, 272), mechanics in the strict sense is not a frequent subject for her poems; she wrote only a few poems and virtually no prose on the subject. Nor, of course, are these few poems limited to the subject of technology. In contrast, Williams in a famous definition wrote in 1944: "A poem is a small (or large) machine made of words." Although Moore would certainly agree with the principle that follows this statement—"When I say there's nothing sentimental about a poem I mean that there can be no part, as in any other machine, that is redundant"[23]— she would not call a poem a machine. Moore's metaphors for poetry, like her subjects for poetry, are more likely to be organic: a snail, "imaginary gardens with real toads in them," the shell of a paper nautilus. Between telling how Moore learned to drive (in her seventies) and how she learned to tango, Elizabeth Bishop expresses succinctly in a memoir of her friend the breadth of Moore's interest: "Marianne was intensely interested in the techniques of things—how camellias are grown; how the quartz prisms work in crystal clocks; how the pangolin can close up his ear, nose and eye apertures and walk on the outside edges of his hands 'and save the claws / for digging'; how to drive a car; how the best pitchers throw a baseball; how to make a figurehead for her nephew's sailboat. The exact way in which anything was done, or made, or functioned, was poetry to her."[24] Thus, what Moore calls "mechanics in general" and Bishop calls "the techniques of things" is hardly limited to machines—Bishop's final sentence is a clear statement of functionalism in the broadest sense of the term.

At least part of the controversy over the definition of "functionalism" (like that over "precisionism") focuses on the degree to which it is or is not a manifestation of the machine aesthetic. By the fifties functionalism had become so associated with machines and with the rallying cry of Le Corbusier, "a house is a machine for living in," that historians felt it necessary to remind readers of the importance of organic analogies for early functionalists. Edward Robert De Zurko describes functionalism as "a

23. Williams, *Selected Essays*, 256.
24. Elizabeth Bishop, *The Collected Prose*, ed. Robert Giroux (New York, 1984), 149.

Figure 31 Georgia O'Keeffe, *The Shelton with Sunspots*

1926. Oil on canvas. 123.2 x 76.8 cm. Gift of Leigh B. Block, 1985.206. Photograph ©
1994 The Art Institute of Chicago, All Rights Reserved.

Figure 32 Georgia O'Keeffe, *Shell no. I*

1928. Oil on canvas. 7 x 7 in. (17.8 x 17.8 cm.). © 1994 Board of Trustees, National Gallery of Art, Washington. © 1995 The Georgia O'Keeffe Foundation / Artists Rights Society (ARS), New York.

value" evident in Western culture since Socrates and shows that early twentieth-century functionalists used organic and moral analogues as well as mechanical ones. Lewis Mumford attributes the "Form follows function" concept to Lamarck, the nineteenth-century biologist, and points out the importance of organicism to Frank Lloyd Wright and other pioneers of the functionalist style.[25] It is also true that organic forms attracted precisionist painters and straight photographers. Georgia O'Keeffe's close-up

25. Edward Robert De Zurko, *Origins of Functionalist Theory* (New York, 1957), 8–14; Lewis Mumford, "Function and Expression in Architecture," *Architectural Record*, CX (November, 1951), 108.

Figure 33 Paul Strand, *Double Akeley, New York, 1922*

Gelatin-silver print. 9 5/8 x 7 5/8 in. The Museum of Modern Art, New York. Gift of Mrs. Armand P. Bartos. Copyright © 1971, Aperture Foundation, Paul Strand Archive.

Figure 34 Paul Strand, *Toadstool and Grasses, Georgetown, Maine, 1928*

Gelatin-silver print. 10 x 8 in. The Museum of Modern Art, New York. Gift of the Photographer. Copyright © 1950, Aperture Foundation, Paul Strand Archive.

paintings of flowers, bones, and shells reveal a functionalist aesthetic by their attention to the unity between the abstract architectural properties of her subjects and their biological accuracy. These paintings resemble the closely cropped photographs that Paul Strand was taking in the twenties of lichens, leaves, and other natural forms. The functionalist aesthetic is present in these works no less than in O'Keeffe's New York skyscrapers and Strand's machine parts of the same period. (In contrast, Stieglitz's "Equivalents," his abstract cloud sequences of the twenties, though also natural forms, are not functionalist to the same degree. The clouds are read as abstractions, not functional clouds. Stieglitz's own remarks concerning these photographs show that he wanted viewers to see "music," in other words to see beyond the clouds themselves.[26])

Organic functionalism is a major theme of Marianne Moore's poetry. Her functionalism is not limited to animals, but her animal poems show it most characteristically. Beginning with "The Labours of Hercules," which praises the mule for "its neat exterior / expressing the principle of accommodation reduced to a minimum,"[27] her animal poems celebrate again and again the beauty with which an animal's physical attributes serve its biological needs. This aesthetic becomes especially pronounced in her poems of the thirties and forties. Also important to Moore is the moral dimension of functionalism, the belief that beauty inheres in architecture (and other things) created honestly and for honest purposes. Again her animals are the most obvious exemplars of this morality.

"The Pangolin" (*CP*, 117–20), for many readers the paradigm of Moore's animal poems, is the one most explicitly functionalist. While the pangolin itself most easily demonstrates organic functionalism, Moore draws machines, architecture, morality, and even spirituality into her poem through the ubiquitous meanings of "grace." The pangolin's physical features, upon which Moore bestows her best rhapsodic wit, demonstrate perhaps the fundamental principle of functionalism: no part of the form is mere "ornament," is "extra."

> Armor seems extra. But for him,
>   the closing ear-ridge—

26. Alfred Stieglitz, "How I Came to Photograph Clouds," *Amateur Photographer and Photography*, September 19, 1923, reprinted in *Alfred Stieglitz*, by Greenough and Hamilton, 207.

27. MM, "The Labours of Hercules," *Dial*, LXXI (1921), 638.

or bare ear lacking even this small
    eminence and similarly safe

contracting nose and eye apertures
    impenetrably closable, are not;

As in Williams' metaphor, no part of this "machine" is "redundant." At first Moore's comparisons to machines in the poem seem merely fanciful, but their frequency—"grit-equipped gizzard," "graceful tool," "machine-like / form," "mechanicked / like the pangolin"—suggests a more pointed use. For the subject of the poem is not strictly the pangolin, but "grace"— the "not unchain-like machine-like / form and frictionless creep of a thing / made graceful by adversities, con- // versities"—a grace replicated by artists such as Leonardo, Thomas of Leighton-Buzzard, and Gargallo, by the "approved stone mullions" of Gothic cathedrals, and by machines.[28] The pangolin, the "artist engineer" with his "graceful tool" of a tail, demonstrates that the engineer and machine are unique neither to the twentieth century nor to humanity: "A sailboat // was the first machine. Pangolins, made / for moving quietly also, are models of exactness, / on four legs." Thus, "the self, the being we call human" may turn to these models of exactness in history and in nature to learn "grace." Nor, Moore reminds us, is this idea new; technology has always imitated animals.

a paper-maker like the wasp; a tractor of foodstuffs,
    like the ant; spidering a length
        of web from bluffs
            above a stream; in fighting, mechanicked
            like the pangolin

By the end of the poem Moore intentionally blurs the distinction between pangolin and "man"—"Consistent with the / formula—warm blood, no gills, two pairs of hands and a few hairs"—in order to demonstrate humans' potential for grace, and she moves from physical grace to morality. The pangolin is not graceful in the usual sense, say, of the gazelle.

---

28. For discussion and photographs of the thirteenth-century wrought iron vine by Thomas of Leighton-Buzzard and of the twentieth-century metal sculpture *Picador*, by Gargallo, see [Patricia C. Willis], "Iron Sculpture Similes in 'The Pangolin,'" *Marianne Moore Newsletter*, IV (Spring, 1980), 2–5. That these two sculptors of metal span the centuries reinforces Moore's point that grace can exist in any age.

His grace is his demeanor. Closely resembling "The Hero" in the poem of that title, the pangolin, "Fearful yet to be feared," "endures / exhausting solitary trips through unfamiliar ground at night." Despite his inherent nakedness and potential for inexactitude, man too is "tread paced to meet an obstacle / at every step" and can achieve "grace" in each sense of the term through a certain "Unignorant, / modest, and unemotional, and all emotion[al]" reverence, a reverence for the rhythms of nature, the "alternating blaze." Thus, while the poem is not about technology per se, it shows that given a moral demeanor on the part of mankind, which the pangolin exemplifies, technology need not preclude aesthetic, moral, or spiritual grace.

"The Icosasphere" (*CP*, 143) more concisely synthesizes the mechanical, organic, and moral aspects of functionalism. The poem begins by admiring birds' nests, "spherical feats of rare efficiency," and then moves to persons. Humans' capacity for crime and greed is contrasted with their ability to engineer in the twentieth century an icosasphere, "steel-cutting at its summit of economy," and in ancient Egypt to "set up seventy-eight-foot solid granite vertically."

"Granite and Steel" (*CP*, 205), the most ambitious of Moore's late poems (1966), presents her own paradigm for resolving the question that confronted artists of her generation: how to redirect technology toward humanistic ends, both aesthetic and moral ones. As in Alan Trachtenberg's book that inspired the poem, the Brooklyn Bridge symbolically "bridges" more than two cities; it also "bridges" granite and steel, materials of the nineteenth and twentieth centuries respectively. It bridges, as emphasized in the final stanza, the "untried expedient" with the "tried," the "mind" with the "eye." "Actuality," according to Hegel (whose ideas influenced the bridge's engineer John Roebling), the word with which Moore's poem ends, "is the unity of essence and existence, of the inner world of life and the outer world of its appearance."[29] The catenary curve, the physical principle that supports the bridge, is itself the perfect "bridge" of form and function; "one of the simplest unities of nature,"[30] it becomes in Moore's poem a "Climactic ornament, a double rainbow, / inverted." Also, Moore's own uncharacteristic poeticisms and direct literary allusions "bridge" art and technology: "O catenary curve."

29. G. W. F. Hegel, quoted in Alan Trachtenberg, *Brooklyn Bridge: Fact and Symbol* (New York, 1965), 68.

30. Trachtenberg, *Brooklyn Bridge,* 69.

But the achievement of the bridge is not strictly formalist. In Moore's poem it becomes a symbol of peace and equality "bridging" Germany and America "in the sea" through the "ingenuity" of its German-American creator, John Roebling, as the Statue of Liberty next to it bridges France and America. Following two world wars that prompted great technological advancements on both sides of the Atlantic, Moore reminds us that technology need not serve tyranny. The one finite verb in the poem, "dominate," is what technology typically does in the twentieth century; as in war, it serves "the mind's deformity, / . . . man's uncompunctious greed / his crass love of crass priority." But in this poem it is the "Enfranchising cable" and "Liberty" that "dominate"; the catenary curve is the "implacable enemy of the mind's deformity." The "chains, / once . . . wrought by Tyranny" are replaced by the "enfranchising cable," the catenary curve. Thus, the bridge is for Moore morally as well as aesthetically functionalist. It is a utopian "actuality" to which American artists can aspire.

Marianne Moore participates with her contemporaries in an American tradition of "emotive factualism," of wanting to uncover "the unknown in the familiar." For precisionist painters and straight photographers this meant uncovering clean geometric forms behind the murk and clutter of urban life. For Moore this meant challenging the murk and clutter of misconceptions in order to see and name an experience precisely. Also important to the precisionists and to Moore (as well as to other poets) was the recognition that "gusto" underlies the cool, patterned surfaces they created. In "Bowls" and in several essays, Moore uses images such as the sport of bowling and the orchestra conductor's signal to show that precision must begin "a long distance ahead" (*Prose*, 396). She finds passion where casual readers least suspect it: in, for instance, Henry James and in the Federal Reserve Board's description of a counterfeit note (*Prose*, 401, 422). She would have concurred with Charles Sheeler's admiration for artists who "conceal the means by which they set forth their statement." "With them," writes Sheeler, ". . . one receives a direct impact from the emotional content, but when one seeks to disintegrate their means of arrival the evidence just isn't there. Means and ends are fused together."[31] Sheeler's statement suggests the "method of conclusions" Moore admires in "To a Snail." Sheeler and Moore resemble one another in this preference more than they do Williams, who usually does not disguise his energy and emotion, his "means."

31. Charles Sheeler, quoted in Constance Rourke, *Charles Sheeler: Artist in the American Tradition* (New York, 1938), 181.

Despite its ambiguities, "functionalism" more accurately describes the aesthetic Moore shared with visual artists such as Sheeler, Demuth, O'Keeffe, and Strand than does "precisionism," for all were interested in the aesthetic relationship between form and function in both nature and technology. The issue of technology per se neither disturbs nor excites Moore to the degree it does some of her contemporaries, for to her the machine demands neither a new morality nor a new aesthetic. What Moore calls grace and others call functionalism has always existed in nature and has for centuries existed in art and technology: that which tyrannizes is deformed; that which is humble, courageous, reverent, and efficient has "grace."

One reason Moore's response to technology was not as urgent as it might have been is that the machine did not threaten literature as intrinsically as the camera threatened painting and mass production threatened the applied arts. The revolution of the printing press was centuries old, and the typewriter, which Hugh Kenner credits with changing the look of the poem on the page, did not undermine the writer's craft.[32] In any case, it did not provoke controversy. On the other hand, the aesthetics of straight photography and of architectural functionalism result directly from the artists' appropriation of materials from technical uses to artistic ones. What threatened poetry was not the machine directly but a machine-age demand for clear, factual (unpoetic) prose. Pound, Eliot, and Williams understood and addressed this challenge to some degree, but none was as radical as Moore in appropriating for poetry the new material of their age, the language of "business documents and /school-books." Moore wrote in 1960: "For anyone with 'a passion for actuality' there are times when the camera seems preferable to any other medium" (*Prose*, 543). While again the terms must not be confused, the development of the straight photography aesthetic provides a useful context for understanding Moore's own "mania for straight writing" (*Prose*, 509, 510).

Following several decades during which painting in America and Europe had moved progressively toward abstraction, certain American artists of the twenties found the camera ideally suited to their own modern but "realist" vision. Although photography had been invented in France and the concept of "art photography" developed first in England, Americans nevertheless felt they had a unique claim to photography as an indepen-

32. Kenner, *A Homemade World*, 98.

Figure 35 Charles Sheeler, *Doylestown House—Stairs from Below*

1914. Gelatin-silver print. 8 x 10 in. The Lane Collection. Photograph courtesy of the Museum of Fine Arts, Boston.

Figure 36 Paul Strand, *Abstraction, Porch Shadows, Twin Lakes, Connecticut, 1916*

Satista print. 33.2 x 23 cm. Alfred Stieglitz Collection, 1949.885. Photograph © 1994, The Art Institute of Chicago, All Rights Reserved. Copyright © 1971, Aperture Foundation, Paul Strand Archive.

dent art form. Not only was it machine-made and hence appropriate to a nation that identified itself with technology, but also, in looking at the development of modern art in America, artists of the twenties saw photography, especially under the sponsorship of Stieglitz, as America's unique contribution to modernism. Paul Strand claimed that in photography "America has really been expressed in terms of America without the outside influence of Paris art-schools." He compared American photographers with the architects of American skyscrapers—both were innocents, working without formulae or precedent.[33] Unlike the dadaists, however, who also extolled the Americanness and the lack of precedent of their machine aesthetic, the straight photographers believed their machine, the camera, did not preclude personal expression.

The Armory Show affected American photography as much as it did painting. During the Armory Show in 1913 Stieglitz showed a retrospective of his own photographs at 291 so that photography could be seen alongside the new developments in painting. Although Stieglitz's own photographs became sharper and more geometrical after the Armory Show, the impact of cubism was even more pronounced in the work of two younger photographers, Sheeler and Strand. Sheeler, whose paintings had been included in the Armory Show and who already had a reputation as an outstanding commercial photographer of architecture and sculpture, took his first noncommissioned photographs in 1914 of stairwells and doorways in his Bucks County house. In 1915 and 1916 Strand experimented with a series of sharply focused, straight photographs which nevertheless appear "abstract" because of his close cropping of the subject. The most famous of these is *Porch Shadows*, where the dominant subject is an abstract pattern of light and shadow and the viewer must look closely to discover the porch itself. All three artists photographed city buildings to bring forth the "cubism" inherent in New York. Their use of "straight photography," which had long been used for documentary purposes, with an eye toward cubist abstraction was unique at this time. During the next two decades it would become the dominant aesthetic for photographers both in America and in Europe.[34]

33. Paul Strand, "Photography," *Seven Arts*, II (August, 1917), reprinted in *Photographers on Photography: A Critical Anthology*, ed. Nathan Lyons (Englewood Cliffs, N.J., 1966), 137.

34. For further information about the relationship between cubism and photography, see John Pultz and Catherine B. Scallen, *Cubism and American Photography, 1910–1930* (Williamstown, Mass., 1981), esp. 16–34.

Although Stieglitz admired the photographs of Sheeler, who had been on the periphery of 291 for some years, he developed a much closer relationship with Strand, possibly because Strand like himself was strictly a photographer, not a painter-turned-photographer, and certainly because Strand shared Stieglitz's views about the importance of photography as an autonomous genre. Stieglitz gave Strand a show at 291 in 1916 and devoted the final issue of *Camera Work* to Strand the following year. Also like Stieglitz, Strand was a gifted writer who became one of the most articulate advocates for photography in the late teens and twenties. Unlike photography's detractors who regarded machine-made art as an impossibility or the dadaists who saw plumbing and bridges as replacing art, Strand describes the photographer's relationship to the camera as a paradigm for the new age: the artist utilizing and controlling the machine for humanistic ends. He writes:

> [Stieglitz's photographs] may also be seen as symbols of the machine used not to exploit and degrade human beings, but as an instrument for giving back to life something that ripens the mind and refreshes the spirit. They give hope of, and perhaps prophesy, a new world, humanly speaking, which is not an absurd Erewhon; but one in which people have learned to use machines with a different attitude towards them and towards each other. In such a world the machine would take its place, not alone as an invaluable tool of economic liberation, but also as a new means of intellectual and spiritual enrichment.[35]

("Granite and Steel" presents a similar utopia.)

By the twenties "straight photography" became not merely a technique but a new aesthetic and even moral cause, and it extended beyond the bounds of its own medium to effect precisionism in painting. This aesthetic evolved from the adaptation of materials from a technical purpose, documentation, to an artistic one. Functionalism in architecture

35. Paul Strand, "Alfred Stieglitz and a Machine," in *America & Alfred Stieglitz: A Collective Portrait,* ed. Waldo Frank *et al.* (New York, 1934), 285. Moore read this essay in 1921, when she visited Strand's studio with Bertram Hartman. She wrote to Strand afterward, praising both the article and his photographs; a later letter praises his photographs in the "Seven Americans" show and thanks him for inviting her to the exhibit. I am grateful to Amy Rule for calling my attention to these letters and sending me photocopies of them. MM to Paul Strand, September 13, 1921, and March 15, 1925, Paul Strand Collection, Center for Creative Photography, University of Arizona, Tucson.

evolved similarly. In the late nineteenth century, innovative architects began to expose the iron supports of their buildings rather than concealing
them behind neoclassical facades. Thus, their buildings initially resembled
the bridges and factories "engineered" for efficiency rather than beauty.
By the twentieth century, iron had been replaced by steel and concrete,
but most architects continued to hide these supporting materials behind
ornamental stone facades, just as initially art photographers tried to make
photographs resemble paintings. Eventually in both cases the new material precipitated a new aesthetic.

Part of this change was due, in both cases, to the emphasis of the
arts and crafts movement upon honest use of one's materials. While the
arts and crafts movement began in England largely in resistance to the machine and especially to the poor design and tawdry quality of mass-pro-
duced furnishings, through the leadership of architects such as Frank Lloyd
Wright and his friend C. R. Ashbee (who changed his mind about machines soon after Moore heard him speak at Bryn Mawr), the machine
came to be the modern craftsman's "tool" and steel simply another material that any true artist-craftsman could use "honestly." In his famous
Hull House Lecture of 1901, "The Art and Craft of the Machine," Frank
Lloyd Wright calls for architects, and artists generally, to be true to their
Machine Age, to accept the challenge of the machine rather than, by resisting it, allow it to dominate American society: "The machine is here
to stay. It is the forerunner of the democracy that is our dearest hope. There
is no more important work before the architect now than to use this
normal tool of civilization to the best advantage instead of prostituting
it as he has hitherto done in reproducing with murderous ubiquity
forms born of other times and other conditions and which it can only serve
to destroy."[36]

While architectural functionalism's indebtedness to William Morris
and the arts and crafts movement is widely assumed, this is not the case
with straight photography. Paul Strand, however, as indicated earlier,
viewed American skyscrapers and American photography analogously. And
the many photographs of skyscrapers, beginning with Stieglitz's and
Steichen's pictorial photographs of New York's Flat-Iron Building,
show an implicit affinity between photography and the new architec-

36. Frank Lloyd Wright, "The Art and Craft of the Machine," in *Frank Lloyd Wright
on Architecture: Selected Writings, 1894–1940,* ed. Frederick Gutheim (New York, 1941),
24.

ture. That arts and crafts publications such as *Craftsman* included articles on photography alongside those on basketry, jewelry-making, and weaving indicates Americans' openness to machine-made crafts.[37] For like other craftsmen, photographers were struggling to overcome the hegemony of painting and to raise the status of photography from that of a mere hobby. Even long after the arts and crafts movement had faded, its language and idealistic fervor prevailed within the Stieglitz circle.

For instance, proponents of photography continually emphasized the *craft* of photography. Sherwood Anderson contrasts "the figure of Alfred Stieglitz as the craftsman of genius" against the tawdriness of the industrial age. This praise pleased Stieglitz, whose letters reveal an obsession with the quality of his materials and long hours working for just the right print.[38] Paul Strand lectured in 1923 for photographers to return to the values of craftsmanship and resist the domination of painting; in 1931 he wrote: "Camera materials, paint, clay, words, all are what they are—material—until they fall into the hands of someone who having lived deeply and beautifully, utilizes them as a craftsman, to put that living into form as vision, as song, as some kind of clear saying."[39] Sheeler's appreciation for early American furniture, architecture, and textiles resulted directly from his early exposure to arts and crafts ideology. Even though T. J. Jackson Lears regards the arts and crafts movement as antimodernist because of its resistance to change, especially technological change, ironically, it prevailed most strongly within the art forms most affected by technology—architecture and photography.[40]

Moore responded enthusiastically, though not extensively, to art photography. During her senior year at Bryn Mawr she wrote home detailed descriptions of the pictorial photographs she saw in *Camera Work*, calling them "way beyond pictures (painted)." Upon her arrival in New York in

37. See, for example, Sadakitchi Hartmann, "The Photo-Secession, a New Pictorial Movement," *Craftsman*, VI (April, 1904), 30–37.

38. Sherwood Anderson, "Alfred Stieglitz," in *Can a Photograph Have the Significance of Art?*, ed. Alfred Stieglitz, special issue of *MSS.*, IV (December, 1922), 15; Alfred Stieglitz to Arthur Dove, October 24, 1922 (Beinecke).

39. Paul Strand, "The Art Motive in Photography," *British Journal of Photography*, LXX (1923), reprinted in *Photographers on Photography*, ed. Lyons, 144–45; Paul Strand to Samuel Kootz, September 11, 1931, in *Paul Strand*, by Sarah Greenough (Washington, D.C., and New York, 1990), 68.

40. T. J. Jackson Lears, *No Place of Grace: Antimodernism and the Transformation of American Culture, 1880–1920* (New York, 1981), 59–96.

1915, she headed straight for what she expected to be a photography studio, 291. The photographs by Stieglitz and Steichen that she saw on this trip, not at 291 but at the Kreymborgs' apartment, elicited superlatives: "some of the most superb pictures of snow and engines and boats that I have ever seen."[41] In her "Comment" on the "Seven Americans" exhibit, she praises the "veracious[ness]" of Strand's photographs and Stieglitz's "profound and penetrating comprehension of character" (*Prose*, 151). And in her retrospective essay on the *Dial* she devotes an entire paragraph to Charles Sheeler's "scientifically businesslike proceedings" while photographing a Lachaise bust, "reminding one of the wonderfully mastered Bucks County barn and winding stair turn" (*Prose*, 362). Her favorite photographer was her friend, the portrait and fashion photographer George Platt Lynes, whom she claimed "contributed to my knowledge of art." She praised "his understanding of light and impatience with retouching as a substitute for focus" (*Prose*, 655), the fundamental principle of straight photography. Anyone who studies the footnotes to Moore's poems or her collections of clippings at the Rosenbach will witness Moore's appreciation for documentary photographs and will see that Moore herself resembles the photographer Susan Sontag describes, who "chooses oddity, chases it, frames it, develops it, titles it."[42]

Stieglitz, Strand, and other advocates of straight photography show a correlative concern for straight prose. Strand wrote Stieglitz that he aimed for "direct statement" in his own prose; he criticized Paul Rosenfeld's and others' critical prose for its lack of "incisive[ness]" and "clear thinking," for its sentimentality and the "too lush . . . slough of language."[43] Georgia O'Keeffe deeply distrusted words and claimed that "colors and shapes make a more definite statement than words."[44] The comparison that at least one writer in the Stieglitz circle made between photography and prose may have been implicit in others' thinking: "Once only poetry could become art, not prose. The whole classical tradition of aesthetic excluded

41. MM to her family, April 4, 1909 (Rosenbach VI:15a:05); MM to JWM, December 12, 1915 (Rosenbach VI:21:13).

42. Sontag, *On Photography*, 34.

43. Paul Strand to Alfred Stieglitz, August 3, 1921, and July 25, 1922 (Beinecke). Quotations are from the 1922 letter.

44. Georgia O'Keeffe, *Georgia O'Keeffe* (New York, 1976), [no pagination]. I compare Moore's and O'Keeffe's resistance to the oppressiveness of imprecise language in "Marianne Moore and Georgia O'Keeffe: 'The Feelings of a Mother—A Woman or a Cat,'" in *Woman and Poet*, ed. Willis, 309–11.

the factual domain." [45] Thus, poetic language, like pictorial photography, began to seem fuzzy whereas direct prose, like straight photography, offered a new challenge to the artist.

This resistance to poetry—especially to the poetic—also prevailed among poets; hence Moore's disclaimer, "I, too, dislike it." What Pound calls "poppy-cock" Moore calls "fiddle." Pound admonished poets to "consider the way of the scientists" and "not [to] retell in mediocre verse what has already been done in good prose." Eliot advocated an art that could "approach the condition of science." [46] Pound, Eliot, and Moore all looked to the prose of Henry James as a model for poetry. Bad poetry, or "half-poets," opposed prose and science; good poetry aspired to them. As it moves away from the influence of French symbolism, the poetry of Pound and Eliot loses its early mistiness, but it continues to be richly suggestive and allusive, resonating with the traditions of Occidental and Oriental poetry in which Pound and Eliot immersed themselves. Williams and Moore, on the other hand, sought an American idiom that is not poetic in the usual sense.

Williams finds that idiom in American speech, in "American speech as distinct from English speech." [47] Moore, however, seeking "plain American which cats and dogs can *read*" (my emphasis), finds it in American prose: not just the artful prose of such writers as James, Whistler, and Poe, whose prose she admired (*Prose*, 165), but also the much more prevalent American prose of "business documents and / school-books." Technical writing, as we now call it, and straight photography were products of an industrial age suited to conveying fact but adopted by Americans such as Paul Strand and Marianne Moore for artistic expression. Moore admired, for instance, the accuracy in a statement like the following description of a counterfeit bill from the U.S. Treasury office.

> $20 FEDERAL RESERVE NOTE . . . faint crayon marks have been used to simulate genuine fibre. . . . In the Treasury Seal, magnification reveals that a green dot immediately under the center of the arm of the balance scales blends with the arm whereas it should be distinctly separate. Also, the left end of the right-hand scale pan extends

45. Waldo Frank, "A Thought Hazarded," in *Can a Photograph Have the Significance of Art?*, ed. Steiglitz, special issue of *MSS.*, 5.

46. Ezra Pound, *Literary Essays of Ezra Pound* (New York, 1935), 12, 6, 5; T. S. Eliot, *Selected Essays* (New York, 1950), 7.

47. Williams, *Selected Essays*, 289–90.

beyond the point where the left chain touches the pan. In the genuine, the pan ends where it touches the chain. The serial numbers are thicker than the genuine, and the prefix letter "G" is sufficiently defective to be mistaken for a "C" at first glance, . . . the letters "ry" in "Secretary" are joined together. In "Treasury" there is a tiny black dot just above the first downstroke in the letter "u." The back of the note, although of good workmanship, is printed in a green much darker than that used for genuine currency. (Moore's ellipses; quoted in *Prose*, 422–23)

And as her readers readily observe, diction from business, science, and technology pervades her poetry: "certain/Ming products," "amanita-white petals," "*leontopodium*," "equidistant three tiny arcs of seeds in a banana" (*CP*, 38, 16, 96, 170). Like Williams and Pound, Moore was interested in common speech; she studied dialects and slang and recorded countless fragments of conversation in her notebooks. But the intricate syntax and specialized diction of her poems, even their carefully researched subject matter and footnotes, typically lack the spontaneity of speech that one finds in Williams' poetry; rather, they bear distinct characteristics of prose. She even admits to Donald Hall: "I . . . am really much interested in dialect and intonations. I scarcely think of any that comes into my so-called poems at all" (*MMR*, 254).

During the twenties, when the "straight," precisionist aesthetic was at its peak, Moore moved further and further away from the poetic. She first abandoned her rhymed stanza in favor of free verse and after January, 1925, published no new poems for seven and a half years. This same month she wrote to an inquirer in Missouri regarding influences on her poetry. She lists first the literary writers she admires, dominated as usual by prose writers: "Sir Francis Bacon, Chaucer, Spenser, Defoe, Bunyan, Sir Thomas Browne, Leigh Hunt, Burke, Dr. Johnson, Anthony Trollope, Hardy, Henry James, W. B. Yeats, W. H. Hudson, and Sidney's The Defense of Poesie." But then she lists influences she had not named before, prose of an unexpected nature: advertisements, criticism, and "technical books."

I have been entertained and instructed by advertisements and book reviews in *Punch*, in the London *Spectator*, in *The London Times*, by reviews in the Fortnightly *Dial*, the present *Dial*, by reviews published in *The English Review* during the years 1907–1911; by Gordon Craig's books and other publications of his. And I have learned I feel, from technical books, which, in addition to being instructive and entertaining, seemed to me, aesthetically accomplished—John McGraw's "How to Play Baseball," Christy Mathewson's "Pitching in a Pinch," Tilden's books on tennis, W. Rhead's "The Earthenware Collector," Harold Baynes's manual on dogs published by *The National Geographic Magazine*, articles in *The Journal of Natural History*. The exactness and esprit of the work mentioned led me to submit to various publications, critical work which has in no case been declined, though I have never in any case, achieved what entirely satisfied me.[48]

While Moore credits this prose with stimulating her to write criticism—of which she wrote a great deal over the next four years—the "exactness and esprit of the work mentioned" can be felt in her poems of the twenties and to an even greater extent in her poems of the thirties and forties. I have said in Chapter 2 that the rhythms of prose characterized Moore's poems from the mid-teens, but not until the twenties did Moore appropriate for poetry "the vocabularies of science," which later she calls "creative, in fact enthralling" (*Prose*, 539).

This is not an abrupt change. Moore had used "Ming products" and "chrysoprase" already (*CP*, 38, 40). But in the free verse poems of the twenties words such as "accreted," "lignum vitae," and "chlorophylless fungi" appear more and more frequently (*CP*, 54, 59, 74); so do numbers, such as "one thousand four hundred and twenty pages make one inch" and "twenty-eight ice fields from fifty to five hundred feet thick," and other kinds of facts, both scientific and fanciful: "a voyager obtained the horn of a sea unicorn / to give to Queen Elizabeth, / who thought it worth a hundred thousand pounds" (*CP*, 55, 71, 77). Scientific terminology and facts are especially prevalent in "An Octopus" and are appropriate to this poem advocating "relentless accuracy." The opening to "Marriage"—hardly a technical subject—typifies Moore's goal at this time to defy misconceptions and misinformation with precision. She replaces a culturally laden term with a precise, businesslike one: "This institution, / perhaps one should say enterprise" (*CP*, 62).

Moore avoids not only poetic language but also the subject matter of conventional lyric poetry, the areas of human experience that to most per-

---

48. MM to Caspar Harvey, January 27, 1925, in *Marianne Moore Newsletter*, IV (Spring, 1980), 15–16.

sons are ineffable (thus the poet's challenge). Rather than death and love, for instance, subjects typically reserved for poetry and myth, she repeatedly turns to the subject matter of prose: persons, animals, places, objects, aesthetics, ethics. Her challenge is not to articulate the wilderness beyond words but rather to glean the precise from a wilderness that consists of words, of information and misinformation. Her working method attests to this. She read copiously—books, magazines, newspapers—and attended lectures and films and visited museums, and from this information she gleaned notebook after notebook of phrases and information as well as files of clippings as a general resource for poems. The phrases that survive in the poems themselves represent only a tiny portion of those preserved in the notebooks. In addition to this general research, she investigated her subject thoroughly before writing a poem about it. This is especially true of her longer poems. To name one of many examples, she took extensive notes (complete with page numbers) from *Peasant Art in Sweden, Lapland, and Iceland* in preparation for her poem "A Carriage from Sweden" and then underlined in red the passages she intended to use in the poem.[49]

Critical attempts to distinguish the poetic from the nonpoetic in verse are nearly as old as poetry itself. Aristotle, Ovid, and Thomas Hobbes all excluded "didactic" poetry, which conveys scientific information or technical instruction, from true poetry. But didactic poetry is the earliest extant form of Greek, Hebrew, and other literatures, and despite its disparagement has reappeared throughout Western literary history, especially during periods of scientific and technical advancement.[50] The low status of didactic poetry, which surely has not risen in the twentieth century, did not prevent Moore from employing its characteristic devices—emblem, fable, and epigram—nor from admiring some of its greatest practitioners, including Chaucer, Spenser, and La Fontaine.

In our own time Roman Jakobson and others have pointed to the po-

49. See Moore's notes with her typescript for "A Carriage from Sweden" (Rosenbach I:01:29). Also see Willis' thoroughly documented account of Moore's research process for "An Octopus" in Willis, "The Road to Paradise," in *Marianne Moore,* ed. Kappel, special issue of *Twentieth Century Literature,* 242–66.

50. S[mith] P[almer] B[ovie], "Didactic Poetry," *Princeton Encyclopedia of Poetry and Poetics,* ed. Alex Preminger (Enlarged ed.; Princeton, 1974), 190–93. Bovie distinguishes between didactic poetry, the aim of which is to inform, and moral poetry or satire, the aim of which is to improve the reader. Moore's poetry has elements of both, the latter often passing for the former.

lar differences between metaphor and metonymy to distinguish poetry from prose. Though according to Jakobson's definitions, metaphor and metonymy are both essential to any discourse, recognizing the domination of one "pole" over the other can help distinguish types of literature. Metaphor, Jakobson claims, based on the principle of substitution, characterizes romantic and symbolist poetry; metonymy, based on the principle of contiguity, characterizes realistic fiction.[51] Marianne Moore's poetry, according to this system, moves closer to the metonymic pole during the late teens and twenties. As shown in previous chapters, her poems of the mid-teens are largely metaphoric ("Critics and Connoisseurs," "To the Peacock of France," "Black Earth"). But the tropes that most distinguish Moore's mature style are not metaphors: "maple-/leaflike feet" (evident already in "Critics and Connoisseurs"), "froglike accuracy," "An Octopus // of ice," "This near artichoke" (*CP*, 38, 43, 71, 117). Maple leaf is not a metaphor for swan feet, nor frog for cat, nor octopus for glacier, nor artichoke for pangolin. When one reads Eliot's famous simile "the evening is spread out against the sky, / like a patient etherized upon a table," although the comparison is unexpected, it resonates with metaphoric significance: the suggestion of illness, of anticipation, of a near-death, dreamlike state, and so forth. In contrast, artichoke does not resonate. Rather there is only one point that connects the artichoke and pangolin, and that is their pattern of "scales" (and the "grace" in both patterns). The comparison between pangolin and artichoke wittily resists the kind of reading one gives to Eliot's conceit. This point of connection is what Jakobson calls contiguity, making Moore's trope metonymic. Most prose, literary and nonliterary, proceeds according to logical points of contiguity. Often in descriptive prose the points of contiguity are spatial; in narrative prose, temporal or causal. Moore's points of contiguity, however, are not the expected ones. They startle with what Moore admires in Lewis Carroll, "a precision of unlogic" (*Prose*, 170). Hugh Kenner calls this device in Moore "optical pun[ning]." Williams describes it thus: "With Miss Moore a word is a word most when it is separated out by science, treated with acid to remove the smudges, washed, dried and placed right side up on a clean surface."[52]

51. Roman Jakobson, "Two Aspects of Language and Two Types of Aphasic Disturbances," in *Fundamentals of Language*, by Roman Jakobson and Morris Halle (The Hague, 1956), 77–78.
52. Williams, *Selected Essays*, 128.

And although there are surely metaphoric elements throughout Moore's poems, her usual subjects during the twenties and afterwards are not symbols or metaphors. Instead of embodying large, complex ideas, her animals, objects, and landscapes illustrate principles in discrete, specific ways. The pangolin does not symbolize or represent grace; rather, it exemplifies it. It is a microcosm, not a macrocosm; it is, in other words, a part of the whole, a synecdoche, as are other things cataloged in the poem. The animal in Lawrence's "The Snake" (a poem Moore admired) is, on the other hand, a macrocosm, a symbol of primal forces, as is the elephant in "Black Earth" a symbolic macrocosm. David Lodge, who elaborates upon Jakobson's theories to form his own typology for reading modern fiction, finds that literature is essentially metaphoric and nonliterature metonymic. But the metonymic literary text is valuable, he argues, because it "run[s] against the grain of literature itself." While the metonymic text he has in mind is primarily the realistic novel, the distinctions he draws between metonymic and metaphoric literature apply to the difference between Moore's mature poems and most lyrics, including most modernist ones: "No message that is decoded without effort is likely to be valued, and the metaphoric mode has its own way of making interpretation fruitfully difficult: though it offers itself eagerly for interpretation, it bewilders us with a plethora of possible meanings. The metonymic text, in contrast, deluges us with a plethora of data, which we seek to unite into one meaning." This difference can readily be seen in how one reads Lawrence's "The Snake" versus how one reads "The Pangolin." And since readers of poetry are more accustomed to the metaphoric mode, they usually find Lawrence's poem more accessible than Moore's. Even Williams' "Young Sycamore," discussed in Chapter 2, suggests a plethora of metaphoric meanings—growth from youth to old age, sexual climax, the process of reading a poem—in contrast to Moore's "The Sycamore," which "deluges us with a plethora of data," a plethora of synecdoches for the principle, "There's more than just one kind of grace." Lodge continues: "Furthermore, it must always be remembered that we are not discussing a distinction between two mutually exclusive types of discourse, but a distinction based on dominance. The metaphoric work cannot totally neglect metonymic continuity if it is to be intelligible at all. Correspondingly, the metonymic text cannot eliminate all signs that it is available for metaphorical interpretation."[53] (Both "The Snake" and "Young Sycamore" have more

53. David Lodge, *The Modes of Modern Writing: Metaphor, Metonymy, and the Typology of Modern Literature* (Ithaca, N.Y., 1977), 111.

narrative continuity than Moore's poems typically have; likewise, the swan and ant in "Critics and Connoisseurs," one of Moore's few narrative poems, are metaphors, as her later animals typically are not.) Lodge's last point may explain why in the thirties Moore returned after more than a decade to her rhymed stanzas. The stanza itself invites a different kind of reading than does expository prose. Indeed, the very title of Moore's first poem sequence published after her seven-year hiatus from poetry announces her return to "literature": "Part of a Novel, Part of a Poem, Part of a Play."

Moore's footnotes are metonymic in Jakobson's sense, too. Unlike in *The Waste Land*, where the sources cited in the footnotes enhance the meaning and scope of the poem, the sources in Moore's footnotes often have little to do with the subject of her poem except by the thinnest thread of contiguity. Usually one must look up the source to discover how thoroughly Moore has removed the "smudges" of the original context; sometimes the footnote itself makes clear the irrelevance of the original context: in her notes to "An Octopus" she cites a remark "overheard at the circus" (*CP*, 273).

Whether they can define "literature" or not, most persons think they can recognize nonliterature. Tolstoy thought it safe to exclude business documents and school books (*CP*, 267); David Lodge thinks it safe (or nearly so) to exclude advertising and travelogues. Marianne Moore excludes none of these. The existence of such categories and their implicit hierarchy in the modern age—nonliterature valued for its unimaginative usefulness, literature for its useless beauty—would surely have been irresistible to her; she relished exceptions. Moore, however, wished not to offer her own distinctions but rather to show the fallaciousness of such distinctions. Poetry is "important not because a // high-sounding interpretation can be put upon [it] but because [it is] / useful" (*CP*, 266–67). For poetry to have any authority in modern times, it must aspire not only to the usefulness but also to the stylistic effectiveness of expository prose: "Pressure of business modifies self-consciousness and genuine matter for exposition seems to aid effectiveness; in for instance, Darwin's scientific descriptions" (*Prose*, 178). A hallmark of Moore's criticism is the use of nonliterary examples to illustrate aesthetic principles. To Moore distinctions between literature and nonliterature distract the critic, whose true purpose is to distinguish stylistic and moral effectiveness.

In one of her late *Dial* "Comments" she commends to the artist the "uses" of one of America's most pervasive forms of prose, advertising (*Prose*, 214–15), but she strips away the usual twentieth-century meaning. Though she does not openly rebuke commercial advertising, she does so implicitly by praising what most of it is not: "Poetry . . . [that] makes a friend of the advocate if not of his client" and "iteration" that is not wasteful. The examples she quotes approvingly come from Sir Philip Sidney, astrologer William Lilly, and P. T. Barnum; the sixteenth, seventeenth, and nineteenth centuries, respectively. The twentieth-century example she approves and to which she devotes nearly half of her essay is another nonliterary form, the travel guidebook, a genre enjoyed by both Moore and her mother. Though the two guidebooks she reviews do not rival "Karl Baedeker's contagious impassivity," she praises them for directing the reader through text and photographs to the treasures of Germany; she enumerates some of these treasures, including such otherwise unremarkable ones as "the domestic interior with the window for cactuses." Thus Moore elicits the etymological meaning of *advertising,* to turn one's attention. Good advertising—and implicitly good literature— is distinguished not by its genre but by its "contagious impassivity" and by, ultimately, its moral purpose. As she does with technology in "The Pangolin" and "Granite and Steel," Moore proves that advertising need not preclude either art or morality. Her essay concludes: "The desire to see good things is in itself good when not degraded by inquisitiveness or predatoriness, and it is not just to regard as rapacity the advertiser's art of educating visualization." By teaching her readers to see that "educating visualization" is artful and useful, Moore here as elsewhere "advertises." Advertising in this sense is the function of the critic, of the exhibitor (she praised Stieglitz for his "arduous" advertising [*Prose*, 646]), and of the poet. In "The Arctic Ox (or Goat)" she admits: "If you fear that you are / reading an advertisement, / you are" (*CP*, 195).

The travel guide "advertiser" appears throughout Moore's poems. In "An Octopus" travel books and brochures are the major sources for the poem, and in poems such as "The Steeple-Jack," "Virginia Britannia," and "An Octopus" the persona herself assumes the role of travel guide— and in other poems museum guide or zoo guide—in "advertising" features of the landscape or town. In "The Hero" a "decorous frock-coated Negro" employed as a guide at Mount Vernon exemplifies heroism. But here the travel guide directs the reader beyond the "sight" to "the rock / crystal thing to see" (*CP*, 9). The hero is a spiritual guide.

Photography, one could argue, is also metonymic in contrast to the metaphoric nature of painting. (Jakobson approaches this idea by calling the close-up in film metonymic.) A photograph connects the viewer contiguously with the moment preserved in the image, whereas a representational painting, executed over time, substitutes the artist's interpretation and reflections upon the subject for the immediate experience. Hence, straight photography is more metonymic than pictorial photography. Again, these are polar differences, not exclusive ones. Synecdoche is the chief device of photojournalism, which can convey in one face a message about an entire war.

It is true that, as Bram Dijkstra points out, Williams' poems often resemble photographs, and in a more obvious way than do the composite images of Moore's poems.[54] Like photographs, "The Red Wheelbarrow," "Nantucket," "Between Walls," and "This Is Just to Say" each seize a bit of the familiar world and frame it, asking readers to regard it in a new way. So does the readymade. This is a fundamental similarity between the straight photograph of the 291 group and the readymade of the Arensberg circle, that both are arts of selection rather than making. Since both undermine the conventional separation between art and life, Dickran Tashjian regards them both as examples of "anti-art."[55] But there is a difference in attitude between the readymade and straight photography that may likewise distinguish Williams and Moore. Inherent in the readymade and in dadaism generally is a wry despair over the uselessness of art, over its inability to mean anything more than itself. Allen Ginsberg interprets Williams' credo "No ideas but in things" to mean "There's no God basically."[56]

But for the straight photographers, especially Alfred Stieglitz, Paul Strand, and later Edward Weston, "photographic seeing" is virtually a religion. Morally it means, in the words of Paul Strand, having "a real respect for the thing in front of him." Spiritually it means, in the words of Edward Weston, seeing "the very quintessence of the thing itself."[57] In one essay Strand advocates cooperation between science and art to create

54. Dijkstra, *The Hieroglyphics of a New Speech, passim.*

55. Tashjian, *Skyscraper Primitives,* esp. 15–28.

56. Interview with Allen Ginsberg in "William Carlos Williams," *Voices & Visions,* television series. The degree to which Williams' poems have such a despair is, of course, arguable.

57. Strand, "Photography," in *Photographers on Photography,* ed. Lyons, 136; Edward Weston, "Photography—Not Pictorial," *Camera Craft,* XXXVII (1930), reprinted in *Photographers on Photography,* ed. Lyons, 155.

"a new religious impulse." With the photographer as its paradigm, this new religion calls for a collapse of resistance between science and art, a recognition that both scientist and artist are "true seekers after knowledge."[58]

Moore, of course, also saw science and art as united in their pursuit of knowledge, knowledge as much spiritual as intellectual. For Moore both scientist and artist share the commitment to what Edward Weston calls "learning to *see photographically*." He explains: "The camera's innate honesty . . . provides the photographer with a means of looking deeply into the nature of things, and presenting his subjects in terms of their basic reality. It enables him to reveal the essence of what lies before his lens with such clear insight that the beholder may find the recreated image more real and comprehensible than the actual object."[59] This statement accords with Moore's views of art generally: "What is more precise than precision?" she asks. "Illusion" (*CP*, 151). In her morality Moore is closer to the photographer and the realistic novelist than to the metaphoric poet (indeed, morality is rarely a concern of lyric poetry). Her morality is learning to see—as protagonists in the novels of Jane Austen and Henry James learn to see. It arises not from a desire for metaphoric unity between disparate things but from a metonymic "respect for the essence of a thing" (*Prose*, 79). Moore never quite adopts the religious language Strand employs, yet her "respect for the essence of a thing" assumes moral and spiritual dimensions. For Moore, as for Stieglitz and Strand, artistic seeing is equivalent to religious vision.

After four years as editor and critic for the *Dial* and eleven years of living in the Village in almost daily contact with innovations in the arts, Moore published her own treatise on seeing in 1932, "Part of a Novel, Part of a Poem, Part of a Play." As it appeared in *Poetry* magazine, this sequence originally consisted of three poems, "The Steeple-Jack," "The Student," and "The Hero," each of which corresponds to the novel, poem, and play, respectively.[60]

58. Paul Strand, "Photography and the New God," *Broom*, III (November, 1922), reprinted in *Photographers on Photography*, ed. Lyons, 143–44.

59. Edward Weston, "Seeing Photographically," *Complete Photographer*, IX (1943), reprinted in *Photographers on Photography*, ed. Lyons, 161, 162–63.

60. MM, "Part of a Novel, Part of a Poem, Part of a Play," *Poetry*, XL (1932), 119–28. In 1935, when she published *Selected Poems*, Moore eliminated "The Student" from the sequence but retained the sequence title for the remaining two poems, which opened the vol-

Despite its flaws, the original sequence demonstrates a progression and unity that has been overlooked in discussions of the three individual poems. It progresses from surface observations to spiritual vision. This progression is evident in the descriptions of the settings of each poem—from a specific New England seaside town in "The Steeple-Jack," to America in "The Student," to an unspecified "where one does not wish / to go" in "The Hero." The flora and fauna of each setting are described in progressively more abstract terms, as are the respective characters, who are specific individuals with names, C. J. Poole and Ambrose, in "The Steeple-Jack," are a type in "The Student," and an archetype in "The Hero." The poems are populated with travelers: Dürer, whose travels to the Tyrol and to see a stranded whale are mentioned; Ambrose, with "his not-native books and hat"; John Bunyan's Pilgrim; the Mount Vernon sightseers; and with a variation of traveler, the expatriate: Goldsmith, Einstein, Audubon, Joseph, El Greco, Moses, and, in a sense, both George Washington and the "frock-coated Negro." Even the "eight stranded whales" are out of their natural element.[61] The non-native has the potential to see what natives do not notice.

The words "see" and "sea" resonate throughout "The Steeple-Jack." This is a poem about the kind of artistic seeing that delights in ordered surfaces—"water etched / with waves as formal as the scales / on a fish"— and in the ironies that such surfaces conceal—"It could not be dangerous to be living / in a town like this." The vantage point is one of "privilege": of the travel-guide persona; of Dürer, the traveler; of Ambrose, a non-native viewing the town from a nearby hillside; and of the steeple-jack himself, who has a unique, superior view from atop the steeple. This privileged distance allows each of them to see ironies and dangers an inhabitant of the town would not see: the "confusion" of the approaching storm (whereas inside "your house" it seems "a fine day"), the element of the tropics beneath the "disguise" of "austerity," and "the pitch / of the church // spire, not true." In the names of the apparently harmless flora lurk ominous animals—"fox-glove, giant snap-dragon," "spiderwort," "crab-claw"

---

ume. Thereafter she eliminated the sequence title, but "The Steeple-Jack" and "The Hero" retained their foremost position in *Collected Poems* and *Complete Poems*. She later revised "The Student," which in its original form had been clumsier and more pedantic than its companions, but she never restored it to the original sequence.

61. In *The Savage's Romance,* John Slatin notes that the plants cataloged in "The Steeple-Jack" are likewise not native (187).

daisies, "toad-plant," "tiger[lilie]s"—and other dangers, as in "poppies"; the fauna include no cobras but the rat population requires control! The "simple people" living here are in greater danger than they think. Yet the playful tone suggests the dangers are not serious ones, as they are in "The Hero." The ironic distance is the "privilege" of the novelist, who knows his subject "by heart," who enjoys the irony of the gilded star and the whitewashed church, and who, if successful, maintains tension between appearance and reality, between order and confusion. This sequence also marks Moore's return after more than a decade to the rhymed, syllabic stanza she had developed in 1915 and 1916. The tension in "The Steeple-Jack" between simplicity and complexity, between safety and danger, between stasis and motion, reflects the tension Moore's stanzas achieve between the formal static pattern of syllables, rhyme, and typography and the uneven kinetic prose rhythms.

The superior, ironic distance is missing in "The Student," who unlike Ambrose is a native, seeking within his own country, America, to learn from travelers and expatriates such as Einstein, Audubon, and the French lecturer. The observations are abstractions—"science is never finished" and "we are / as a nation perhaps, undergraduates not students"—rather than the tangible things cataloged in "The Steeple-Jack." Like "England" and "An Octopus," this poem links America with precision; it is devoted to intellectual seeing, the kind of seeing required of the scientist and, according to Moore, of the poet. It is the poet's task, as it is the scientist's, as it is the American's, to be a student, to make distinctions.

> . . . to learn—the difference between cow
>   and zebu; lion, tiger; barred and brown
>   owls; horned owls have one ear that opens up and one that opens
>   down.
>
> The golden eagle is the one with feathered legs. The penguin wing
>   is
>
> ancient, not degenerate.

And to master words:

> . . . It is a
>   thoughtful pupil has two thoughts for the word
>   valet; or for bachelor, child, damsel; though no one having heard

213

them used as terms of chivalry would make the mediaeval use of them.

It is the student's task (though one which, like science, is never finished) to name what is knowable, the facts of "science—/theology or biology," to form and "hold opinions that fright//could [not] dislocate."

"The Hero," however, travels in a world where fright *can* dislocate opinions. It is the realm of the invisible, the unknowable. As in "New York" and "An Octopus," Moore moves from a privileged vantage, that of "The Steeple-Jack," down into a wilderness where "to go in is to be lost." [62] The first twenty-one lines of "The Hero" describe an unspecified but forbidding place "where the ground is sour" and "love won't grow." Here, we have not "the diffident/little newt" of "The Steeple-Jack" nor the "cow/ and zebu" of the "The Student" but "what it is fl[ying] out on muffled wings . . . until the skin creeps," something that cannot be named or fully seen. This place does not attract travelers like Dürer and Ambrose or even heroes; it is a place "where one does not wish/to go"—no stranded whales nor facts of science here. The traveler here is deprived not only of the physical distance of the steeple-jack and the intellectual distance of the student, but even of seeing what is immediately before him. Indeed, to attain spiritual vision, the hero must have a kind of blindness to the "sights":

> . . . He's not out
> seeing a sight but the rock
> crystal thing to see—the startling El Greco
> brimming with inner light.

One hero in the poem, Jacob, is physically blind. The "fearless sightseeing hobo," intently looking for George Washington's grave, is oblivious to what the Negro guide, "not seeing her," does see. The hero knows fear because of his "reverence for mystery," because he *can* see beyond the sights. Other kinds of blindness are required: the hero sees hope when "all ground for hope has / vanished" and looks "upon a fellow creature's error with the / feelings of a mother—a / woman or a cat." Even the reader learns to see beyond George Washington, the anticipated hero, to the Negro "standing like the shadow / of the willow."

Reflecting the progression in the three poems from direct observa-

62. This phrase originally appeared in "New York," but Moore appropriated it three years later for "An Octopus."

214

tion, to intellectual discrimination, to spiritual vision, is each poem's artist-in-residence: Dürer in "The Steeple-Jack," Audubon in "The Student," and El Greco in "The Hero." Dürer is closest to Moore herself. Like her, he was an innovator, heralding a new period in art history; also like her, he was fascinated by detail and influenced by technology. Printing was still a new invention, and Dürer made the woodcut and copper engraving respectable art forms. He even invented a device for mechanically recording perspective, a kind of primitive camera. What Moore emphasizes in "The Steeple-Jack" is his travels: the only artist of the three to achieve early success and popularity in his own country, he was a traveler by choice, never an expatriate. Audubon is the appropriate transition figure, since he was both an extensive traveler throughout the United States and an expatriate from Santo Domingo. Self-trained in both naturalism and watercolor and noted for his scientific discriminations as much as for his art, he aptly exemplifies the American student described in the poem. El Greco, never the traveler that Dürer and Audubon were, was an expatriate several times over. Born in Crete of Greek parents and trained in Venice, he moved to Spain at age thirty to seek financial support for his work. Even in Spain he never earned the success or fame he deserved but nevertheless remained true to his oddly individualistic style and spiritual vision. Thus is the hero linked with the expatriate, the exile.

The uncongenial environment itself demands the hero's vision—hence making the hero a tragic figure, as in a play. The hero, like the student and steeple-jack, is more "at home" in the New England seaside town. The presence of Mount Vernon in "The Hero" suggests that this poem too is about America, though more subtly so than "The Student" or even "The Steeple-Jack." Whether to stay in one's native country or move to Europe, an environment considered more congenial to artists, was an issue that confronted many American artists during the twenties. Despite Moore's decision to stay home, she took no pride in this and never, as others did, admonished Eliot, Pound, or other expatriates for living abroad. Finding freedom within the inevitable constraints of one's environment is an enduring theme in her poetry; a favorite image for this is the sea in a chasm.

> . . . He
> sees deep and is glad, who
>   accedes to mortality
> and in his imprisonment rises
> upon himself as

the sea in a chasm, struggling to be
free and unable to be,
    in its surrendering
        finds its continuing. (*CP*, 95)

Perhaps Moore identified with the hero because of the constraints of her own filial responsibility, within which she nevertheless found the necessary freedom for her work. More likely, however, "The Hero" pays tribute to Moore's mother, for whom living in Greenwich Village had surely been a kind of exile. A liberating maternal love—"the / feelings of a mother—a / woman or a cat"—is one of the hero's main virtues. The greatest artist or hero, the poem implies, is necessarily something of an expatriate even in her own country. Elsewhere, Moore writes of Blake: "his home [is] not the age nor the house in which he lived, but his mind" (*Prose*, 184).

The same "Comment" on Blake begins with a quotation from Ruskin, which seems virtually a paradigm for at least the second and third poems in Moore's sequence: "Thousands of people can talk . . . for one who can think; but thousands can think for one who can see. To see clearly is poetry, prophecy, and religion all in one" (*Prose*, 184). The steeple-jack's way of seeing is less specialized than the student's; the hero's rarer still. In "The Steeple-Jack" "The hero, the student, / the steeple-jack, each in his way, / is at home," and in "The Student" the "scholar must have the heroic mind," but "The Hero" includes neither steeple-jack nor student. A clear hierarchy exists among the three poems.

Yet Moore typically resists hierarchies, which is important to recognize in interpreting this one. For Moore seems to identify most strongly with "The Steeple-Jack." As several critics have noted, this poem was written shortly after Moore's move to Brooklyn and in various ways pays tribute to her new hometown. Like Dürer, she does see "reason for living / in a town like this." There is no indication that Moore regarded herself as a hero or even as an expatriate (though she did surely regard herself as a student). Together the poems exemplify three kinds of seeing, three modes, in Moore's poetry. The playful, ironic delight in surfaces and oddities that characterizes "The Steeple-Jack" is Moore's most original and distinctive mode, the one most natural for her. This is the usual mode of her letters. That the original version of "The Student" was the least successful of the three poems reveals the greater difficulties of her intellectual, didactic mode. However, she could not justify the "delight" of her poetry without its "teaching" too: only thus does poetry become useful, does it educate visualization, refine the language, and, by threatening the tyranny of imprecision, liberate the individual. The spiritual mode occurs only occasionally in Moore's work and is so unobtrusive that readers sometimes overlook it or interpret it ironically; nevertheless, it appears often enough and forcefully enough to demonstrate its earnestness. As the echoing internal rhymes of "The Hero" indicate,[63] this is Moore's most lyrical mode.

Despite the obvious importance to Moore of all three modes, there are certain inconsistencies, even contradictions, among them. How can the author of "The Steeple-Jack" advocate a blindness to physical sights? And yet they are prismatic variations of Moore's most consistent theme. She challenges her readers to *see*—as the artist, the student, and the hero do, as Henry James's American does, with a mind " 'intrinsically and actively ample . . . reaching westward, southward, anywhere, everywhere,' with a mind 'incapable of the shut door in any direction' " (*CP*, 321–22).

63. Miller, "Marianne Moore's Black Maternal Hero," points out the many long *e* and *o* sounds in the poem, echoing "Hero" (809).

BIBLIOGRAPHY

Note: The following includes works cited in the text plus a few others that were especially useful. For a complete listing of the first published versions of each of Moore's poems, see Holley, *The Poetry of Marianne Moore*, 195–202. For a thorough bibliography of recent works about Moore, see Bonnie Honigsblum, "An Annotated Bibliography of Works About Marianne Moore, 1977–1990," in *Woman and Poet*, ed. Willis, 443–620.

Manuscripts and Special Collections

Beinecke Rare Book and Manuscript Library, Yale University, New Haven
    Yale Collection of American Literature.
        Gaston Lachaise Archive.
        Alfred Stieglitz Archive.
Center for Creative Photography, University of Arizona, Tucson
    Paul Strand Collection.
Miriam Coffin Canaday Library, Bryn Mawr College, Bryn Mawr, Pennsylvania
    Bryn Mawr College Archives.
Rosenbach Museum and Library, Philadelphia
    Marianne Moore Papers.
Smith College Library, Northampton, Massachusetts
    Sophia Smith Collection.

Principal Works by Marianne Moore

Poems. London, 1921.
Observations. New York, 1924; 2nd ed., 1925.
The Selected Poems of Marianne Moore. New York, 1935.
The Pangolin and Other Verse. London, 1936.
What Are Years. New York, 1941.
Nevertheless. New York, 1944.
Collected Poems. New York, 1951.
The Fables of La Fontaine [translation]. New York, 1954.
Predilections. New York, 1955.
Like a Bulwark. New York, 1956.

O to Be a Dragon. New York, 1959.

A Marianne Moore Reader. New York, 1961.

The Arctic Ox. London, 1964.

Tell Me, Tell Me: Granite, Steel, and Other Topics. New York, 1966.

The Complete Poems of Marianne Moore. New York, 1967; rev. ed., 1981.

The Complete Prose of Marianne Moore. Edited by Patricia C. Willis. New York, 1986.

Interviews and Works About Marianne Moore

Abbott, Craig S. *Marianne Moore: A Descriptive Bibliography.* Pittsburgh, 1977.

Altieri, Charles. *Painterly Abstraction in Modernist American Poetry: The Contemporaneity of Modernism.* Cambridge, England, 1989.

Bishop, Elizabeth. *The Collected Prose.* Edited by Robert Giroux. New York, 1984.

Borroff, Marie. *Language and the Poet: Verbal Artistry in Frost, Stevens, and Moore.* Chicago, 1979.

A Celebration of H.D. and Marianne Moore. Special issue of *Poesis*, VI, nos. 3/4 (1985).

Costello, Bonnie. *Marianne Moore: Imaginary Possessions.* Cambridge, Mass., 1981.

Doolittle, Hilda [H. D.]. "Marianne Moore." *Egoist*, III (August, 1916), 118.

Erikson, Darlene Williams. *Illusion Is More Precise than Precision: The Poetry of Marianne Moore.* Tuscaloosa, 1992.

Goodridge, Celeste. *Hints and Disguises: Marianne Moore and Her Contemporaries.* Iowa City, 1989.

Goodridge, Celeste, ed. *Marianne Moore.* Special issue of *Sagetrieb*, VI (Winter, 1987).

Hartman, Geoffrey. Jacket notes to *Marianne Moore Reads from Her Works.* Yale Series of Recorded Poets, n.d. [*ca.* 1960].

Heuving, Jeanne. *Omissions Are Not Accidents: Gender in the Art of Marianne Moore.* Detroit, 1992.

Holley, Margaret. *The Poetry of Marianne Moore: A Study in Voice and Value.* Cambridge, England, 1987.

Joyce, Elisabeth W. "Complexity Is Not a Crime: Marianne Moore, Modernism, and the Visual Arts." Ph.D. dissertation, Temple University, 1991.

Kappel, Andrew J., ed. *Marianne Moore.* Special issue of *Twentieth Century Literature*, XXX (Summer/Fall, 1984).

Kenner, Hugh. *A Homemade World: The American Modernist Writers.* New York, 1975.

Marianne Moore Newsletter, I-VII (1977-1983).

Martin, Taffy. *Marianne Moore: Subversive Modernist.* Austin, 1986.

Miller, Cristanne. "Marianne Moore's Black Maternal Hero: A Study in Categorization." *American Literary History*, I (1989), 786-815.

Molesworth, Charles. *Marianne Moore: A Literary Life.* New York, 1990.

Moore, Marianne. "Conversation with Marianne Moore" (Interview with Grace Jan Schulman). *Quarterly Review of Literature,* XVI (1969), 154–71.

————. "Interview with Donald Hall." In *A Marianne Moore Reader.* New York, 1961.

————. "Some Answers to Questions Posed by Howard Nemerov." In *Poets on Poetry,* edited by Howard Nemerov. New York, 1966.

Parisi, Joseph, ed. *Marianne Moore: The Art of a Modernist.* Ann Arbor, 1990.

Sargeant, Winthrop. "Humility, Concentration, and Gusto." *New Yorker,* February 16, 1957, pp. 38-77.

Schulman, Grace. *Marianne Moore: The Poetry of Engagement.* Urbana, 1986.

Slatin, John M. *The Savage's Romance: The Poetry of Marianne Moore.* University Park, Pa., 1986.

Stapleton, Laurence. *Marianne Moore: The Poet's Advance.* Princeton, 1978.

Steinman, Lisa M. *Made in America: Science, Technology, and American Modernist Poets.* New Haven, 1987.

Tomlinson, Charles, ed. *Marianne Moore: A Collection of Critical Essays.* Englewood Cliffs, N.J., 1969.

Vendler, Helen. *Part of Nature, Part of Us: Modern American Poets.* Cambridge, Mass., 1980.

Wescott, Glenway. "Miss Moore's Observations." *Manikin,* no. 3 (1923), 1–4.

Willis, Patricia C. *Marianne Moore: Vision into Verse.* Philadelphia, 1987.

Willis, Patricia C., ed. *Marianne Moore: Woman and Poet.* Orono, Me., 1990.

Other Primary and Secondary Sources

Abrahams, Edward. *The Lyrical Left: Randolph Bourne, Alfred Stieglitz, and the Origins of Cultural Radicalism in America.* Charlottesville, 1986.

Apollinaire, Guillaume. *Apollinaire on Art: Essays and Reviews, 1902–1918.* Edited by Leroy C. Breunig. Translated by Susan Suleiman. New York, 1972.

Bachelard, Gaston. *The Poetics of Space.* 1958. Translated by Maria Jolas. Boston, 1969.

Besant, Annie. *The Ancient Wisdom: An Outline of Theosophical Teachings.* 1897; rpr. Adyar, India, 1949.

Burgard, Timothy Anglin. "Charles Demuth's *Longhi on Broadway: Homage to Eugene O'Neill.*" *Arts Magazine,* LVIII (January, 1984), 110–13.

Burke, Doreen Bolger, *et al. In Pursuit of Beauty: Americans and the Aesthetic Movement.* New York, 1986.

Camfield, William A. *Francis Picabia.* New York, 1970.

Carr, Carolyn Kinder, and Margaret C. S. Christman. *Gaston Lachaise: Portrait Sculpture.* Washington, D.C., 1985.

Cohn, Sherrye. "Arthur Dove and the Organic Analogy: A Rapprochement Between Art and Nature." *Arts Magazine,* LIX (Summer, 1985), 85–89.

Davidson, Abraham A. "Demuth's Poster Portraits." *Artforum*, XVII (November, 1978), 54–57.

———. *Early American Modernist Painting, 1910–1935*. New York, 1981.

De Zurko, Edward Robert. *Origins of Functionalist Theory*. New York, 1957.

Dijkstra, Bram. *The Hieroglyphics of a New Speech: Cubism, Stieglitz, and the Early Poetry of William Carlos Williams*. Princeton, 1969.

Eddy, Arthur Jerome. *Cubists and Post-Impressionism*. Chicago, 1914.

Eliot, T. S. *Selected Essays*. New York, 1950.

Elliott, Emory, ed. *Columbia Literary History of the United States*. New York, 1988.

Frank, Joseph. *The Widening Gyre: Crisis and Mastery in Modern Literature*. New Brunswick, N.J., 1963.

Frank, Waldo, *et al. America & Alfred Stieglitz: A Collective Portrait*. New York, 1934.

Friedman, Martin L. *The Precisionist View in American Art*. Minneapolis, 1960.

———, *et al. Charles Sheeler*. Washington, D.C., 1968.

Green, Jonathan, ed. *Camera Work: A Critical Anthology*. Millerton, N.Y., 1973.

Greenough, Sarah. *Paul Strand*. Washington, D.C., and New York, 1990.

Greenough, Sarah, and Juan Hamilton. *Alfred Stieglitz: Photographs & Writings*. Washington, D.C., and New York, 1983.

Hartley, Marsden. *Adventures in the Arts*. New York, 1921.

———. *The Collected Poems of Marsden Hartley*. Edited by Gail R. Scott. Santa Rosa, 1987.

Hartmann, Sadakitchi. "The Photo-Secession, a New Pictorial Movement." *Craftsman*, VI (April, 1904), 30–37.

Haskell, Barbara. *Arthur Dove*. San Francisco, 1974.

Hilton, Timothy. *The Pre-Raphaelites*. New York, 1970.

Hoffman, Katherine, ed. *Collage: Critical Views*. Ann Arbor, 1989.

Hoffman, Malvina. *Yesterday Is Tomorrow: A Personal History*. New York, 1965.

Hoffman, Marilyn Friedman. *William and Marguerite Zorach: The Cubist Years, 1915–1918*. Manchester, N.H., and Hanover, N.H., 1987.

Homer, William Innes. *Alfred Stieglitz and the American Avant-Garde*. Boston, 1977.

"The Iconoclastic Opinions of M. Marcel Duchamps [*sic*] Concerning Art and America." *Current Opinion*, LIX (1915), 346–47.

Jakobson, Roman. "Two Aspects of Language and Two Types of Aphasic Disturbances." In *Fundamentals of Language*, by Roman Jakobson and Morris Halle. The Hague, 1956.

Johnson, Ellen H. *Modern Art and the Object: A Century of Changing Attitudes*. London, 1976.

Joost, Nicholas. *Scofield Thayer and "The Dial": An Illustrated History*. Carbondale, Ill., 1964.

Kandinsky, Wassily. *Concerning the Spiritual in Art.* 1911. Translated by M. T. H. Sadler, 1914; rpr. New York, 1977.

Kandinsky, Wassily, and Franz Marc, eds. *The "Blaue Reiter" Almanac.* 1912. Translated by Henning Falkenstein and edited by Klaus Lankheit. New York, 1974.

Kreymborg, Alfred. *Troubadour: An Autobiography.* New York, 1925.

Lachaise, Gaston. "A Comment on My Sculpture." *Creative Art,* III (August, 1928), xxiii–xxvi.

Lears, T. J. Jackson. *No Place of Grace: Antimodernism and the Transformation of American Culture, 1880–1920.* New York, 1981.

Lessing, Gotthold Ephraim. *Laocoön: An Essay on the Limits of Painting and Poetry.* 1766. Translated by Edward Allen McCormick. Baltimore, 1984.

Levin, Gail. "Wassily Kandinsky and the American Avant-Garde, 1912–1950." Ph.D. dissertation, Rutgers University, 1976.

Lodge, David. *The Modes of Modern Writing: Metaphor, Metonymy, and the Typology of Modern Literature.* Ithaca, N.Y., 1977.

Lyons, Nathan, ed. *Photographers on Photography: A Critical Anthology.* Englewood Cliffs, N.J., 1966.

MacLeod, Glen. *Wallace Stevens and Modern Art: From the Armory Show to Abstract Expressionism.* New Haven, 1993.

Marling, William. *William Carlos Williams and the Painters, 1909–1923.* Athens, Ohio, 1982.

Mumford, Lewis. "Function and Expression in Architecture." *Architectural Record,* CX (November, 1951), 106–12.

M[unson], G[orham] B. "Exposé No. 1." *Secession,* no. 1 (Spring, 1922), 22–24.

Newhall, Beaumont. *The History of Photography.* Rev. ed. New York, 1982.

Newton, Douglas. *The Nelson A. Rockefeller Collection: Masterpieces of Primitive Art.* New York, 1978.

Nordland, Gerald. *Gaston Lachaise: The Man and His Work.* New York, 1974.

Norman, Dorothy. *Alfred Stieglitz: Introduction to an American Seer.* New York, 1960.

O'Keeffe, Georgia. *Georgia O'Keeffe.* New York, 1976.

Pound, Ezra. *Literary Essays of Ezra Pound.* New York, 1935.

———. *Personae: The Collected Poems of Ezra Pound.* New York, 1926.

———. *The Selected Letters of Ezra Pound, 1907–1941.* Edited by D. D. Paige. New York, 1950.

Preminger, Alex, ed. *Princeton Encyclopedia of Poetry and Poetics.* Enlarged ed. Princeton, 1974.

Pultz, John, and Catherine B. Scallen. *Cubism and American Photography, 1910–1930.* Williamstown, Mass., 1981.

Rosenblum, Robert. "Picasso and the Typography of Cubism." In *Picasso, 1881–1973,* ed. Roland Penrose and John Golding. London, 1973.

223

Rourke, Constance. *Charles Sheeler: Artist in the American Tradition.* New York, 1938.

Rubin, William, ed. *"Primitivism" in 20th Century Art: Affinity of the Tribal and the Modern.* 2 vols. New York, 1984.

Sanders, Emmy Veronica. "America Invades Europe." *Broom,* I (November, 1921), 89–93.

Saunders, Susanna Terrell. "Georgiana Goddard King (1871–1939): Educator and Pioneer in Medieval Spanish Art." In *Women as Interpreters of the Visual Arts, 1820–1979,* edited by Claire Richter Sherman. Westport, Conn., 1981.

Sayre, Henry M. *The Visual Text of William Carlos Williams.* Urbana, 1983.

Scott, Gail R. *Marsden Hartley.* New York, 1988.

The Sculpture of Gaston Lachaise. New York, 1967.

Sontag, Susan. *On Photography.* New York, 1977.

Spears, Monroe K. *Space Against Time in Modern Poetry.* Fort Worth, 1972.

Steinberg, Leo. *Other Criteria: Confrontations with Twentieth-Century Art.* London, 1972.

Steiner, Wendy. *The Colors of Rhetoric: Problems in the Relation Between Modern Literature and Painting.* Chicago, 1982.

———. *Exact Resemblance to Exact Resemblance: The Literary Portraiture of Gertrude Stein.* New Haven, 1978.

Stewart, Rick. "Charles Sheeler, William Carlos Williams, and Precisionism: A Redefinition." *Arts Magazine,* LVIII (November, 1983), 100–14.

Steiglitz, Alfred, ed. *Can a Photograph Have the Significance of Art?* Special issue of *MSS.,* IV (December, 1922).

Tarbell, Roberta K. *Marguerite Zorach: The Early Years, 1908–1920.* Washington, D.C., 1973.

Tashjian, Dickran. "Engineering a New Art." In *The Machine Age in America, 1918–1941.* New York, 1986.

———. *Joseph Cornell: Gifts of Desire.* Miami Beach, 1992.

———. *Skyscraper Primitives: Dada and the American Avant-Garde, 1910–1925.* Middletown, Conn., 1975.

———. *William Carlos Williams and the American Scene, 1920–1940.* New York, 1978.

Torgovnick, Marianna. *Gone Primitive: Savage Intellects, Modern Lives.* Chicago, 1990.

Trachtenberg, Alan. *Brooklyn Bridge: Fact and Symbol.* New York, 1965.

Tsujimoto, Karen. *Images of America: Precisionist Painting and Modern Photography.* San Francisco and Seattle, 1982.

Tuchman, Maurice, *et al. The Spiritual in Art: Abstract Painting, 1890–1985.* Los Angeles and New York, 1986.

Vendler, Helen, ed. *Voices & Visions: The Poet in America*. New York, 1987.

Voices & Visions. Television series produced by the New York Center for Visual History, 1987.

Weber, Max. *Cubist Poems*. London, 1913.

Wheeler, Monroe, to the author, August 7, 1988.

Whistler, James McNeill. *The Gentle Art of Making Enemies*. New York, 1890.

Wight, Frederick S. *Arthur G. Dove*. Berkeley, 1958.

Williams, William Carlos. *The Autobiography of William Carlos Williams*. New York, 1951.

———. *The Collected Poems of William Carlos Williams*. Edited by A. Walton Litz and Christopher MacGowen. 2 vols. New York, 1986.

———. *I Wanted to Write a Poem: The Autobiography of the Works of a Poet*. Reported and edited by Edith Heal. New York, 1958.

———. *A Recognizable Image: William Carlos Williams on Art and Artists*. Edited by Bram Dijkstra. New York, 1978.

———. *Selected Essays*. New York, 1969.

———. *The Selected Letters of William Carlos Williams*. Edited by John C. Thirlwall. New York, 1957.

Wilson, Edmund. "An Imaginary Conversation: Mr. Paul Rosenfeld and Mr. Matthew Josephson." *New Republic*, April 9, 1924, pp. 179–82.

Wright, Frank Lloyd. *Frank Lloyd Wright on Architecture: Selected Writings, 1894–1940*. Edited by Frederick Gutheim. New York, 1941.

Zorach, Marguerite. "Embroidery as Art." *Art in America*, XLIV (Fall, 1956), 48–51.

Zorach, William. *Art Is My Life: The Autobiography of William Zorach*. Cleveland, 1967.

INDEX

Italicized page numbers indicate illustrations.

Abrahams, Edward, 140

Abstraction: in painting, 47, 58, 80–81, 103, 118, 142–43, 168, 174, 190, 194; in poetry, 73–74, 88–89, 91; in collage, 97, 98; in photography, 197

Academic art, 61, 136, 153, 161, 163

Advertising, 54, 203, 208–209

Africans: art by, 135, 137, 139, 141, 145, 148, 154, 174, 179; MM's treatment of, 161–62

Aldington, Richard, 26, 44

Altieri, Charles, 4

America: expatriation from, 11, 215; and nationalism, 118, 170; modernists define, 170–72, 174; MM defines, 173, 179–84, 213

American Indians: Carlisle Indian School, 20, 145; MM's treatment of, 124, 145, 154, 181; art by, 137, 138, 141, 142*n*, 147; and Hartley, 144–45

American Place, An, 34

American tradition in art, 118, 173–80, 193, 194–97. *See also* Folk art

Anderson, Sherwood, 35, 172, 200

Anderson Galleries, 34, 35

Animal poems: progress toward, 81, 111; and Bachelard, 83; values in, 154–68, 190–92; mentioned, 9, 120, 166, 207

Antiacademic art, 17n, 61, 65, 135–36, 137, 153

Antihierarchical values. *See* Pluralism

Apollinaire, Guillaume, 66, 96, 107

Architectural form. *See* Spatial form; Stanza

Architecture, 81, 170, 178, 185–87, 194, 197, 198–200

Arensberg, Louise, 2, 31

Arensberg, Walter C., 2, 29, 31, 32

Arensberg circle, 2, 31–33, 46, 102*n*, 172, 174

Aristotle, 119, 205

Armory Show: MM's awareness of, 21, 64; and photography, 197; mentioned, 5*n*, 32, 34, 37, 57, 142

Arts and crafts movement: MM's exposure to, 15–16, 138–39; ideology of, 16, 117, 129, 138–39, 164*n;* and book design, 65; and architecture, 199; and photography, 199–200; mentioned, 1, 141

Ashbee, C. R., 108, 138, 199

Assemblage: MM's use of, 3, 7, 102–103, 112–34, 156, 164; and Cornell, 7, 50–53; synthetic cubism, 62–63; three-fold objectification in, 96–100; object portraits, 100–108. *See also* Selection

Assyrian art, 139, 142*n*

Audubon, John James, 54, 56, 212, 213, 215

Bachelard, Gaston, 81–83, 115, 130–31, 132

Barr, Alfred H., Jr., 127

Barton, George A., 139

Baxter, Sylvester, 141

Benét, Laura, 13

Benét, William Rose, 13

Besant, Annie, 143, 152

227